Relationships Between Canadian-American Wage Settlements

Relationships Between Canadian-American Wage Settlements

An Empirical Study of Five Industries

by

BRYAN M. DOWNIE

INDUSTRIAL RELATIONS CENTRE
QUEEN'S UNIVERSITY
AT KINGSTON, ONTARIO
1 9 7 0

FOREWORD

The influence of international unions, bi-national labour agreements, and wage parity, have all been subjects of continuing debate in Canada. Paradoxically, as the author indicates, these areas are perhaps the least understood phenomena in Canadian industrial relations. Against this background, Professor Downie's study is particularly timely. His analysis and extensive empirical data should contribute greatly to a better understanding of the issues in this field.

The author is Associate Professor of Industrial Relations in the School of Business, and Faculty Associate in the Industrial Relations Centre at Queen's University. His undergraduate work was done at Concordia College and his doctorate at the School of Business, University of Chicago.

The Director wishes to express his appreciation to Professor Downie for preparing this excellent study for publication, and to Mrs. C. Williams and Centre staff for their valuable editorial work.

> W. DONALD WOOD, Director,
> Industrial Relations Centre,
> Queen's University at Kingston, Ont.

November, 1970.

PREFACE

The importance of an issue can often be gauged by the amount of public debate it generates. Against this criterion, bi-national wage patterns and United States wage parity for the Canadian labour force are of major concern. Both aspects, of course, involve the extension of United States' practices and standards to the Canadian scene. It is not surprising, therefore, that these two essentially interrelated practices have been intensively discussed during the past decade. Not only labour and management but also government officials and academics have put their views on record. At this point in time, their positions have been fairly clearly established. In general, however, more heat than light has been generated. Paradoxically, wage parity and joint U.S.-Canadian labour agreements are perhaps the least understood phenomena in Canadian industrial relations.

The purpose of this book is threefold — (1) to develop the theoretical underpinnings for an understanding of bi-national wage patterns and, concurrently, of similar domestic phenomena; (2) to provide some public policy inputs on the issue; and (3) to provide more empirical data on the Canadian industrial relations system. The value of the manuscript may ultimately reside with the latter. Perhaps the greatest need in Canadian industrial relations is more information on our wage setting institutions. Regrettably, publication of the study has been delayed and, to some, this may reduce its value, It is part of my Ph.D. dissertation which was undertaken at the University of Chicago but the pressures of teaching and the performance of less productive academic activities have caused its delay. While the study has been modified and reduced somewhat, it has not been completely updated. Time will be the final arbiter of its worth.

There are numerous acknowledgements which should be made in a work of this size. However, the value of acknowledgements, it seems to me, is an indirect function of the number that are made. Therefore, only a few will be listed. My dissertation committee — Arnold R. Weber, Robert B. McKersie and Joel Seidman — provided not only useful criticism and insight but also encouragement, particularly when the size of the project became apparent. Their incisive comments always contained a positive flavour and were a source of inspiration. Also, I am particularly indebted to Arnold Weber for introducing me to the industrial relations area and interesting me in the topic at hand. The usual disclaimer, of course, is in order. The shortcomings of the manuscript clearly are personal. The financial aid of the University Research Program of the Canada Department of Labour provided the initial impetus for the study. Indeed, without its help the study could not have been initiated. Therefore, I am indebted to that body and also to the Queen's University Industrial Relations Centre for its continuing financial and moral support and, in particular, to its Director for his patience. Lastly, my wife and mother and father who put up with my moods, strange hours and other peccadillos while I worked on the study, deserve special mention. Their forebearance was remarkable and it is hoped that this visible evidence of endurance and labour will be a source of comfort and satisfaction to them.

BRYAN M. DOWNIE

Kingston, Ontario.
November, 1970.

CONTENTS

LIST OF TABLES

CHAPTER 1

INTRODUCTION

A broad variety of collective bargaining practices precipitated the search for new insights into union behavior and union-management negotiations. One of the most important of these has been the well-known phenomenon of pattern bargaining. This refers to the practice of using one agreement (often called the "key bargain") as a standard and model for many others. The existence of well-developed wage contours generated the familiar "political" construct of union wage policy by Arthur Ross.[1] The locus and boundaries of union wage comparisons and their role in negotiations are an important aspect of that theory. The notion is that pressures for following a pattern or to close a differential develop in situations where there is common ownership, centralized union bargaining, and where intra- and inter-union political struggles are important. A criterion of equity becomes the *sine qua non* in such situations. Wage comparisons and pattern following within an institutional orbit are the result. There are several aspects to this construct that merit investigation. The two that are of concern to this study are discussed below.

First, whether the political framework is an adequate explanation of the internal mechanisms of union decision-making and of wage patterns has not been thoroughly examined. While the industrial relations field is fairly replete with *a priori* argumentation, empirical contributions in the area of pattern bargaining have been quite rare, fairly limited in scope, and by no means definitive. Second, there has been little in the way of empirical investigation regarding the effect of structural aspects on the bargaining process itself. The substantive issues selected for comparison, the behavior of constituent groups, the procedural arrangements chosen to facilitate uniformity, and the implications for conflict resolution under various institutional variables, require further analysis and elaboration.

To this point, attention has been focused on bargaining relationships within conventional groupings — intra-industry, inter-industry and inter-area — within a domestic setting. Despite the existence of international unions with locals in both the United States and Canada, a detailed empirical investigation has yet to be made of the relationship between union policy and bargaining activity in the

---

1. Arthur M. Ross, *Trade Union Wage Policy* (Berkeley: University of California Press, 1948).

two countries.[2] The structural connection presents the interesting possibility of examining the practice and process of bargaining within a bi-national dimension. The focus of this study is solely on the above aspects.

The next two sections of this introductory chapter are devoted to the significance of this research and to a literature review, respectively. This is followed by a discussion of the orientation of the study.

THE SIGNIFICANCE OF THIS STUDY

Union wage policy and the collective bargaining process could be made more intelligible by an examination of specific wage patterns and the process through which changes are channeled. The implications for constructs of union wage policy are somewhat different from those enunciated in the political theory if well-developed wage contours develop where internal and external political pressures are relatively unimportant. A study of collective bargaining within a bi-national dimension, therefore, serves the purpose of extending and enriching theory and research on union wage policy and the key bargain phenomenon. Second, the systematic study of wage comparisons in the bargaining process is critical to an understanding of union-management negotiations. This is not to argue that wage comparisons determine wage rates. They may be, however, a major influence with regard to the bargaining agenda, strategies selected, the limits of the negotiating unit, and industrial peace. These all have implications for the bargaining theories that are beginning to emerge. Insights that have been derived thus far can be sharpened through a broader empirical base.

This study is of significance at an additional level. The existence in Canada of unions which have their headquarters in the U.S. has precipitated considerable national debate. This revolves around the question as to the relationship between U.S. and Canadian bargaining activity. Basically, a question of sovereignty is involved.[3] The discussion intensified before this study was com-

2. Shortly after the inception of this study an investigation of internationals was undertaken by Professor J. H. G. Crispo. The subject of collective bargaining is, however, treated in a general manner. Interviews were the primary source of information. See J. H. G. Crispo, *International Unionism: A Study in Canadian-American Relations* (Toronto: McGraw-Hill, 1967), Chapter 6.

3. There are a multitude of issues raised by the presence of internationals in Canada that are beyond the scope of this study. There is the question of their economic impact, Canadian unionism developing national objectives, union dues leaving the country, Canadian union members receiving adequate representation, and so on.

pleted with the signing of the 1967 UAW-Chrysler agreement. It purports to give Canadian workers parity of wages with their U.S. counterparts. The agreement was negotiated in the United States by officials in that country. An analysis of bargaining activity by internationals can produce valuable public policy inputs with regard to the issue. The locus of decision-making, the wage benchmarks chosen, the issues selected for transference, the structural arrangements devised, and the function of wage patterns in the bargaining process under international unionism, are all critical issues in the public policy context.

A Review of the Literature

The particular issue at hand, i.e. wage patterns, fits into a long-standing controversy with regard to union wage policy and collective wage determination. The issue revolves around a diverse, and essentially opposing, set of factors that have been designated as central in the formulation of union wage policy. The writings of two authors generated the controversy. The Dunlop approach stresses "economic" ("impersonal" or "market") forces as the primary determinant of union behavior.[4] This is opposed to the "political" ("institutional" or "structural") approach of Ross.[5] As others have pointed out, these are not mutually exclusive but can be clearly differentiated.[6] The purpose of this section is to define and discuss in a systematic manner the variables subsumed in each of these, and to review the contributions of other authors. A reading of the literature indicates that U.S.-Canada wage relationships can be viewed or analyzed in a number of different ways.

The Ross-Dunlop Controversy

The Ross construct, which was published in 1948, was a reaction against two streams of thought — traditional wage theory and a theory of union wage policy which has an economic rationale as its base. According to the marginal productivity theory, in the long run and under competitive conditions, wage levels will tend to equality, reflecting only differences in "skill mix" and differences in the cost-of-living in various communities. Movement of capital

4. John T. Dunlop, *Wage Determination Under Trade Unions* (New York: Augustus M. Kelley, 1950).

5. Ross was not the first to develop this treatment but his is the most lucid statement of the political approach. See also Fredrick Harbison, "A Plan for Fundamental Research in Labor Relations," *American Economic Review*, XXXVII, Supplement (May 1947), pp. 379-82.

6. See Walter Galenson and Seymour Lipset, *Labor and Trade Unionism* (New York: John Wiley and Sons, 1960), p. 1.

and labor is the mechanism which eliminates differentials and in the process the output of the economy is increased. Thus, *ceteris paribus,* if wages in an area are relatively low, workers will move to higher wage areas where their marginal contribution is greater. Such movements if large enough will eliminate existing wage differentials. Ross rejected this as a viable explanation of equalizing tendencies.

Secondly, he rejected the Dunlop thesis that unions consider the employment effect of their wage demands. The latter, in 1944, was the first to analyze trade union wage policy in a comprehensive manner. Extrapolating from the theory of the firm, he argued that a union must be trying to maximize some wage or employment dimension of its membership, or some optimum combination of both. This implied that, with the exception of simply maximizing the wage rate, the union had to make some estimation of the elasticity of demand for membership services. Dunlop, like Ross, did not argue that his assertions applied to all cases but only to most of the cases. In a second edition six years later, he allowed some scope to political pressures but emphasized that the principal determinants of union wage policy are found in the interrelations of wages, costs, product prices and employer profits.[7]

During the postwar years the economy experienced a number of major wage "rounds" and it was against this background that Ross proposed a theoretical reconstruction.[8] The central proposition was that a trade union is a political agency operating in an economic environment.[9] In this environment the interests of various constituent groups must be resolved. The union leadership is concerned with reconciling these conflicting pressures for two reasons — (1) to maintain their political position, and (2) to maintain a viable organization. He did not argue that the goals of the leadership and membership were in conflict. Instead, the framework rests on the premise that real policy-making resides with the leadership who are responsible for maintaining a political equilibrium. Union policy, then, is strongly influenced by political considerations and it is this environment that leads to wage equalization tendencies and well-developed wage contours.

Political pressures are engendered by membership "orbits of coercive comparison" with the comparisons doubly coercive in the

---

7. Dunlop, *Wage Determination Under Trade Unions,* pp. iii-vi.
8. He did not argue that market forces have no significance, but only that they do not have a compelling effect. For a restatement see Arthur M. Ross, "The External Wage Structure," in *New Concepts in Wage Determination,* George W. Taylor and Frank C. Pierson, eds. (New York: McGraw-Hill, 1957), pp. 173-205.
9. Ross, *Trade Union Wage Policy,* p. 18.

face of institutional rivalry. There is, according to Ross, an internal and external aspect to both of these. He proposed several dimensions along which workers make their equity comparisons — (1) wages paid in the local labor market; (2) wages paid in the same product market; (3) bargains negotiated at other locals in the same union, with the comparisons far more compelling if there is centralized bargaining within the union; (4) wages paid in other establishments of the same firm; and (5) wages paid by closely related unions.[10]

As far as the orbits are concerned, Ross de-emphasized the importance of the local labor market as a union consideration.[11] In addition, the product market is of secondary importance.[12] By far the most compelling forces for equalization, he hypothesized, are institutional — centralized union bargaining, common ownership of establishments, and union rivalry.[13] With regard to the first of these, when an international union not only requires the submission of a settlement for ratification, but actively participates in negotiations, uniform settlements are the likely result. Common ownership makes differentials less tolerable and the "equal pay for equal work" slogan becomes compelling. Union rivalry can take the form of intra-union strife, jurisdictional rivalry, and rivalry among the leaders of the labor movement. There is an offensive and defensive aspect to the comparisons, particularly in the case of jurisdictional rivalry. In order to preserve his position a union leader may break the equilibrium and move out in front. Alternatively, if a rival union has taken the offensive, the union leader must restore the equilibrium at the higher level.

Ross also argued that equalizing tendencies are directed toward equalization of adjustments as often as equalization of rates.[14] In any case, the more coercive the comparisons, the greater the pressure on union leaders to achieve at least wage increases comparable to the reference group and the more likely is pattern bargaining.[15] That is, the pressures must be reconciled in the bargaining process with the traditional market forces of supply and demand playing a secondary role. In short, invidious comparisons

10. Ross, *Trade Union Wage Policy*, pp. 53-64.

11. *Ibid.*, p. 53.

12. *Ibid.*, pp. 54-5.

13. *Ibid.*, pp. 18 and 55. He hypothesized further that there would be more uniformity with government participation.

14. *Ibid.*, p. 46. For a concurring opinion see William G. Bowen, *The Wage-Price Issue: A Theoretical Analysis* (Princeton, N.J.: Princeton University Press, 1960), p. 130.

15. No attempt has been made to account for the actions of pattern originators.

by the union based on institutional factors will be manifested in union policy and will play a central role in the negotiation process and in the development of wage patterns.

The two basic theories were originally treated as distinct and fairly comprehensive explanations of union wage policy. Others[16] have rejected this bifurcation and have argued that both forces are operative; that an eclectic approach is more appropriate. Writing in a later period the issue was partially joined by the two originators. Dunlop noted — "It is indeed appropriate to study the processes, procedures, and influences which determine decisions in these organizations and the techniques they employ in agreement making . . . but this subject does not pre-empt the theory of wages."[17] Ross conceded that a purely political theory of wages was not implied but that institutional pressures operate within a given periphery.[18]

Empirical and Theoretical Contributions

The empirical record is not clear despite a substantial number of studies on union wage policy and related topics. Major studies have been conducted which support, or partially support, both authors. In studies by Shultz of union policy in the shoe industry, Shultz and Meyers of the shoe and textile industries, and Rees of the steel industry, it has been maintained that union leaders are sensitive to the employment effects of their wage policies.[19] Reynolds incorporates both sets of influences in explaining his findings on wage structure in the New Haven labor market.[20] Economic forces affecting the relative ability of firms to pay, explain persisting wage differentials. Coercive comparisons, however, generalize wage adjustments within the local labor market after the application of a national pattern to a local employer. In a more recent empirical

---

16. See Melvin W. Reder, "The Theory of Union Wage Policy," *The Review of Economics and Statistics*, XXXIV (February, 1952) and Albert Rees, "Union Wage Policies," *Interpreting the Labor Movement* (Madison: Industrial Relations Research Association, Publication No. 9, 1952), pp. 130-48.

17. John T. Dunlop, "The Task of Contemporary Wage Theory," in *New Concepts in Wage Determination*, p. 127.

18. Ross, "The External Wage Structure," p. 187.

19. George P. Shultz, *Pressures on Wage Decisions: A Case Study in the Shoe Industry* (New York: John Wiley and Sons, 1950); George P. Shultz and Charles A. Meyers, "Union Wage Decisions and Employment," *American Economic Review*, XL (June, 1950), pp. 362-80; and Albert Rees, "Post-War Wage Determination in the Basic Steel Industry," *American Economic Review*, XLI (June, 1951). pp. 389-404.

20. Lloyd Reynolds, *The Structure of Labor Markets* (New York: Harper and Brothers, 1951).

contribution on the subject, Levinson[21] concentrates on the impact of political, economic, and "pure power" variables on money wage levels, in six West Coast industries. He concludes from a detailed case analysis that all three forces had an impact.

Two noteworthy studies[22] have approached the question by examining collective bargaining within the jurisdictions of two major unions in the United States. Seltzer examined pattern bargaining by the Steelworkers while Levinson analyzed the same phenomenon as practised by the United Auto Workers. The early postwar period was the focus of both studies. The findings were essentially complementary. Each found considerable flexibility in the union's approach to pattern bargaining. Levinson stressed that neither the economic nor the political hypotheses alone provides an adequate frame of reference. Seltzer took particular issue with the Ross hypothesis that the influences determining wages run in political more often than geographical or industrial orbits. Both emphasized that, when economic conditions were generally favorable, the key bargain was widely emulated. It was, however, rarely exceeded. In addition, Seltzer found that, while union policy built in greater degrees of uniformity, wage patterns pre-date unionism in the basic steel industry. This he attributes to a larger business strategy that includes price as well as wage synchronization. It can be explained as inherent in the economic nature of the industry — the concentration of production in a small number of firms, the tradition of price leadership, wide cyclical fluctuations in production, and the importance of the labor cost ratio because of integration of production. This results in wage and price changes being considered together. In a later study, Reynolds and Taft offer a similar explanation.[23]

With the empirical record unclear some authors[24] stress that bargaining activity takes place within a range of discretion. That is, there are limits that survival conditions impose upon the wage rate a firm can pay. Within those limits or margin of choice, disputes are settled or strikes called, wages are equalized or differentiated, and so on. The political framework may or may not be an appropriate

21. Harold M. Levinson, *Determining Forces in Collective Wage Bargaining* (New York: John Wiley and Sons, 1966).

22. George Seltzer, "Pattern Bargaining and the United Steelworkers," *Journal of Political Economy,* LIX (August, 1951), pp. 319-31; and Harold M. Levinson, "Pattern Bargaining: A Case Study of the Automobile Workers," *Quarterly Journal of Economics,* LXXIV (May, 1960), pp. 296-317.

23. Lloyd Reynolds and Cynthia H. Taft, *The Evolution of Wage Structure* (New Haven: Yale University Press, 1956), p. 51.

24. For the best treatment see Reder, "The Theory of Union Wage Policy".

explanation of union policy and wage patterns within the designated range. The limits may be narrow or fairly broad. They will not uniquely determine the wage rate but the narrower the limits the more decisive will economic considerations be. The lower limit is placed by the minimum wage the union needs to hold together its membership, and the firm to hold its labor force. The upper limit will be higher the more inelastic the labor demand, i.e., the smaller the ratio of labor costs to total costs, the greater the market power a firm possesses, the smaller the extent of non-union competition, and the greater the difficulty of substituting other factors of production for union labor. Under the first condition a large wage increase will have little effect on the price of the product and, therefore, on sales and employment. Under the second, when the firm possesses some product market power a wage increase may be passed on to the consumer with a smaller loss in revenue. Non-union firms may not experience the same factor price increases, however, and therefore the third condition may assume importance. Non-union firms would expand to the detriment of production and employment in unionized firms. Under the fourth condition, if union labor is essential, perhaps because the technology requires fixed manning, a given wage increase will have a smaller effect on employment, at least in the short run. These will all influence the upper limit, therefore, and the margin of discretion within which the parties negotiate.

Significantly, Slichter, Livernash, and Healy[25] note that wage standardization takes place under the following favorable circumstances — substantial union organization, a homogeneous product or fairly simple product structures, a limited degree of price competition in the product market, locational stability as contrasted with locational fluidity, national instead of local product markets, and large multi-unit companies versus small companies. These describe conditions where the upper limit would be relatively high. This is supplemented by the research on pattern bargaining by Levinson and Seltzer which revealed that the diversity in wage levels and wage changes is greatest for firms that lie farthest, geographically and industrially, from the heart of the union's jurisdiction. Also, it was found that small firms experience greater deviations from the key bargain.

Bowen[26] draws an important distinction between two types of "wage leadership". Two equivalent changes in wage rates may be "barometric" or "coercive". Equivalent wage adjustments may result

25. Sumner Slichter, James Healy, and Robert Livernash, *The Impact of Collective Bargaining on Management* (Washington: The Brookings Institution, 1960), pp. 607-21.
26. Bowen, *The Wage Price Issue*, pp. 129-41.

either because the firms are subject to the same economic pressures and respond in the same way, or because an equivalent wage adjustment at a key firm is granted even though the wage pressures are dissimilar. It is in the latter case, where exogenous wage pressures are not the same, that an independent influence on the wage adjustment process can be attributed to wage comparisons. He also notes that, while wage comparisons take place in a non-union setting, the appearance of a union extends the avenue and boundaries of impact. In the case of collective bargaining, the local labor market is of relatively less importance, while industry and even inter-industry comparisons may gain in importance. Wages being paid by the firm's competitors in the product market serve as the relevant comparison for determining the feasibility or opportunity cost of a comparable wage increase. The local labor market will be most relevant in determining the pressures exerted on the firm. In the same vein, Cartter[27] notes that pattern bargaining is common in industries which meet the following three conditions — (1) the industry is composed of a relatively small number of firms; (2) the product is sold on a national basis, so that relative unit labor costs are vitally important to the companies; and (3) there is a high degree of centralized decision-making within the union organization.

Broader approaches or different lines of development have been undertaken which also circumvent the issue of political versus economic forces. There is, nevertheless, a relationship to the controversy. Chamberlain[28] views bargaining as a power relationship and has attempted to develop an understanding of the bargaining process through a concept of bargaining power. For each party this is the ratio of the other party's costs of disagreement to their costs of agreement. The higher the ratio the greater the bargaining power, i.e., the greater the willingness of the other party to agree to one's own terms. Both the economic and political environment will affect the ratio for each side. If a union leader is motivated to obtain a pattern increase, as Ross indicates, a below pattern settlement will entail very high costs of agreement. This will reduce the bargaining power ratio for management. At the same time, the union power position would be strengthened because management's costs of disagreement would presumably be high due to the willingness of the membership to strike for a considerable duration over a below-pattern offer.

27. Allan Cartter, *Theory of Wages and Employment* (Homewood, Ill.: Richard D. Irwin, 1959), pp. 132-33.
28. Neil Chamberlain, *Labor* (New York: McGraw-Hill, 1958), pp. 97-126 and 377-78; also Neil Chamberlain and James Kuhn, *Collective Bargaining* (New York: McGraw-Hill, 1965), pp. 162-190. For a more sophisticated treatment see J. Pen, "A General Theory of Bargaining," *American Economic Review*, XLII (March, 1952), pp. 24-42.

In a more useful approach Walton and McKersie[29] analyze union and management preferences within a range of uncertainty. They focus on why particular issues are selected and how union-management differences are handled and settled. The economic environment will determine the range of choice and may affect the utility curves of both parties. An external wage pattern, similarly, may influence each negotiator's preference function. The economic and political parameters within this framework, however, are taken as given. The emphasis is then on manipulative behavioral tactics that are used to ascertain the other party's resistance point and to change his perceptions. A pattern settlement may serve as a focal point to one side or the other, or both, and describe a small positive or negative range. In some studies[30] it has also been observed that well-developed pattern relationships may be an important structural factor in union-management accommodation. Such studies do not suggest that pattern bargaining is the major factor in union-management accommodation. The major causes of industrial peace undoubtedly go much deeper.[31] In some industries, for example, it has been found that the application of external patterns may be a source of conflict.[32] The important point is that patterns may be an important aspect in this context.

Another line of development has been the analysis of bargaining structure. This area has received some detailed attention and is directly related to this study. Pattern bargaining (domestic or bi-national) is simply one dimension along a continuum of wage relationships. Of concern is the fact that bargains may be extended beyond the unit certified by government agencies and beyond those within which formal collective bargaining takes place. This extension can take the form of multi-plant bargaining, pattern bargaining, multi-employer bargaining, or some other consolidated form. According to the literature, the factors that circumscribe the unit of direct impact vary. Generally, however, in order to "take wages out of competition" industrial unions have pressed for bargaining structures which encompass a given product market either through in-

29. Richard Walton and Robert McKersie, *A Behavioral Theory of Labor Negotiations: An Analysis of a Social Interaction System* (New York: McGraw-Hill, 1965).

30. See, for example, F. H. Harbison and J. R. Coleman, *Goals and Strategy in Collective Bargaining* (New York: Harper and Row, 1951).

31. For the major study in this area see C. S. Golden and V. D. Parker, eds., *Causes of Industrial Peace under Collective Bargaining* (New York: Harper and Row, 1955).

32. Robert McKersie, "Structural Factors and Negotiations in the International Harvester Company," in *The Structure of Collective Bargaining,* Arnold R. Weber, ed. (New York: The Free Press of Glencoe, 1961), pp. 279-306.

creasing the scope of the negotiating unit or by increasing the area of direct impact of a settlement.[33] The locus of decision-making among different units may, however, vary with the issue being considered by the parties.

A brief summary is in order. Internal organizational pressures, according to the political construct, are the mechanisms linking one bargain with another. The pressures come from the union side and patterns run in political or institutional, more often than geographic and industrial, orbits. Those stressing economic forces emphasize that patterns may exist but that those patterns which persist will be compatible with the economic survival conditions of the firms involved. If not, they will be terminated or attenuated in some way. The economic variables that seem to be of significance in establishing limits are — the scope of the product market, industrial structure, union membership strength, and the labor cost ratio.[34] Further, the propensity for wage leadership may be inherent in the economic nature of some industries. Even according to this view, however, political factors may be important in terms of bargaining structure, behavioral tactics, conflict resolution, and so forth.

Research Orientation

Despite the synthesis of the Dunlop-Ross controversy, pattern bargaining remains an important issue. Different approaches and a more comprehensive empirical base are essential. Accordingly, this study explores and evaluates the reasons for and existence of bi-national wage contours. The focus is on the practice and process of collective bargaining in five Canadian industries in which international unions have jurisdiction.

The political approach, although couched in terms of a national framework, could conceivably be extended to North American dimensions. By extension of the theory there are three independent variables which are adaptable to U.S.-Canada dimensions. Firstly, the existence or absence of U.S. subsidiary plants in a Canadian industry. Secondly, the degree to which union bargaining is centralized in the U.S.-Canada context. Thirdly, the degree of intra- and

---

33. For a discussion of the importance of market factors on bargaining structure see Arnold R. Weber, "Stability and Change in the Structure of Bargaining," in *Challenges to Collective Bargaining*, Lloyd Ulman, ed. (Englewood Cliffs, N.J.: Prentice-Hall 1967), pp. 15-17.

34. The labor cost ratio is important in two ways. If it is low a firm may put up less resistance to union demands. If it is fairly high, firms may prefer a standardization policy. Indeed, unions negotiating in industries where labor costs are a large part of total costs often press for uniform rates or labor costs. If concessions were made at one firm other firms would insist on concessions, as well.

inter-union rivalry in a Canadian industry. An international may press for the U.S. pattern to reduce this rivalry. Or, this type of pressure should intensify comparisons which find their source in some other factor(s).

The approach used entailed analyzing the bargaining process in a selected sample of industries over a long period of time and within the framework of the political and economic variables. The industries were examined in terms of U.S. control, union structure, and union rivalry to determine the orbits of coercive comparison that ought to be manifested in collective bargaining. They were analyzed as well to determine at what periods political rivalry was strongest. Then, the process and practice of collective bargaining in the industries was examined to determine if comparisons manifested themselves in negotiatons, on the bargaining agenda, and in negotiated settlements. In selecting tnis approach the basis of judgment was the nature of the problem and availability of data. It was selected because it offers important advantages. It suffers some important disadvantages, as well, which will be noted below. For the purposes at hand, however, it is a fruitful approach. Firstly, data was available in a number of large unions for their major sets of negotiations. Secondly, it allowed an intensive investigation of the importance of union coercive comparisons in the bargaining process, the behavior of constituent groups (including employers and government), and the issues selected for comparison. To this point, these aspects have often been ignored. Thirdly, it was possible to evaluate and assess any evolution or change in the bargaining process through time. That is, it emphasizes interactions through time including an evaluation of the pre-union period. Fourthly, it was particularly amenable to preserving the unitary character between relationships and processes. This is important in the Ross framework. Finally, it was the most promising approach in terms of uncovering all possible interrelationships.

The major disadvantage is that the approach falls back on a qualitative appraisal and, to a considerable extent, on an intuitive "feel" of the forces in operation. This does not prevent value insights, however. The following sections discuss research methods, the data used and the sample.

Research Methods

A theoretical framework was developed at the beginning of the research to avoid, in so far as possible, speculations made on the spot to fit the peculiarities of each case. The schema was used to help assess — (1) the importance of the political and economic factors in the bargaining process, (2) the circumstances under which each set is of paramount importance, and (3) the combination of these which is especially potent. Those in the political classification were the three discussed above. The variables included in the economic environment were — the scope of the product market, product market structure, union membership strength in Canada, the significance of labor costs, and plant location (the local labor market). Cases were selected and assessed against this frame of reference.

Chapters 2 to 6 undertake the kind of analysis suggested above for five industries — pulp and paper, autos, meat packing, steel and iron ore — which have good qualitative data and which contain a variety of organizational and economic situations. During the period under review, the international unions having jurisdiction in these industries were — the United Packinghouse Workers; the United Steelworkers (in both steel and iron ore); the United Automobile Workers; the International Brotherhood of Pulp, Sulphite and Paper Mill Workers and the United Papermakers and Paperworkers.

In each case, detailed analyses of collective bargaining are presented. The time period selected for the most intensive analysis was 1953 to 1962. This period was long enough to include a number of bargaining rounds in each case and, therefore, to assess any evolution in the bargaining relationships. In those cases where binational relationships existed, the time perspective was broadened to encompass the pre-union period. Post 1962 developments were also included when of importance.

In each case, every effort was made to develop an understanding of the potentially important environmental variables plus such factors as the homogeneity and militancy of the membership, the relationship between the U.S. and Canadian branches of the union, and employer and government policy. To give perspective, in each chapter the nominal U.S.-Canada differential in common labor and skilled wage rates in both countries was presented. It should be stressed, however, that this was done solely as a convenient frame of reference.

A detailed analysis of settlements in the five industries in comparison with the key bargain in the relevant U.S. industry was undertaken. The objective of this part of the analysis was to determine whether or not an "organic" connection existed between the relevant settlements on the two sides of the border. Of concern were the uniformities and deviations from the key bargain(s) in the U.S. with respect to — (1) the amount of the increase; (2) fringe benefit and wage related increases; and (3) the timing of settlements. Key bargains in the U.S. were identified largely on the basis of policy statements made by union officials and/or by past collective bargaining history. Both absolute and percentage changes were compared.[35] Fringe benefits were considered separately. A similar settlement could be one consisting of either identical benefits or an equivalent total "package" of benefits regardless of their specific form. There are grounds for supporting either point of view. It is often difficult,

—13—

however, to obtain an accurate estimation of the cost of fringe items and even when available they are sometimes misleadingly manipulated. When available, nevertheless, cost data were included.

The following were used as criteria in assessing the existence and strength of connections:

1. The degree to which percentage and/or absolute wage increases secured in Canada conform to the key bargain in the U.S.
2. The degree to which the nature of fringe changes conform.
3. The extent to which Canadian bargains are linked to their U.S. counterpart by a perceptible temporal chain.
4. The extent to which qualitative analysis substantiates the existence of any connection.

The following dimensions of the bargaining process were considered — (1) the formulation of union demands; (2) the locus of union pressure, if any, for U.S. patterns; (3) the timing and length of Canadian negotiations in relation to those in the U.S.; (4) the role of U.S. union and corporate officials in Canadian negotiations; (5) the issues that were introduced into negotiations and an assessment of the barriers to settlement; (6) the effect of U.S. standards being introduced into negotiations; and (7) the role of the Canadian conciliaton process as it relates to this study.[36]

---

35. The data were not adjusted for differences in the cost-of-living. The movement of comparable price indexes in the two countries has been very similar throughout the postwar period. Further, on the matter of price relationships between the two countries a Canadian study dealing with the comparable economic performance of the two countries stated — "On balance, it is not likely that a price adjustment would materially alter the results." See J. Brecher and S. Reisman, *Canada - United States Economic Relations* (Ottawa: Queen's Printer, 1957), p. 225.

36. Canadian public policy toward labor resembles, indeed reflects, the United States approach. As in the U.S., there is a multiple loci of public policy, both the federal and provincial governments being separate and distinct jurisdictions. Unlike the United States, however, the major locus of policy for constitutional reasons is at the provincial rather than the federal level. With the exception of a few industries, the provinces are responsible for certification, unfair labor practices, and dispute settlement in industries within their boundaries. Another major difference in Canadian legislation has been the inclusion of dispute settlement procedures which must be complied with before legal strike or lockout action can take place. In theory, the parties generally must go through a two stage conciliation process — a conciliation officer followed by a conciliation board. Thus, conciliation complicates negotiations even when there is single-plant bargaining and the problem becomes magnified when the negotiations involve plants which are located in more than one province. Just as vital is the fact that conciliation boards make and report recommendations for settlement. The parties are not required to accept the recommendations but they are designed to bring public opinion to bear on a dispute. In many cases board recommendations have had a substantive effect on settlements. For any union attempting to follow a U.S. pattern the procedures could act as a barrier.

At the end of each industry analysis, an overall assessment was made with regard to the relationships, union policy, and the role of U.S. standards in the bargaining process. An evaluation was made of the apparent reasons for the relationships. The concern was with analyzing, to the extent possible, the relevant charactetristics as they appeared in interaction. The final chapter draws on the five case studies and the available literature for an appraisal of the relationships and the bargaining process. The dimensions and strength of the bargaining relationships were consolidated in a single table to obtain an overall view. The data on the behavior of constituent groups were tied together and assessed.

Sources and Quality of Data

In each case, data were obtained on negotiated base rates and fringe benefits for each major settlement from World War II to 1962. A significant body of evidence was accumulated for years previous to this. The data in Canada came largely from the actual memoranda of agreement. These were contained in union files. U.S. data and information came from the *Monthly Labor Review,* Bureau of Labor Statistics *Wage Chronologies* and similar sources. In some cases this was supplemented by data contained in union files in both countries.

Information on the institutional environment and the bargaining process was derived from transcripts of record, conciliation briefs and reports, minutes of union meetings, proceedings of Canadian and international union conventions, union and management correspondence and, to some extent, from secondary sources. The reliability of the data recorded and the analysis of data were checked through personal interviews with management and union officials. Despite this, a caveat is in order. The data is a highly qualitative type of supporting evidence. The reader can only be assured that the data was selected and analyzed with great care. Tentative conclusions constructed in light of the data are construed to be no more than that.

The Industries Selected

One major problem was keeping the analysis within narrow enough limits to be researchable while at the same time broad enough to be useful. A sample containing a variety of organizational and economic situations between and within the industries was the desideratum. The following criteria were used when selecting the mix of industries — (1) variation from case to case in political and economic factors; (2) the existence of some potential for a bi-national orbit in each case; (3) the representation of important Canadian sectors; and (4) data availability and access. After intensive preliminary work, the five industries noted above were selected. They represent various sectors with a potential range of experience.

Table 1-1 reveals the strengths and weaknesses of the selection. It presents in capsule form the nature of each of the political and economic factors. There is some variation from case to case. There is some potential for bi-national relationships in each industry. The selection of the basic steel and iron ore industries allowed an assessment of policy in a common union (the Steelworkers) in two industries where the environment is not precisely the same.

In the meat packing industry, one major firm (Swift Canadian) is U.S. owned. It accounts for approximately 15 per cent of Canadian output. Centralized union bargaining in the U.S. - Canada context was absent and internal and external rivalry fairly weak. One small fabricating plant in the steel industry is owned by Republic Steel. Centralized bargaining and union rivalry are relatively unimportant, however. The same holds true of the iron ore industry with one exception. It is highly dependent upon and, in some cases, vertically integrated with the U.S. steel industry. Most of the major firms are U.S. controlled. Marmoraton Mine is owned and managed by Bethlehem Steel. At most of the other mines, however, there are a multiplicity of interests or they are operated by a managing firm. In the auto industry, moderate internal rivalry existed just prior to 1953. The situation stabilized thereafter, however. Centralized bargaining was not of great importance during the early postwar years. The firms are, however, the same on both sides of the border. There is a mix of Canadian, U.S., and foreign owned companies in the pulp and paper industry. External rivalry is present. There are three major unions in the industry — the two internationals plus one Canadian union (the Pulp and Paper Workers' Federation). The latter is a Quebec-based union and is affiliated with a rival federation of labor. U.S. officials in the international unions have traditionally participated in and supervised Canadian negotiations.

Two of the industries are in the non-durable goods sector, two in durable goods, and one in the mining sector. With regard to plant location, the iron ore and newsprint industries, by and large, are located in isolated communities with company towns being a fairly common characteristic. Local labor market conditions, therefore, vary fairly widely. In both industries, there are cases where the facilities are in close proximity to those in the United States. In the other three industries plants are located for the most part in heavily populated areas. Historically, the Canadian auto industry was centered in Windsor which is contiguous to Detroit. Labor costs

Table 1-1—POTENTIAL FACTORS SHAPING BI-NATIONAL RELATIONSHIPS

Industry	Political Factors			Economic Factors				
	U.S. Ownership	Centralized Union Bargaining	Union Rivalry	Product Market Scope	Industrial Structure	Labor Costs	Non-union Competition	Plant Location
Meat Packing	One firm — Swift Canadian (15% of mkt.)	No	External — weak; Internal — moderate	Local or Regional	Highly Competitive	Significant	Yes	Diffuse; high and low wage areas
Steel	One peripheral firm — Union Drawn	No	External — weak; Internal — moderate	Essentially Domestic — some U.S. imports and exports	Small no. of large firms	Significant	Yes	Diffuse; generally high wage areas
Iron Ore	90%	No	External — weak; Internal — little	Substantial exports to U.S.	Small no. of firms; integrated with U.S. steel industry	Low	No	Diffuse; high and low wage areas
Autos	100%	Yes — after 1950	External — weak; Internal — strong prior to 1953	Domestic (until 1965)	Small no. of large firms	Significant	No	Geographically concentrated high wage area
Pulp and Paper	40%	Yes	External — strong; Internal — moderate	Substantial exports to U.S.	Small no. of large firms	Fairly Significant	No	Diffuse; high and low wage areas

are extremely low in the iron ore industry, fairly significant in the paper industry, and significant in the other three industries.

It should be noted that the sample represents a fairly narrow range in terms of union strength and product market constraints. The industries are all high in union strength. The degree ranges from 75 to 80 per cent in basic steel and meat packing, to 100 per cent in the other industries. The steel, auto, and paper industries are highly concentrated and the iron ore industry is largely "captive". The major firms are relatively large and the scope of the product market is national or international. Almost all of Canada's paper production goes to the United States. Steel exports to and imports from the U.S. are fairly sizeable in terms of the Canadian industry. They have been in the order of 10 to 15 per cent of Canadian output. The market for Canadian auto production, up to the 1960's, was largely domestic; in 1965, however, the Canada-U.S. auto pact allowed Canadian producers to rationalize production and export duty free to the United States. Only meat packing represents an industry where there are few barriers to entry and the product market is generally local or regional in scope. Four of the industries, therefore, represent situations where the economic environment would suggest some overlap in negotiated settlements.

The sample, then, falls short of representing the full perspective of bargaining environments. It is a very small sample of Canadian industry and, if time and data permitted, it would have been desirable to explore a variety of other industries. Leading candidates would be local product market-craft union industries such as construction, plus industries in the service and transportation sectors. As it is, rigorous testing is prohibited and broad extrapolations are unwarranted. The depth of insight afforded, however, is substantial. From the analysis, plausible conclusions can be formulated and yield at least some preliminary hypotheses.

CHAPTER 2

THE PRIMARY PULP AND PAPER INDUSTRY

INDUSTRIAL BACKGROUND

One of the difficulties in examining collective bargaining in pulp and paper is the broad scope of the industry. It actually encompasses a number of separate, but in some cases overlapping, and related industries. All plants engaged in the manufacture of pulp, paper and board, and specialty and fine papers make up the industry. But thousands of grades of paper and board can be distinguished as to character and quality, and wood pulps can be identified according to their method of production. The paper component can be broken down into a few broad categories with newsprint, book, tissue, wrapping, and writing papers constituting the basic types. Faced with the problem of keeping the analysis within manageable proportions, the study only deals with what can be called the primary or basic pulp and paper industry, i.e., those firms engaged primarily in the manufacture of groundwood, sulphite, sulphate and soda pulp, newsprint, wrapping, building and miscellaneous heavy papers, and paperboards. It will exclude those firms engaged principally in converting paper stock into specialty and fine paper products. Further, within the basic industry, the focal point of the analysis will be on the pulp and newsprint sector because of the continental trade pattern which has evolved for those two products and, secondly, because newsprint production is by far the largest component of Canadian paper production.

While an analysis concentrated on the primary sector in general and the pulp and newsprint component in particular is advisable for research purposes, a distinct dichotomy cannot always be easily drawn between the basic and converting ends of the industry. The essential similarity of production techniques and basic raw materials, together with the prevalence of multi-product producers and the possibilities of grade shifting, makes any division difficult. Some overlapping, therefore, is unavoidable.

While the Canadian industry dates back to the 1800's, it was not until after 1910 that it began to grow to significant proportions. The mold of the North American market was, however, cast by 1920. The series of events which shaped the industry are of more than mere historical interest; they are important as a determining factor with regard to U.S. capital investment in the Canadian industry and in the expansion of two U.S. paper unions to international dimensions. A few historical aspects should therefore be noted.[1]

In the late 1900's American forests, which were providing the raw material for U.S. paper mills, were in the initial stages of depletion. The Canadian industry was small and, by and large, producing for domestic consumption. At this point U.S. newspaper publishers foreseeing a critical shortage of newsprint saw expansion of the Canadian industry as a solution but, faced with substantial import duties, the Canadian industry could not compete in the U.S. market. To remove this barrier U.S. newspaper publishers began lobbying Washington for the complete removal of duties on Canadian pulp and newsprint imports. Predictably U.S. producers strongly opposed such a move. After a battle of considerable length the American newspaper publishers emerged completely victorious in 1913 with the passage of the Underwood Tariff by the Wilson Administration. Under the terms of the bill and one passed two years earlier, Canadian newsprint, wood pulp, and pulpwood were admitted to the U.S. free of any tariff regulations. The free entry situation was the primary factor accounting for the spectacular growth of the Canadian industry. Free access to the large U.S. market made expansion on a new scale possible and also shaped the expansion predominantly along newsprint and pulp lines.

The free entry provision, plus the policies of provincial governments, also radically affected the development and structure of the U.S. industry. Faced with the depletion of forests in the Eastern United States, free entry of Canadian newsprint, and provincial embargoes on pulpwood, the large American newsprint companies began to realize that it was impossible for them to compete effectively with Canadian newsprint and converted the machines to the manufacture of various types of fine papers and kraft, on which they still enjoyed high tariff protection from Canadian competition. At the same time many of these U.S. companies built newsprint mills in Quebec, Ontario, and to a lesser extent in some other provinces, exporting most of their production to the American market. The newsprint segment of the U.S. industry, while it diminished, did not disappear. Production shifted not only to Canada but to the U.S. West Coast, as well, because of its large and relatively cheap forest reserves. Additionally, some companies continued to produce news-

---

1. The historical information was obtained from the following sources: W. E. Greening, *Paper Makers in Canada: A Record of Fifty Years' Achievement* (International Brotherhood of Paper Makers, 1952); John A. Guthrie, *The Economics of Pulp and Paper* (Pullman, Washington: State College of Washington Press, 1950); Royal Commission on Canada's Economic Prospects, The Forest Study Group, *The Outlook for the Canadian Forest Industry* (Ottawa: Queen's Printer, 1957).

print in the Eastern and Lake States. With the exception of an expansion of the industry in the U.S. South in later years, the configuration and structure of the North American industry had been determined by the 1920's. It featured U.S. companies operating on both sides of the border with the Canadian industry dominating the newsprint market.

There are several important features with regard to the size and production patterns of the basic industry in both countries which must be noted. Statistics released by the Canadian Pulp and Paper Association for 1954 are descriptive and typical of Canada's position for the entire post World War II period.[2] Canadian newsprint production in 1954 totalled almost 6 million tons. This comprised about 60 per cent of the total end-product of the entire Canadian industry and was five times as great as the newsprint production of the U.S. industry. In terms of markets, about 7 per cent of the shipments went to domestic consumers, almost 82 per cent to the U.S. market, and the remaining 11 per cent were exported to about 65 other countries. Wood pulp accounted for 22.6 per cent of production in 1954 with almost 77 per cent going to the United States. The remainder of the industry's products, made up of a wide range of papers and paperboards, comprised only about one-fifth of its end-product output.

Two facts are clear from this. Firstly, newsprint and pulp production in Canada dominate the country's pulp and paper industry and, secondly, not only is the export of newsprint and pulp large in terms of Canadian dimensions, but it also makes up a large portion of U.S. consumption. Table 2-1, U.S. Newsprint Supply and Sources, indicates the importance of Canadian newsprint in the U.S. market.

Because of continental specialization and varying tariff regulations, the product structure of the Canadian pulp and paper industry is somewhat unlike that of the U.S. industry. The Canadian and U.S. sectors do produce all major paper products. The comparative structures of the industries are worth noting, however, because of the importance of this on the type of continental competition that exists. From Table 2-2 it is clear that the U.S. industry has evolved to a position where paperboard and fine and wrapping papers constitute the largest portion of the industry with newsprint production of secondary importance. A diametrically opposite situation exists in Canada. Despite these differences in product structure, Canadian and U.S. mills in the basic portion of the industry are in competition

---

2. Canadian Pulp and Paper Association, *Submission to Royal Commission on Canada's Economic Prospects,* January 1956, p. 15.

Table 2-1

SUPPLY AND SOURCES OF NEWSPRINT, UNITED STATES, SELECTED YEARS, 1913-62
(tons)

Year	Canada	U.S.A.	Europe	Total
1913	218,000	1,255,000	——	1,473,000
1930	2,145,471	1,272,168	134,180	3,551,819
1950	4,748,228	1,002,125	171,033	5,921,386
1962	5,228,624	2,085,881	185,830	7,078,272

SOURCE: Newsprint Association of Canada, *Annual Newsprint Supplement, 1964* (April, 1965).

Table 2-2

COMPARATIVE STRUCTURE OF UNITED STATES AND CANADIAN PULP AND PAPER INDUSTRIES, 1955
(Estimated)

	Canada		U.S.	
	Thousands of tons	Percentage	Thousands of tons	Percentage
Newsprint	6,191	59.7	1,456	4.7
Fine Papers	321	3.1	5,318	17.0
Wrapping Papers	258	2.5	3,721	11.9
Paperboard	788	7.6	13,872	44.3
All other grades	400	3.8	5,491	17.6
Wood Pulp	2,419	23.3	1,422	4.5
Total	10,377	100.0	31,280	100.0

SOURCE: *The Outlook For The Canadian Forest Industries*, The Forest Study Group (Royal Commission on Canada's Economic Prospects, 1957).

with one another, particularly with grade shifting always being a possibility. While it is true that one of the notable features since the early 1900's has been a decline of U.S. newsprint production, the post World War II expansion of newsprint and pulp production in the U.S. South has acted as a catalyst, intensifying continental competition in the pulp and newsprint fields.

As noted, in the U.S. the major producing areas are the West Coast and the South, but lesser amounts are also produced in the Northeastern and Lake States. Canadian output comes essentially from four regions — the Atlantic Provinces, Quebec, Ontario and British Columbia (see Table 2-3). From 1950 to 1962 approximately 40 per cent of Canadian newsprint capacity was in Quebec.

Table 2-3

CANADIAN NEWSPRINT CAPACITY BY REGION, 1950-1962
(thousands of tons)

Year	Quebec	Ont. & Man.	Atlantic Provinces	B.C.	Total
1950	2,723	1,308	813	383	5,227
1956	3,192	1,541	921	589	6,243
1962	3,727	2,087	1,088	1,078	7,980

SOURCE: Newsprint Association of Canada, Newsprint Data, 1964: *Statistics of World Demand and Supply.*

The Ontario-Manitoba region over the period ranked second, followed by the Atlantic Provinces and British Columbia. The bulk of Canadian newsprint exported to the U.S. was produced in the Quebec and Ontario regions. There were no dramatic regional shifts, as was the case in the U.S., but one of the notable features was the rapid growth in B.C. capacity. The expansion in British Columbia was, in part, due to the fact that, during the period, there had been no continuous operation permitted in Quebec, and very little existed in Ontario and the Atlantic Provinces. It was normal practice for many years in British Columbia.[3]

While Canadian paper is consumed in almost all sections of the United States, certain producing sections in Canada traditionally

3. The existence of 7-day operations in B.C. compared to a 6-day operation at most other Canadian mills has had a decided effect on wage structure.

have supplied specific U.S. regions. Mills in Quebec and the Atlantic Provinces supply the eastern part of the United States and some parts of the South. Ontario shipments go down the Great Lakes to such states as Illinois, Ohio, Michigan, and Indiana. Newsprint from British Columbia mills goes principally by water to Pacific Coast ports and by water and rail to Texas, Oklahoma, and inland points of the Pacific Coast States.

Throughout North America there are two market outlets which Canadian mills use. Some companies sell their newsprint independently on the open market. A number of Canadian firms have their own selling companies and maintain sales offices and a sales force in the principal American cities. A few sell through American firms. A second group of firms are referred to as "captive" mills. Such mills produce entirely, or substantially, for the consumption of their United States parent or controlling corporation, or ship pulp directly to their United States parent for final processing. Also, a substantial amount of integration exists between Canadian paper mills and U.S. newspaper publishers. Many American publishers have controlling stock in Canadian pulp and paper companies, or contractual arrangements exist between a newspaper and a newsprint company.

Individual plants in the industry are of moderate size employing from less than 500 employees up to a maximum of 2000. The industry is a highly mechanized one with skilled and semi-skilled employees comprising a substantial proportion of the labor force. In the United States, investment per employee amounted to approximately $23,000 in 1957 — more than three times the investment per employee in manufacturing.[4] Capital intensity is approximately the same in Canada. It was almost $25,000 per mill employee in 1947.[5] The high capital expenditures have resulted in industry wage costs being a fairly small proportion of total costs. The ratio is in the order of 10 to 25 per cent, depending on the type of mill.[6] Industry output is relatively stable and therefore there is considerable stability in employment. Continual growth of the industry has minimized union fears of unemployment due to technological change.[7]

---

4. "Impact of Automation in the Pulp and Paper Industry, 1947-60," *Monthly Labor Review*, LXXXV (October, 1962), p. 1114.

5. T. H. Robinson, *Industrial Relations in the Pulp and Paper Industry* (The Sixth of a Series of Seven Lectures on Pulp and Paper at McGill University under the sponsorship of The Pulp and Paper Research Institute of Canada, delivered on February 21, 1960), p. 3.

6. Robert M. MacDonald, "Pulp and Paper," in *The Evolution of Wage Structure*, Lloyd G. Reynolds and Cynthia H. Taft, eds. (New Haven: Yale University Press, 1956), p. 103.

7. The major advances in the industry have come primarily from the speeding up and modernization of machines. By this means output per man hour has increased significantly without a heavy displacement of workers.

There are geographical wage differentials in both countries. Up until the post World War II period, wages at Quebec mills were below those in Ontario, and throughout the analysis period rates at British Columbia have been higher than those at mills east of that province. U.S. West Coast rates are the highest in North America.

As far as the ratio of U.S. to Canadian ownership is concerned, the pulp and paper industry is the "median" industry in terms of the five analyzed. Dominion Bureau of Statistics data reveals that, in 1953, 30 per cent of the Canadian pulp and paper mills were controlled by U.S. firms.[8] In terms of percentage of employees and percentage of production, the degree of U.S. control was 36 per cent and 39 per cent, respectively. The ratio is higher in the iron ore and auto industries but the ratio in pulp and paper far surpasses that for meat packing and basic steel. Also, two of the Canadian output leaders — C.I.P. and Crown Zellerbach — are U.S. owned. There are, however, very large Canadian owned firms as well.

In both countries the industry is widely dispersed geographically. The majority of its production units are located in small, semi-rural communities. The companies in a number of cases are located in company towns remote from other populated areas. For the most part, Canadian mills are substantial distances from those in the U.S. There are a number of significant situations to note. Firstly, the B.C. mills are relatively close to those in Oregon and Washington State. Secondly, some Quebec mills and those in the Maritime provinces are a short distance away from New England mills. Thirdly, there are two mills owned by the Ontario-Minnesota Pulp and Paper Company located right across the border from each other. One is located in the U.S. city of International Falls, the other in Canada at Fort Frances, Ontario. Of further significance, the two mills have had different and strongly competing unions as bargaining agents. By and large, however, because of the dispersion of the industry in both countries, only a few cases exist of significantly close proximity.

This is the only industry of the five selected where a situation of inter-union competition prevails. Two of the three unions are internationals — the United Papermakers and Paperworkers and the International Brotherhood of Pulp, Sulphite and Paper Mill Workers. Both are members of the AFL-CIO in the United States and the Canadian Labour Congress and, as a general rule, have followed a course of co-operation in their organizing and negotiating functions. The third union, however, while confined to Quebec during the

---

8. Canada, Dominion Bureau of Statistics, *Canada's International Investment Position, 1926-54* (Ottawa: Queen's Printer, 1955).

analysis period, injects a very significant union competitive element to this case. An affiliate of the Confederation of National Trade Unions (CNTU), the Pulp and Paper Workers' Federation (Federation Nationale des Travailleurs de la Pulpe et du Papier) is opposed to international unionism and is a serious immediate threat to the Internationals in Quebec.[9]

UNION BACKGROUND AND THE COLLECTIVE BARGAINING PROCESS

The pulp and paper industry is highly unionized in both countries. In the U.S. it has been estimated that more than 90 per cent of the industry's production workers are covered by agreements.[10] The ratio in Canada is higher. In a 1949 survey covering 87 mills, including all of the big producing units, not a single mill was reported without a labor agreement.[11] The dominant unions by far are the three mentioned above — the two Internationals and the Catholic "syndicate". There are a handful of international craft unions in the industry as well, which have bargaining rights for small groups of skilled workers in some plants. In such cases the two major Internationals have the bulk of the mill organized and in all of the major mills the craft groups bargain jointly with the Pulp and Sulphite Workers and the UPP. An intensive analysis of their activities is beyond the scope of this study and would add little with regard to the findings because their policy has been immersed in, and adapted to, the bargaining policy of the two major Internationals.

Of the three major unions in Canada, the Pulp and Sulphite Workers are the largest with approximately 35,000 members, with the UPP and the Catholic syndicate having memberships of about 10,000 and 8,000 respectively. The numerical position of the UPP vis-à-vis the Pulp and Sulphite Workers in Canada is chiefly a reflection of the fact that there are a smaller number of employees within the historical jurisdiction of the former. The antecedents of the UPP were the International Brotherhood of Paper Makers, the oldest union in the industry, originating in 1893, and the United Paperworkers of America. The UPA was an industrial union formed in the 1940's (affiliated with the CIO). The IBPM was a craft union, which had primarily organized the paper machine tenders.

---

9. A fourth union has been formed in British Columbia. Although comprised of a handful of locals and confined to that province, it is also a future threat to the two Internationals, particularly because it is a purely Canadian union. This is also true of a faction on the U.S. West Coast which broke away and formed the Association of Western Pulp and Paper Workers.

10. *Monthly Labor Review,* LXXXV (October, 1962).

11. Robinson, *Industrial Relations in the Pulp and Paper Industry,* p. 4.

With the merger of the AFL and CIO in 1956, the two unions merged to form the UPP and claimed a jurisdiction which over-lapped that of the Pulp and Sulphite Workers. In Canada, however, the traditional jurisdictional lines have largely been maintained, essentially because the UPA had not organized any workers in Canada prior to the merger. The UPP's Canadian arm, therefore, is largely confined to machine tenders and some other skilled groups.

A long history of collective bargaining in both countries has been a feature of the pulp and paper industry and distinguishes it from the other four cases. One of the greatest contrasts between conditions today and conditions some fifty years ago, when the first locals were established in Canada, is the peaceful state of union-management relations. Since the 1920's, with the exception of jurisdictional battles with the Quebec syndicate, the industrial relations scene has been remarkably peaceful.[12] The leadership of both international unions has shown a great reluctance to call a strike. This aversion to the strike weapon stems from a number of factors,[13] but early historical events were one factor which played a large role in facili-tating industrial peace in the industry. A strike called in 1921 failed and almost destroyed the Internationals. It was an experience that the unions' leadership did not forget.

The impetus for unionism in the Canadian industry came from the U.S. By 1910 many locals had sprung up at such widely-separated points as Sault Ste. Marie, Espanola, and Sturgeon Falls in Ontario, and Grand'Mere, Shawinigan, and Hull, in Quebec. The Internationals jointly organized the mills, dividing up the member-ship along their established jurisdictional lines. Upon successfully organizing the labor force, they ran up against stiff employer oppo-sition, but by 1920, despite a number of set-backs, they had received recognition and had signed agreements with a number of major Canadian paper companies. This success, however, was confined for the most part to Ontario, the Maritimes, and Newfoundland. In Quebec, effective union organization only became a reality after the Great Depression. A major event occurred in 1937 when the Inter-national Paper Company decided to recognize the unions. By sign-ing an agreement with the Canadian International Paper Company covering its mills in Quebec, the union acquired in one move a large number of members. This became a solid foundation on which to build its Quebec membership. By 1939, the entire newsprint field

---

12. An executive in the industry has stated " . . . no industry has been freer of strikes, neither has there been a Canadian industry with a better history of relations between management and labor." (*Ibid.*, p. 2.)

13. See Clark Kerr and Roger Randall, "Crown Zellerbach and the Pacific Coast Pulp and Paper Industry: A Case Study," *Causes of Industrial Peace Under Collective Bargaining.*

in Ontario was organized. Organization in B.C. during this period also went on at a rapid pace and was, to a large extent, a result of the great expansion of unionism on the U.S. West Coast during the 1930's.[14] By 1940 the unions had locals throughout Canada and were bargaining with companies in every part of the country.

Organization of Quebec-based mills by the Catholic syndicate did not become intensive until the early 1940's. Central to their organizing drives was a claim that the Internationals were America "dominated". Aided by this propaganda plus the direct involvement of Catholic parish priests, they obtained a considerable degree of success but only after very bitter battles with the Internationals.[15] It is unlikely that the Internationals' hands were entirely clean, but the important fact is that even though the animosity lessened somewhat with the passage of time, the two union forces developed a deep dislike for each other. The two groups are affiliates of two opposing federations — the Canadian Labour Congress and the Quebec-based Confederation of National Trade Unions.

The breakdown of union membership in Quebec, as of 1952, was this — union membership was divided about equally between the two Internationals and the Federation; the former had bargaining rights in the majority of large mills including the mills of Canadian International Paper; the Federation was more successful in smaller mills but was the bargaining agent in a handful of larger firms as well, the two most notable ones being Price Brothers and Consolidated Paper. In the rest of Canada, during the 1953 to 1962 period, the Internationals had all of the important companies organized.

With regard to union structure, both Internationals have Canadian representation on their respective executive boards in the U.S. and Canadian delegates attend the internationals conventions. The UPP has two vice-presidents directing union affairs in Canada and a Canadian office in Ottawa. This office supervises all the locals from Newfoundland to British Columbia. One of the international vice-presidents also acts as Canadian director. Head office for the union is in Albany, New York. The Pulp and Sulphite Workers have four international vice-presidents in Canada, two for Ontario, one each for Quebec and British Columbia. Up until 1966 there was no provision for a Canadian director. At their 1965 convention, however, in response to the threat of the CNTU, a resolution was passed establishing such an office. The international vice-president for the Quebec region now also acts as Canadian director. With headquarters in Fort Edward, New York, the union had the distinction

14. Greening, *Paper Makers in Canada*, p. 69.
15. *Ibid.*, p. 50.

of being the only international union with a Canadian as president. This was only a momentary phenomenon, however. John Burke, perennial president-secretary of the union was forced to retire in 1965 and appointed William Burnell, a Canadian vice-president, as his temporary successor. Burnell declined to run for office in 1965 and at the union's convention the international vice-president for the New York region was elected president-secretary.

Certainly the formal framework of the unions promotes the spread of U.S. wage developments into Canada. The Canadian executives are in close contact with American officers, principally through periodic executive board meetings in the U.S. Also, because of the large size of the Canadian membership, negotiations and wage rates in Canada warrant close scrutiny by the U.S. executive. While Canadian membership is not large in terms of total international membership, it is larger than the membership in many of the union's individual U.S. regions.[16] While a balance of authority is maintained in both Internationals by the requirement that all agreements must be approved by the local unions concerned, and by the International, disciplinary powers rest exclusively with the latter and strikes must be authorized by the executive board.

Wage policy formulation is carried out in Canada, however, by delegates from the Canadian locals. The international unions, it has been noted, bargain jointly and in order to present a united front and a uniform program to all companies in a region, they have organized district councils in different sections of the country which correspond to the areas of major production. Prior to negotiations with the companies, which generally begin in the spring, the unions hold regional conferences to which local unions within the respective regions send delegates. The delegates draft tentative proposals for revisions in the existing contracts. These determine the proposals which the international officers make to the companies when negotiations begin in April. One of these conferences covers the locals in British Columbia; another (the Central Canada Council) which meets in Toronto embraces newsprint and sulphite mills in Manitoba and Ontario; and a third (the Quebec and Eastern Canada Council), covering companies in Quebec, the Maritime Provinces, and Newfoundland, holds an annual conference in Montreal. The locals in the fine and specialty paper mills have a separate conference, and have little influence on the demands presented to the major newsprint producers. The international craft unions generally take part at the pre-negotiation conferences. The demands are submitted to the companies on behalf of all parties concerned.

---

16. The Canadian membership of the UPP constitutes approximately 1/13 (a ratio of 10,000 to 131,000) of total membership while the ratio is about 1/5 (36,000 to 180,000) for the Pulp and Sulphite Workers.

In negotiations the vice-presidents of the participating companies usually present the case for management, while the presidents of the two major Internationals often lead the discussion for the union side but this is not a fixed rule. In mills where there are more than two unions, it is determined prior to the commencement of bargaining whether all delegates are prepared to negotiate the renewal of the contract and whether they have the power to sign agreements. When that is determined, the company or companies and the unions deal with the uniform agenda.

Bargaining structure varies from region to region and, additionally, has been somewhat unstable through time. Primarily because of price uniformity and the homogeneous nature of the product, multi-employer bargaining has been quite prevalent. Briefly, in British Columbia the mills operate under a Standard Labor Agreement, which is negotiated periodically between the two Internationals and half a dozen paper companies. This practice is patterned after the procedure on the U.S. West Coast where a Uniform Labor Agreement encompasses a large number of mills. After 1955, pattern bargaining rather than multi-employer bargaining has, by and large, been the practice in the industry east of British Columbia. In the years following World War II the Internationals submitted proposals to most of the paper manufacturers as a group and multi-employer negotiations took place on a regional basis. The multi-employer negotiations covered only wages and related matters. Separate agreements were signed with each firm. The two multi-employer units are the Ontario Newsprint group and the Quebec Newsprint group, with the major mills in eastern Canada (CIP being the exception) included in one of these. Canadian International Paper has always insisted on negotiating alone. Up to 1955, it was the practice for the Ontario settlement to serve as a guide in negotiations in Quebec, the Maritimes, and Newfoundland. This method of bargaining was abandoned when the employers insisted on negotiating on a company basis, although a few of the smaller firms still bargain together.

The only other negotiations of importance are those which involve the Federation of Pulp and Paper Workers in Quebec. Thus far, single company negotiations have been the rule. These negotiations have not been of major significance as far as the pattern-setting aspect is concerned. "What has usually happened is that when the international unions have secured a wage increase in a certain region of Quebec, the Federation of Pulp and Paper Workers has tried to follow their lead, sometimes without success."[17]

While any settlement in the U.S. industry may influence collective bargaining in Canada four pattern settlements are most likely

_____

17. Greening, *Paper Makers in Canada*, p. 64.

to do so — the multi-employer settlement on the West Coast, the settlements at International Paper's southern and nothern divisions, and the settlement at Great Northern in New England. The latter company, while it has no Canadian subsidiary, accounts for approximately 4 per cent of combined U.S. and Canadian newsprint production and 18 per cent of total U.S. newsprint output.

U.S.-Canada Wages

An earnings differential between U.S. and Canadian mills has consistently been in evidence but it seems to have narrowed over time. The differential between U.S. and Canadian production workers in terms of average hourly earnings narrowed significantly from 1947 to 1962, in both percentage and absolute amount. In 1947 there was an absolute differential of 27 cents or 23.5 per cent. By 1962 the differential had become 16 cents or 6.7 per cent.[18]

In the 1947 to 1962 period the declining earnings differential was supported by negotiated increases. Canadian common labor increases ranged from 62 cents in Ontario to 68 cents in Quebec and British Columbia. In the U.S. the increases amounted to only 45 and 48 cents in the South and Northeast, and 63 cents on the West Coast. The generally larger Canadian increases simply restored Canadian rates to their approximate position vis-à-vis those in the U.S. prior to World War II.

The relative advance of the Canadian to the U.S. industry from 1953 to 1962, however, could be exaggerated by looking only at trends in gross hourly earnings.[19] During these years, negotiated general increases in most of the companies amounted to 62 cents in Ontario and Quebec and 56 cents in British Columbia, compared with 59 cents on the U.S. West Coast and approximately 70 cents in the Northeast and South. Of similar significance is the fact that over the 1953 to 1962 period inclusive the growth in earnings in each of the major Canadian producing regions was far greater than the increases in negotiated wages at the common labor rate level (Table 2-4). In Ontario, Quebec, and British Columbia average

---

18. The earnings data were obtained from the following sources — U.S., Department of Labor, Bureau of Labor Statistics, *Employment and Earnings Statistics for the United States, 1905-1965* (Bulletin No. 1312-3); Canada, Dominion Bureau of Statistics, *Review of Man-Hours and Hourly Earnings, 1945-64.* The figures have not been adjusted for changes in the exchange rate.

19. It should be noted in passing that U.S. pulp and paper earnings may have been held down by the rapid growth of the industry in the lower-paying South after World War II. The Canadian average, on the other hand, may have been increased somewhat by industry expansion in the high-wage West Coast region.

hourly earnings in pulp and paper mills increased by 89, 92, and 88 cents, respectively. It is doubtful that the entire 27 to 32 cent excess over general increases could be accounted for by increases in wage related items or, as the data below shows, by increases to skilled workers. Table 2-5 lists the U.S.-Canada differential for 1952 and 1962 in terms of wage rates for semi-skilled and skilled jobs. There was a positive differential in favor of the United States industry in absolute and percentage terms for the listed jobs in both 1952 and 1962 and there was no significant change in the differentials over the period.

Table 2-6 indicates that the configuration of the regional wage structure throughout the continent has changed very little. It will be shown that Canadian wages in the 1930's were probably equal to or approached those in the United States east of the Pacific Coast, at least at the common labor rate level. Ontario rates were above those in the South. In 1962, rather than having wage equality with the Northern United States mills, Eastern Canada mills were 5 cents below them, and the advantage over Southern mills was only 1.5 cents. The U.S.-Canada common labor rate differential on the West Coast was 19.5 cents in 1962. On the whole, the position of Canadian to U.S. wages had changed very little since the 1930's.

Table 2-4

INCREASES IN AVERAGE HOURLY EARNINGS AND NEGOTIATED GENERAL WAGE INCREASES, PULP AND PAPER MILLS, ONTARIO, QUEBEC, AND BRITISH COLUMBIA, 1953 - 62

	Ontario	Quebec	British Columbia
Increase in average hourly earnings	89	92	88
Negotiated general wage increases	62	62	56
Difference	27	30	32

SOURCES: Canada, Dominion Bureau of Statistics, *Review of Man-Hours and Hourly Earnings, 1945-63* and *Man-Hours and Hourly Earnings* (monthly); the files of the Department of Research and Education, IBPSPMW, Montreal, Quebec.

The one exception has been Quebec. The unions were successful in gaining wage equality for Quebec mills with those in Ontario
and, therefore, indirectly with mills in the U.S. South and North.
The Catholic Syndicate also was able to obtain the same increases
and levels as were obtained by the Internationals.[20] In some cases
the increases were unilaterally extended by management.

It is important to note that the continental wage structure in
pulp and paper conforms to what one would expect on economic
grounds. The industry is more efficient on the U.S. West Coast than
for any other region in the United States and it is in a high wage area.
At the same time, the growth in the U.S. South has been prolific.
Therefore, the very significant relative advantage of U.S. West Coast
rates to those in the rest of the United States, and the relative

Table 2-5

ABSOLUTE AND PERCENTAGE DIFFERENTIALS FOR
AVERAGE WAGE RATES IN SELECTED OCCUPATIONS
PULP AND PAPER INDUSTRY, UNITED STATES AND
CANADA, 1952-1962

Occupation	1952		1962	
	¢	%	¢	%
Chipperman	13	8.8	14	6.3
Millwright	13	7.2	17	6.1
Machinist	13	7.1	17	6.0
Pipefitter	15	8.1	21	7.3
Electrician	14	7.5	20	7.2

SOURCES: Canada, Dept. of Labour, *Wage Rates, Salaries and Hours of
Work in Canada* (annual); U.S., Department of Labor, Bureau of
Labor Statistics, *Monthly Labor Review*, LXXV (November,
1952) and LXXXV (September, 1962).

20. The fact that the syndicate consistently followed the pattern of the
International unions in Quebec is reflected by the fact that in 1962 the two
major mills where it had jurisdiction had the same common labor rate as the
other major eastern Canada mills — $2.03.

Table 2-6

COMMON LABOR RATES, MAJOR PULP AND PAPER
COMPANIES, UNITED STATES AND CANADA, 1953-62

Year	United States				Canada		
	Great Northern	IP North	IP South	West Coast	CIP	Ontario	B.C.
1953	$1.43	$1.50	$1.37	$1.765	$1.41	$1.41	$1.57
1954	1.47	1.55	1.44	1.80	1.46	1.46	1.59
1955	1.55	1.53	1.51	1.845	1.53	1.53	1.67
1956	1.67	1.65	1.64	1.94	1.65	1.65	1.72
1957	1.76	1.73	1.73	2.01	1.73	1.73	1.85
1958	1.81	1.78	1.77	2.06	1.78	1.78	1.89
1959	1.81	1.90	1.84	2.12	1.85	1.78	1.95
1960	1.92	1.98	1.92	2.195	1.93	1.93	2.03
1961	2.02	2.04	1.955	2.24	1.98	1.98	2.03
1962	2.08	2.08	2.015	2.295	2.03	2.03	2.10

SOURCE: The files of the Department of Research and Education,
IBPSPMW, Montreal, Quebec.

improvement of Southern rates, was to be expected. Similarly, the
industry in British Columbia is in a high wage environment and is
more efficient than the industry in other parts of Canada and the
United States (excluding the U.S. West Coast). It is not surprising,
therefore, to see British Columbia rates higher than any on the continent east of the Pacific Coast. Also, the industry in Eastern
Canada is technologically very similar to and apparently just as
efficient as the U.S. industry in the Northern and Southern regions.
In his study of the pulp and paper industry Guthrie has indicated that
the continental differentials have persisted for many years.[21] Collective bargaining has essentially preserved the traditional differentials.

It is not possible to make any definitive conclusions with regard
to U.S. and Canadian fringe benefit levels and the relative trend

---

21. Guthrie, *The Economics of Pulp and Paper*, p. 135.

of fringes over time. Firstly, there are a great variety of fringe benefits in the industry in the two countries even though they all fall into several broad classifications (e.g. health and welfare plans). Secondly, in Canada some fringe benefits were not a part of the collective agreement over the entire analysis period. To illustrate, 1963 was the first time that CIP's retirement plan was subject to negotiation and included in the collective agreement. Thirdly, there are marginal benefits at some companies, such as company housing whose cost cannot be estimated. The problem was aptly stated by Canadian International Paper.

> One thing has stood out in all our studies, namely, the complexity of these matters. Another thing that has struck us is the lack of information to enable us to make meaningful comparisons with competitor companies in the way that we can with wage rates . . . . When someone tells us that his retirement plan is better than ours in one respect, we can usually counter by pointing out how ours is superior in another respect. This situation holds true for virtually all our plans.[22]

If consideration is given to two pieces of evidence, however, it would appear that fringe benefit levels between the two countries, at least on a regional basis, have always been quite close and the increases up to 1962 in both countries have not resulted in a major difference in favor of one country or the other. Two studies by the Newsprint Service Bureau in the United States, one in December, 1950, the other in April, 1954, presented wage and fringe benefits data for more than thirty Canadian and American newsprint firms. In 1950 all made similar provisions for vacations with pay, the same rate for overtime on Sundays, holidays, and after an 8 or 10 hour day. Most provided four paid holidays and very similar shift differentials, although the typical practice in Canadian mills was a 2 cent differential for the second shift and 3 cent premium for the third, while in the United States the provision was for 3 cents and 4 or 5 cents for the second and third shift. The study in 1954 indicated basically the same thing with regard to the above benefits, the only difference being that shift differentials had gone up by 1 cent for the second shift and 2 cents for the third shift in both countries. That study also presented some very general information on health and welfare, and pension plans. It revealed that most companies examined in both countries provided for group insurance and that all but a few provided hospital, medical, and surgical benefits, and a sickness and accident plan. Also, of those included in the survey, all but two companies in Canada and two in the United States had a pension plan, although no information was reported to allow an estimate of the relative cost.

---

22. Minutes of Canadian International Paper Labour Conference, October 5, 1961, Montreal, Quebec (in the files of the Department of Research and Education, IBPSPMW, Montreal, Quebec).

It does seem likely, given the above information, that the levels were about the same.[23] Company and union statements during negotiations indicated, as well, that the cost of fringes in various regions were very close to one another. If a company was below other companies on the continent with regard to one fringe, it would usually have some other benefit which would make up the difference. This was often stressed in negotiations by management. The one area where there appeared to be a significant difference was in shift differentials. By 1962 the premiums were higher on the U.S. West Coast than in any other region on the continent, while they were essentially the same in Eastern Canada, the U.S. South and Northeast. B.C. shift differentials fell midway between those of the U.S. West Coast and the other major mills on the Continent.

In examining the settlements from 1953 to 1962 it was apparent that, considering the entire period, general changes in fringes were very similar from region to region in North America. For example, if there was a 1 cent increase in shift premiums in one region this would also be provided for in other regions during the same negotiating round, or, if not in the immediate wage round the union would bring them into line the following round. In conclusion, the very loose analysis indicates a very close correspondence between provisions by American and Canadian companies with little change in relative position over the period.[24]

---

23. An executive at CIP indicated that fringe benefit levels have always been quite similar at that company and the U.S. parent, although their various plans are not identical. "Initially, they were the same. Now we have different plans, partly through bargaining and partly through our own initiative. An example is life insurance which was instituted in 1920. It was very costly so CIP opted out by increasing another benefit." Anonymous interview at the Canadian International Paper Company, September 9, 1965.

24. There is an additional piece of evidence which indicates that fringe benefit levels are very similar in the two countries. In a study done in 1961 by the Department of Research and Education of the IBPSPMW in Washington and Montreal of the Kimkerly-Clark pension plans in the United States and Canada, it was revealed that the plans were very similar and provided approximately the same level of benefits. The Canadian plan closely resembled the plan at the parent company with only a few principal differences. The retirement age for women was two years earlier in Canada than in the United States. Pensions were vested in Canada after twenty years, at age 55 for men and age 50 for women. The Canadian plan provided a supplementary benefit between retirement and the payment of government old age benefits, and it provided a slightly higher minimum monthly benefit. The monthly benefits in the United States were higher than comparable benefits under any other U.S. plan which operated without payroll deductions, and the benefits were higher than some of those offered under plans with payroll deductions. On the other hand, compared with other Canadian plans, the Kimberly-Clark plan showed somewhat lower monthly benefits, probably because most of the other plans were financed in part by employee payroll deductions.

THE COLLECTIVE BARGAINING RECORD

Pre-1953 Experience

The long record of collective bargaining in the pulp and paper industry makes an examination of union-management developments before the 1953-62 period not only desirable but necessary. The central analysis period, unlike the other cases, is a relatively short period in the context of the total collective bargaining experience. Major developments in labor-management relations, as they relate to this study, have taken place over the entire period. Some attempt has been made, therefore, to piece together the relationship between U.S. and Canadian labor developments in the industry particularly prior to World War II.

The Pre-World War II Period

Isolated cases which illustrate some interrelatedness of labor developments between each country, almost as far back as the genesis of unionism in the Canadian industry, have been reported. Despite the flimsy nature of the evidence, it would appear that the continental scope of the product market infused an international approach to labor problems. For example, with the removal of the U.S. tariff on newsprint the Canadian industry grew rapidly and many of the skilled workers had to be recruited in the United States. As early as 1912, for example, when a mill was opened at remote Grand Falls, Newfoundland, by the Anglo-Canadian Company, union men from the U.S. were hired to tend the machines. Greening in discussing the early organization of the eastern Canadian mills made the following observation:

> The men who staffed the machines in these new mills in most cases, had previous experience in the industry in the United States. There was quite a large migration from the mills in Massachusetts, Maine, and New York State as well as from other regions of the Eastern States to the pulp and paper centers in Northern Ontario and Quebec. Many of these men had already been members in the United States, and as Canada at this time was about twenty years behind her southern neighbor in union organization, they served as transmitters of the union idea to regions of Canada where previously it had been almost unknown.[25]

Available information allows at least a speculative conclusion with regard to U.S. influences on Canadian bargaining in the years prior to the 1920's. It suggests at least some influence. The initial demands by the Internationals, for example, followed the U.S. pattern. The first objectives of the IBPM in Canada, as was the case in the U.S., were a reduction of hours and a tour system, dividing the

---

25. Greening, *Paper Makers in Canada,* p. 10.

twenty-four hour working period into three shifts of eight hours each.[26] There is no definitive evidence, however, to indicate that specific demands and patterns set in the U.S. were followed in Canada in the very early years. If there was an influence it would appear to have been of a very weak nature.[27] Both Internationals were quite impotent at that time. Rather than being on the offensive, more typically they were fighting for their existence.

It seems plausible that, given the existence of U.S. corporations, the entrance of U.S. skilled workers into the Canadian industry, and the continental scope of the industry, some U.S. influence would have been manifested regardless of the presence of international unions. Just before and during World War I large mills were being erected on the Pacific Coast of the United States and Canada with the Internationals organizing mills in both countries. They had successfully organized a mill at Ocean Falls, British Columbia — Pacific Mills — a subsidiary of the largest west coast company on the American side of the border, the Crown Willimette Company. Relations with the company were apparently good. The company granted its employees the rates set up in the Paper Makers Schedule, although no formal written agreement had been signed. In 1918, the unions began organizing the mills of Crown Willimette in Washington and Oregon but in these cases they met stiff resistance. The company imported strike-breakers from the eastern United States. After a great deal of violence the company decided to use the paper from its Canadian mill at Ocean Falls which was still operating. The Canadian employees were, in effect, strike-breakers so that the President of the IBPM ordered the members of the Ocean Falls local to walk out. The Pacific Mills Company responded by using its influence with the Canadian Government. They successfully had union members on the paper machines called up for military duty. Following this the Canadian walk-out collapsed as did the strike in the U.S.[28]

---

26. *Ibid.,* p. 11.

27. Another example of this type of influence was the introduction into Canada of the Standard Minimum Wage Schedule originally designed by the IBPM in 1915. Initially it was intended as a wage scale for skilled paper-machine operators in the newsprint branch of the industry. Under this plan, the wage rates for machine tenders, back tenders and third hands were graduated according to the width and speed of paper machines, so that the large and/or faster the machine, the higher the rates for the three occupations. In the thirties there was an extension of the "graduation" principle to the wage rates for unskilled machine crew members and subsequent revisions gradually brought other occupations under the scale. The use of the schedule spread throughout the pulp and paper industry in both countries.

28. See Greening, *Paper Makers in Canada,* pp. 17-18.

The second instance, demonstrating that action on an international front was a compelling attraction in the industry, occurred three years later. Rather than demonstrating American influence by either international companies or unions, it seems to point to the fact that interconnected activity (for dealing with a situation on both sides of the border) followed naturally from the continental scope of the industry. In 1921, during a recession in the industry, the unions presented demands calling for a 5 per cent increase to all companies on the continent. This was rejected by all the major American and Canadian companies who counterproposed a 30 per cent wage cut. A strike ensued. Finally, both U.S. and Canadian companies agreed to an arbitration. A committee was set up consisting of representatives from the two unions and the companies involved in both countries. The award called for a minimum cut of 10 per cent which most of the companies accepted but the strike continued for five years at International Paper and its Canadian subsidiary.

From the small amount of information available, then, it would appear that there was some U.S. orientation on the part of both companies and unions during the early years of the relationship. Before the growth of the Canadian industry, the International Brotherhood of Paper Makers realized the potential importance of the Canadian industry to employment conditions in the U.S. if pulp and newsprint were allowed to enter the U.S. duty free. Their official policy with regard to the removal of duties was one of modified opposition.[29] Once the tariff barrier had been removed and the Canadian industry experienced spectacular growth the two Internationals were drawn into Canada for essentially two reasons — it was a natural extension of their organization efforts (particularly where the same companies were involved) and many of the U.S. workers, who were recruited by Canadian mills, already had trade union experience in the U.S. Following the extension of unionism into Canada a continental approach seemed to naturally impinge upon the relationship. The initial demands of the IBPM in Canada; the spread of the Paper Maker's Wage Schedule across the U.S.-Canada boundary; the 1918 power struggle on the West Coast involving U.S. and Canadian employees; and the continental arbitration in 1921 were all events and developments which suggest this.[30] Both the unions and the companies operating in a continental context seemingly took a North American approach in dealing with each other.

---

29. *Ibid.,* p. 4.

30. This type of influence was manifested in British Columbia in the form of the Standard Labor Agreement covering a number of firms in that province. It was the same approach to collective bargaining as that used on the U.S. West Coast under the Uniform Labor Agreement.

There is additional evidence, which indicates a more specific and definitive relationship between U.S. and Canadian wages and collective bargaining during the period before World War II. Greening, for example, states (although he supplies no evidence) that the B.C. locals "have enjoyed most of the benefits which have been gained by the union on the American side of the Pacific Coast region . . . ".[31] A more enlightening statement was made by W. H. Burnell, an international vice-president of the IBPSPMW, at the 1948 negotiations with Quebec newsprint companies.

> Now as far back as I can remember, before the war, the Ontario group of organized mills always had the same organized rate as the newsprint mills of the United States. I know when I worked in the mills before 1929 I used to attend wage conference after wage conference and some of these were joint conferences held right in this hotel. Whatever was agreed upon by the American companies was agreed upon by the Ontario companies and we always had standard wage rates.[32]

The above indicates that the U.S. industry was not only used as a benchmark for Canadian rates and increases but also, prior to the war years, much of the Canadian newsprint industry had at least common labor rates equivalent to those in the U.S. counterpart. The statement, along with Greening's description of the 1921 continental negotiations indicates that the Canadian companies went along with such an arrangement, ostensibly without any resistance. There is other evidence which substantiates this finding. The president of the IBPSPMW at the 1949 Ontario newsprint negotiations made the statement below in describing how and why multi-employer negotiations began in Ontario. It indicates that international pattern bargaining may have existed as far back as World War I.

> The history of collective bargaining in this province goes back to the first World War. At that time we had a strike, and the War Labour Board at Washington asked us to submit our differences to them. We did so in the U.S. There was a war on, and how could we refuse? And the Canadian Companies agreed to follow the decision of the Board.[33]

Collective agreements published by *Labour Gazette* in the 1930's substantiate Burnell's claim of a link between U.S. and Cana-

---

31. Greening, *Paper Makers in Canada*, p. 70.

32. The Quebec Newsprint Conference Highlights, 1948 (in the files of the Dept. of Research and Education, IBPSPMW, Montreal, Quebec), pp. 3, 4.

33. Ontario Newsprint and Pulp Conference, July 13, 1949 (in the files of the Dept, of Research and Education, IBPSPMW, Montreal, Quebec), p. 25.

dian settlements prior to World War II. The following are examples of the type of arrangement he discussed. Such provisions disappeared in 1939 and thereafter.

Agreement between Kenora Paper Mills Ltd., the Fort Frances Pulp and Paper Co. Ltd., Kenora and Fort Frances, Ont. and IBPSP-MW and IBOE, May 12, 1934 to April 30, 1935.

> . . . with the further provision that when wage increases are made in comparable newsprint mills in the United States that similar increases will be made in the mills at Kenora and Fort Frances. Under this clause, a further wage increase of approximately 7 to 9 per cent was made, with a minimum of 43 cents per hour for the lowest paid classes of workers . . . .[34]

Agreement between Abitibi Mills, Ontario and Manitoba and IBPSPMW, May 1, 1934.

> These rates to remain in effect until such date as any general increases in the rates being paid in newsprint paper mills in the U.S. which are comparable to the mills of the Abitibi Power and Paper Co. Ltd. are made generally effective, at which time the Co. agrees to meet such general increases so far as minimum rate and percentage increases are concerned, and such increases to be made effective from the date on which they come into effect in such U.S. mills.[35]

Therefore, it can be inferred that there was a direct impact of U.S. on Canadian settlements up to World War II at the very least sporadically.

The 1946 to 1952 Period

The unions, having consolidated their gains during the war years and with broad-based organizations, were in a position to pursue wage standardization on a national and international basis after World War II. With the return to free collective bargaining it is important to consider Canadian negotiations within the context of three sets of differentials — those between the Canadian industry as a whole in relation to the U.S. industry; the one between B.C. mills and mills east of British Columbia; and the one between Quebec and Ontario mills. These differentials repeatedly played a role in the negotiations which took place in the years 1946 to 1952.

Four sets of negotiations in Canada — B.C., Ontario Newsprint, Eastern Canada Newsprint (Quebec), and CIP — essentially cover

---

34. *Labour Gazette*, XXXIV (December, 1934), p. 1149.
35. *Ibid.*, XXXIV (July, 1934), p. 701.

the entire industry.[36]   These four groups set wages for all of the Canadian basic pulp and paper industry. Actually, because of the multi-product firm, there can be no breakdown of negotiations by specialized product in the industry (other than a division between basic producers and those producing fine and specialty papers) and the unions approach negotiations not strictly from the standpoint of "competitive" producers but on the basis of "comparable" producers.[37]   Within this context, the four sets of negotiations to be analyzed were the major ones in Canada and all agreements reached apart from the four major ones were based on them.

The extent to which U.S. base rates were used by the unions as arguments for higher wages was striking. The American pulp and paper wage structure played an extremely important role in all

---

36. Although the make-up changed from time to time, the companies involved in the four sets of negotiations were as follows:

British Columbia
MacMillan, Bloedel & Powell River Ltd.
Crown Zellerbach Canada Ltd.
Columbia Cellulose Company Ltd.
Sorg Pulp Co.
British Columbia Pulp and Paper Co.
Rayonnier Canada Ltd.
Canadian Forest Products Ltd.

Eastern Canada Newsprint
Anglo-Canadian Pulp & Paper Mills Ltd.
Gaspesia Sulphite Company, Ltd.
St. Lawrence Paper Mills Company Ltd.
Lake St. John Power & Paper Co. Ltd.
James Maclaren Company, Limited

Canadian International Paper
Canadian International Paper Co.
New Brunswick International Paper Co.
International Fibre Board Ltd.
Masonite Company of Canada, Ltd.

Ontario Newsprint
Abitibi Power & Paper Co. Ltd.
Manitoba Paper Company Ltd.
Thunder Bay Paper Co. Ltd.
Ste. Anne Paper Company, Ltd.
The Beaver Wood Fibre Co. Ltd.
Brompton Pulp & Paper Co. Ltd.
The Great Lakes Paper Co. Ltd.
The K.V.P. Company, Limited
Marathon Paper Mills of Canada, Ltd.
The Ontario Paper Company, Ltd.
The Ontario-Minnesota Pulp & Paper Company Ltd.
Provincial Paper Limited
Spruce Falls Power & Paper Co. Ltd.
Kimberly Clark Corp. of Canada, Ltd.

37. MacDonald, "Pulp and Paper," p. 132.

Canadian negotiations over the entire six-year period. The comparisons made all took much the same form, were interspersed throughout all the negotiations, and were not limited to common labor rates. The entire wage structure of various U.S. companies or for U.S. papermaking regions was placed before the Canadian companies.

It was primarily in this regard that U.S. officers or international vice-presidents brought their influence to bear. Comparisons with the United States were made repeatedly, with U.S. officers being the most facile in that area. President Burke, for example, in support of union demands would often run down current wage changes or wage rates, not only in Canada but in the United States as well. As leader of the union he was well aware of developments and labor standards at all of the major companies on the continent. The following taken from Ontario negotiations in 1949 was typical:

> Mr. Burke: Let us take two of the newsprint companies in the U.S. — Great Northern and St. Croix. These companies are in direct competition with Ontario newsprint mills. The Great Northern gave shift differentials of 3 and 5 cents per hour, liberalized vacations by giving 2 weeks after 3 years, instead of after 5 years of service as formerly. It also gave a long list of adjustments which averaged an increase of 3½ cents per hour for 250 mechanics. It also gave a pension plan with the company paying all premiums.[38]

There were other statements of a similar nature, too numerous and lengthy to list. The U.S. officers, however, were certainly not the only parties who brought U.S. conditions into play. The Canadian delegates did as well, and most interestingly, so too did the companies when it suited their purpose. What constantly occurred in all four sets of negotiations, during the entire six-year period, was a series of comparisons using conditions of work and recent settlements within the industry on the Continent, with the party on the defensive declaring that the comparisons used were invalid and then turning round and using their own comparisons to put their case in its most favourable light.

Table 2-7 demonstrates that there was some pattern-following between the countries from 1946 to 1950. In 1946, for example, the same wage increase in the Southern Kraft industry was granted by Quebec and Ontario mills. The same situation existed in 1947 but in that case Northeastern mills were granted the same increase as occurred in Quebec and Ontario. In 1950 the South and Northeast set a pattern which was closely followed in all regions of Canada. However, with wage controls in effect in the U.S. in 1951 and 1952 there was no similarity between the settlements in the two countries.

---

38. Ontario Newsprint and Pulp Conference, April 8, 1949, Toronto, Ontario (in the files of the Department of Research and Education, IBPSPMW, Montreal, Quebec).

Table 2-7

WAGE CHANGES IN VARIOUS PULP AND PAPER REGIONS, UNITED STATES AND CANADA, 1945-52[a]

Year	Canada			United States		
	Quebec and Eastern Canada	Ontario	British Columbia	North East	South	Pacific Coast
1946	10¢	10¢	15¢	10¢ 5¢	10¢	4¢
1947	14¢[b]	14¢	12¢	14¢	15¢	11¢ 7.5¢
1948	10%(10¢)[c]	10%(10¢)	11%(12¢)	11¢	5¢	9%(15¢)
1949						
1950	5% 6%	5% 6%	6¢ 5%	5% 5%	7¢(7%) 5¢(4%)	3%(4.5¢) 4%(6.0¢)
1951	15¢(12½%)	17½%	16½%(22¢)	3¢ 2¢	8¢	12.5¢
1952	10%(13¢)[d]	8¢	10¢	6¢	5¢	4.5¢ 2.5¢

a. The wage increases represent the settlements of wage leaders in each region.

b. In addition, adjustments of 3¢, 2¢ and 1¢ on lower-paid jobs.

c. A minimum of 10¢ with adjustments of 3¢, 2¢ and 1¢ on lower-paid jobs.

d. Work week reduced from 48 to 44 hours.

SOURCE: The files of the Department of Research and Education, IBPSPMW, Montreal, Quebec.

The use of coercive comparisons undoubtedly accounted for the exact or close uniformity between some U.S. and Canadian regions from 1946 to 1950. At the same time, however, it seems likely that wage increases between regions on the continent would have been quite similar because most producers faced similar competitive problems and economic conditions. The importance of market conditions on all negotiations on the continent was illustrated in 1949 when the unions agreed to postpone negotiations in all regions because of uncertainty caused by devaluation of European and Canadian currencies.

This is not to deny that U.S. patterns had an effect on Canadian negotiations, but U.S. rates and rate changes were essentially an expectation that never dominated the final stages of negotiations. In Canadian negotiations during the period, there were too many other important demands by the unions — ones domestic in nature. During the early postwar years the unions were much more concerned with obtaining the 40-hour week, reducing the Quebec-Ontario differential, and reducing the British Columbia-Ontario differential. It seems more likely that once a pattern was set either in Canada or the U.S. (except in the West Coast region) this became a mutually acceptable standard to both parties. The major criterion of whether the unions inordinately pursued identical patterns or wage rates on the Canadian side of the border can only be, in the final analysis, whether they struck for them. They never did. Also, there is no evidence to suggest that Canadian companies strongly resisted the type of international pattern-following which existed.

By 1952 common labor rates in Quebec and Ontario mills were on a par with those in the Northeastern United States, and ahead of those in the South, and the British Columbia rate was ahead of all regions on the continent except the U.S. West Coast (see Table 2-8). The relatively high level of the British Columbia rate, however, was simply a return to the situation in the years prior to World War II. The level of the Ontario rate vis-à-vis rates in the U.S. also was not surprising if consideration is given to the wage rate data for the late 1930's. Common labor rates in the Ontario region were consistently ahead of those in the South and slightly higher than Northeastern rates, at a time when the unions were relatively weak. The Ontario and British Columbia rates had fallen behind Northeastern and Southern rates during the war years and by 1952 simply regained their former position in the North American industry. The only major shift after the war was the ascendency of Quebec rates to a level equal to those in the South and Northeast. This was not the result of a formal union program of pushing for wage parity with those two U.S. regions. Rather, union policy was to equilibrate Quebec wages with those in Ontario and this had been successfully achieved during the postwar years. When Ontario achieved wage parity with the two mentioned U.S. regions, so too did Quebec.

Table 2-8

COMMON LABOR RATES IN VARIOUS PULP AND PAPER
REGIONS, UNITED STATES AND CANADA, 1937-52

Year	Canada			United States		
	Quebec Mills	Ontario	British Columbia	North East	South	Pacific Coast
1937	$ .43	$ .51	$ .51	$ .52	$ .44	$ .625
1938	.43	.54	.54	.49	.42	.625
1939	.43	.54	.54	.49	.44	.625
1940	.45	.56	.56	.54	.47	.65
1941						
1942			WAGE CONTROLS IN BOTH COUNTRIES			
1943						
1944						
1945	.57	.63	.67	.75	.75	1.05
1946	.70	.76	.82	.90	.85	1.09
1947	.87	.90	.94	1.04	1.00	1.275
1948	1.00	1.00	1.06	1.15	1.05	1.425
1949	1.00	1.00	1.06	1.15	1.05	1.425
1950	1.10	1.11	1.18	1.27	1.17	1.53
1951	1.25	1.30	1.40	1.32	1.25	1.655
1952	1.38	1.38	1.50	1.38	1.30	1.72

SOURCE: The files of the Department of Research and Education, IBPSPMW,
Montreal, Quebec.

In summation, prior to World War II it appeared that the parties had introduced a policy of closely, sometimes directly, following American settlements in Canada. The war years, accompanied by wage controls in both countries, resulted in a break with this practice and a decline in Canadian wages relative to those in the U.S. With the end of wage controls the parties to some extent re-established international pattern bargaining up to 1950. Wage controls in the U.S. during the Korean conflict again eliminated the bi-national influence.

Collective Bargaining 1953 to 1962

From 1953 to 1962 there were major wage rounds in both countries in every year with the exception of 1954. In that year there were settlements in the United States industry but not in Canada. In many instances there was a close similarity in the dates of signing and the terms of wage settlement in some Canadian and U.S. mills. Two tables have been constructed to reveal the relationship which existed with regard to those two factors. Table 2-9 lists the dates of signing of major agreements in the two countries, while Table 2-10 shows the size of the wage increases in each negotiating round. For the United States the following were used for comparison purposes — Great Northern, International Paper (North and South), and the Uniform Labor Agreement on the U.S. West Coast. For Canada, Canadian International Paper, the B.C. Standard Labor Agreement, and the first key settlement signed by an Ontario mill, were used. The specific dates of settlement could not be determined in every instance and, therefore, in such cases only the month in which signing occurred is presented.

An examination of the two tables reveals a number of cases where Canadian agreements were signed shortly before or shortly after a key agreement in the United States with very similar wage adjustments being involved. This was particularly so between Canadian mills east of British Columbia and International Paper's Northern and Southern Kraft mills. In 1953, for example, mills east of British Columbia signed six months after agreement was reached in I.P. mills and for a similar wage increase (3 per cent — minimum 5 cents). In 1955, 1956, and 1958 the same thing was true but with the dates of signing being only about a month apart. While that much is readily apparent from an examination of the tables, the closeness in timing, and the correlation between and interdependence of, U.S. and Canadian settlements cannot be presented in tabular form.

Table 2-9

TIMING AND LENGTH OF CONTRACT OF MAJOR PULP AND PAPER WAGE ROUNDS, UNITED STATES AND CANADA, 1953-62

Year	United States				Canada		
	Great Northern	IP North	IP South	West Coast	C.I.P.	Ontario	B.C. Standard
1953	April 23 (1 yr.)	April (1 yr.)	May (1 yr.)	Aug. 19 (1 yr.)	Nov. 13 (2 yrs.)	Nov. 6 (2 yrs.)	Sept. (2 yrs.)
1954	June (1 yr.)	May (1 yr.)	July 2 (1 yr.)	May 22 (1 yr.)			
1955	April 13 (1 yr.)	May (1 yr.)	April (1 yr.)	April 23 (1 yr.)	April 8 (1 yr.)	June (1 yr.)	June (2 yrs.)
1956	May (1 yr.)	May (2 yrs.)	May (2 yrs.)	May 18 (1 yr.)	April 10 (2 yrs.)	May (2 yrs.)	
1957	April (1 yr.)			June 25 (1 yr.)			Strike
1958	Dec. (2 yrs.)	May (1 yr.)	June (1 yr.)	Nov. 3 (2 yrs.)	June 13 (2 yrs.)	June (2 yrs.)	Feb. 4 (2 yrs.)
1959		June 20 (2 yrs.)	June 18 (2 yrs.)	May 29 (reopening)	Nov. 14 (reopening)		June 28 (1 yr.)
1960	May (14 mos.)			May (2 yrs.)		April (1 yr.)	June (1 yr.)
1961	July (2 yrs.)	June 27 (1 yr.)	July 5 (1 yr.)	May 31 (reopening)	Oct. 8[a] (2 yrs.)	Sept. (1 yr.)	Aug. (1 yr.)
1962		June 4 (1 yr.)	May 29 (1 yr.)	May 17 (2 yrs.)		May 4 (1 yr.)	June 2 (1 yr.)

a. Eastern Canada Newsprint settled first in Quebec, May 16, 1961.

SOURCE: The files of the Department of Research and Education, IBPSPMW, Montreal, Quebec.

Table 2-10

MINIMUM ABSOLUTE AND PERCENTAGE WAGE CHANGES[a] EACH NEGOTIATING ROUND, PULP AND PAPER INDUSTRY, UNITED STATES AND CANADA, 1953-62

Year	United States				Canada		
	Great Northern	IP North	IP South	West Coast	C.I.P.	Ontario	B.C. Standard
1953	2.5% (4¢)	3% (5¢)	3% (5¢)	2.5% (4.5¢)	3% (5¢)	3% (5¢)	5¢ 2¢
1954	3% (4¢)	5¢	7¢	2% (3¢)			2¢
1955	4% (8¢)	5% (8¢)	5% (7¢)	4.5¢	5% (7¢)	5% (7¢)	5% (8¢)
1956	7% (12¢)	12¢	13¢	6% (9.5¢)	12¢	12¢	5¢
1957	5% (9¢)	5% (9¢)	5% (9¢)	3.5% (7¢)	5% (8¢)	5% (8¢)	
1958	5¢	5¢	4¢	2.5% (5¢)	5¢	5¢	7.5% (13¢) (retro-active to July 1/57)
1959		3.5% (12¢)	3% (7¢)	reopening 3% (8¢)	reopening 7¢		3% (6¢)
1960	5.5% (11¢) 2% (4¢)	4% (8¢)	4% (8¢)	3.5% (7.5¢)	4¢ 4¢	11¢ 4¢	4% (8¢)
1961	6¢	6¢	3.5¢	reopening 2% (4.5¢)	5¢	4¢	0¢
1962	5.5% (6¢)	4¢	3% (6¢)	2.5% (5.5¢)	5¢	5¢	3.5% (7¢)

a. The wage changes are listed as expressed in the settlement. Figures in brackets denote the minimum absolute changes if the settlement was expressed in percentage terms.

SOURCE: The files of the Department of Research and Education, IBPSPMW, Montreal, Quebec.

1953

On April 23, 1953, the union signed the first major agreement in the United States with Great Northern which called for a 2½ per cent (4 cent minimum) increase. At the end of April and the beginning of May the two divisions of International Paper settled for a slightly higher pattern of 3 per cent (5 cent minimum). On the U.S. West Coast the unions had started to negotiate on April 30 but by May 11 had still not reached an agreement. At that point they broke off negotiations and did not resume until August 17. Agreement was reached on August 19. The Great Northern 2½ per cent pattern was followed.

In Canada the major negotiations had started in April but broke down in every region with all of the major companies going to conciliation. The British Columbia mills were the first to settle, signing an agreement in September approximately a month after the one signed by U.S. West Coast mills. Despite the closeness in timing, however, the evidence does not indicate that the Canadian West Coast settlement was influenced in a major way by its U.S. counterpart. The wage settlement in British Columbia was for a series of three increases over a two-year period (5 cents and 2 cents in 1953 and 2 cents in 1954). Additionally the unions in British Columbia indicated during negotiations that they were concerned, not with following the U.S. settlement, but with establishing parity with the IWA-lumber industry rates in the Pacific Coast province.

> During negotiations in 1937, with two of the major Pulp and Paper producers in British Columbia, (these being our first negotiations), we accepted wage rates comparable with those being paid by the Great Northern Paper Company in the State of Maine . . . .
>
> From 1937 to 1940 it was recognized in the Pulp and Paper Industry that our base rate was higher than that being paid in the Lumber and Sawmill Industry . . . .[39]

The unions' brief then went on to demonstrate that rates of pay for the B.C. pulp and paper industry had been higher than those in the province's lumber industry until the Regional War Labor Board came into existence in 1940. IWA rates were then placed on the same level as pulp and paper rates and remained so up to 1952. The unions concluded this argument with the following statement:

> Our members operating the mills in the Pulp and Paper Industry in the Province of British Columbia are required to perform work of a higher degree than that required in the Sawmill or Logging industries.

---

39. Conciliation Brief Submitted to the Members of the Conciliation Board in the Matter of Disputes Between British Columbia Pulp and Paper Companies and the IBPSPMW, August 21, 1953 (the files of the Department of Research and Education, IBPSPMW, Montreal, Quebec), p. 14.

Consequently, the members of these two International Unions feel that the increase requested (10¢) is warranted this year.[40]

The unions then turned their attention to rates of pay in the pulp and paper industry in the rest of Canada, but at no time were U.S. rates or settlements discussed. This, plus the differences in the length and content of the contracts, indicates quite clearly that Canadian negotiations in that case proceeded and concluded with little direct U.S. influence.

For Canadian mills east of British Columbia, agreements were not signed until November of 1953. The first key settlement was arrived at with the Ontario Newsprint Group on November 6. CIP followed that pattern on November 13 and all other major mills in Eastern Canada settled shortly thereafter. The Ontario settlement clearly followed the IP Northern and Southern pattern. As indicated, negotiations for all of Eastern Canada proceeded in the spring, parallel to those in the United States, but were delayed when the parties found it necessary to go to conciliation. The unions rejected the Conciliation Board's report which recommended no change in wage rates. They began negotiating with the Ontario Newsprint Group once more on November 2, 1963, and reaffirmed their original proposals.[41] When the companies rejected the unions' demands negotiations continued several more days without a settlement until the unions, after a caucus on November 5, proposed the United States settlement of 3 per cent (minimum 5 cents) at International Paper.[42] The details of the agreement were worked out with settlement officially arriving the following day. Management agreed to accept the proposal on wages if, in return, the union delegates accepted the balance of management's program. Negotiations at CIP which had also been greatly delayed were resumed on November 11, and on November 13 the parties agreed to follow the Ontario pattern. It is important to note that a U.S. pattern was first followed by companies in Ontario. Many of the companies in the Ontario Newsprint Group had no U.S. corporate connection. In two later wage rounds the CIP settlement was the key bargain in Eastern Canada with the parent company's pattern being followed.

A most interesting aspect of the U.S. settlements was that Great Northern granted special adjustments for a great number of jobs to correct inequities created during the period of wage controls. "During

40. *Ibid.*, p. 18.
41. Minutes of Ontario Newsprint and Kraft Wage Negotiations, November 2, 1953, Royal York Hotel, Toronto, Ontario (in the files of the Department of Research and Education, IBPSPMW, Montreal, Quebec).
42. Minutes of Ontario Newsprint and Kraft Wage Negotiations, November 3-6, 1953, Royal York Hotel, Toronto, Ontario (in the files of the Department of Research and Education, IBPSPMW, Montreal, Quebec).

this period Canadian newsprint manufacturers were able to grant larger increases. Adjustments bring Great Northern in line with Canadian rates."[43]

1954

With only U.S. agreements expiring this year, there were no developments of interest on a continental scale with the exception that the Great Northern settlement resulted in common labor rate parity with Quebec and Ontario Mills. It also included special adjustments to machine room rates to equalize them with rates in Eastern Canada.[44]

All U.S. companies had signed one-year agreements and all major agreements in North America were scheduled to open at essentially the same time in 1955.

1955

Up to this point the Ontario Newsprint Group invariably set the pattern for mills east of British Columbia. In 1955, however, multi-employer bargaining was abandoned in that province and the pattern-setting role passed to CIP. Not only did the CIP settlement of April 8 set the pattern for mills in Canada east of British Columbia, but it became the key settlement for the entire continent. It was the first major agreement signed and it was followed precisely at the mills of the parent company and by most Canadian mills east of British Columbia. The only area where a significantly different pattern prevailed was on the U.S. West Coast. In British Columbia the 5 per cent CIP pattern was followed but a two-year rather than a one-year contract was negotiated, with an additional 5 cent increase being provided for in the second year. One additional interesting feature was that a sick leave plan was established at CIP and this too was included in the parent company agreement.

1956

The 1956 round was very similar to the one in the previous year. The key bargain was again at CIP which was settled on April 10. A two-year agreement was signed, calling for 12 cents in 1956 and 5 per cent (minimum 8 cents) in 1957. Approximately a month later an almost identical settlement was reached in the Southern Kraft industry and the Northern Division of International Paper. The major difference was that at IP South a 13 cent increase rather than a 12 cent increase was provided for in 1956, and a 9 cent rather than 8 cent minimum was provided for in the second

---

43. *Pulp and Paper Worker* (IBPSPMW, Washington), May, 1953, p. 1.
44. *Ibid.,* July, 1954, p. 8.

year at both divisions of the parent company. At both CIP and IP mills shift differentials were also raised — by 2 cents to 3 cents at CIP, by 1 cent to 2 cents in the company's Northern Division, and by 2 cents to 3 cents in the Southern Division. Also, there was a slight liberalization of health and welfare benefits at both the U.S. and Canadian mills although the changes were not the same. This pattern spread to most other mills in Eastern Canada but, due to the fact that B.C. mills were in the second year of a two-year contract, the pattern had no impact in that case. At Great Northern, a one- rather than a two-year contract was signed, but it provided for the same wage increase as at CIP and when a new agreement was nego- tiated in 1957 the 5 per cent pattern established for the second year in the CIP agreement was followed. The settlement on the U.S. West Coast, arrived at three weeks after the CIP pattern, did not appear to be directly influenced by it. A one-year agreement was signed providing for a 6 per cent increase. In 1957, another one- year agreement was signed which called for a 3½ per cent increase rather than the 5 per cent pattern for 1957 established at CIP.

1958

The major settlements in the United States in 1957 have been dealt with above. In Canada, with all major mills east of British Columbia signing two-year agreements in 1957, there were no negotiations in that area until 1958. The two-year agreement signed in B.C. in 1955 opened in June 1957 but, because of protracted negotiations and a three months' strike, settlement did not come until February 4, 1958. The B.C. agreement, which was retroactive to July 1, 1957 did not follow or set a pattern in the pulp and paper industry. The provision for a 7½ per cent increase was quite unlike any of the other settlements in the North American pulp and paper industry. It was based on a 7½ per cent management offer which came out of Conciliation Board proceedings. This followed the pattern established by the IWA in British Columbia's lumber industry.

The settlements which followed in the late spring of 1958, showed no similarity to the B.C. settlement. Negotiations in all regions of North America, B.C. excepted, began in April. Because of poor market conditions, however, negotiations on the U.S. West Coast were postponed until the fall of 1958. Similarly, at CIP talks opened April 3, but were adjourned to June 9 to give union leaders an opportunity to analyze market conditions. In April, the company had asked for an extension of the contract with no wage increase but the unions continued to seek a 15 cent increase. In May the unions had settled at the parent company's Northern Division for a 5 cent increase. The contract was for one year. When talks resumed at

CIP the unions used this settlement and similar ones in the Lake States as a standard.

> The unions claim they have been given an hourly boost of 5¢ in some of the Lake States and are disposed to use this as a lever for prying something out of the companies in the way of higher pay.[45]

CIP settled with little resistance on June 13 for the 5 cent pattern but a two-year agreement was signed. A most significant feature, however, was a reopening provision which fell at essentially the same time that the parent company's contracts were due to expire in 1959.

Some Canadian industry spokesman apparently objected to the pattern being established when economic conditions in the industry were poor.

> A spokesman for the newsprint industry said in Montreal today there was no justification for a wage increase in the industry at present and union demands should be resisted . . . .
> The Montreal industry spokesman said a wholly-owned subsidiary of a U.S. Corporation "has elected to import a foreign wage pattern, which will probably be unacceptable to the majority of Canadian-owned newsprint companies, who will endeavor to create a pattern of their own more suited to the best interests of Canada."[46]

Up until the point at which CIP settled, Canadian companies east of British Columbia were providing a solid wall of resistance to the unions. Once CIP settled, however, the resistance collapsed for the most part and other Eastern Canadian companies followed the pattern.

The 5 cent pattern spread to other companies in the United States, as well. The U.S. West Coast employers settled in November and Great Northern in December. Great Northern, as the Eastern Canadian companies had, signed a two-year agreement.

1959 to 1960

The United States agreements at International Paper expired in the spring of 1959 while those in Canada in all regions were not to expire until the spring of 1960. Great Northern and the U.S. West Coast contracts, also, were not to expire until the spring of 1960. Despite this dissimilarity in contract length, once again there was international pattern-following in the industry.

The companies on the Pacific coast of the United States decided to open their contracts in 1959 and on May 29 agreed to a 3 per

---

45. *Canada Labour Views* (Toronto), May 28, 1958, p. 1.
46. *Montreal Star*, June 16, 1958, p. 3.

cent (minimum 8 cents) increase. In June, International Paper signed two-year agreements at their Northern and Southern Divisions. The contract called for a 1959 increase of 3½ per cent (minimum 12 cents in the North and a 3 per cent (minimum 7 cents) increase in the Southern Division. In both Divisions a 4 per cent (minimum 8 cents) increase was scheduled for 1960.

The British Columbia employers also settled in June on a one-year basis providing a 3 per cent increase. In percentage terms the settlement was identical to the increase under the re-opener on the U.S. West Coast. There can be little doubt that the U.S. West Coast pattern was being followed in this case. In addition to the identical wage increase and the fact that the U.S. settlement was reached shortly before the one in B.C., the U.S. settlement provided for a seventh paid holiday which was also included in the British Columbia settlement.

Developments in Eastern Canada clearly established the fact that the IP South settlement became the key bargain for mills east of British Columbia. In June of 1959 the unions invoked the wage reopener clause in the two-year agreements in eastern Canada. They approached most of the newsprint companies in the summer asking for a wage increase but all of the companies refused to consider an increase at that time. Two later meetings were held at CIP under the 30-day reopening clause which allowed either side to ask for a wage conference at any time after April 30, 1959. One conference was held on July 28 and 29, another on October 20 and 21. In both cases the company refused to increase wages despite the fact that the parent firm had done so. At the close of the October talks, President Burke asked the company if it would be willing to consider the negotiation of a new agreement on the basis that it would replace the current one for the balance of the time the latter would be in effect, and for an additional period of one year. If agreed to by the company this would have resulted in the CIP and IP contracts expiring at the same time in 1961. The company replied that it would consider such a proposal.[47] With this understanding CIP held another conference with the unions in the early part of November.

It is important to note that as soon as the United States settlements at International Paper had been signed in June of 1959, the unions used them as a benchmark in Canada. The following is an excerpt from union correspondence to several Ontario locals:

---

47. Minutes of Canadian International Paper Labour Conference, November 9, 1959 (in the files of the Department of Research and Education, IBPSPMW, Montreal, Quebec).

At the convention of the Quebec and Eastern Canada Council of Paper Mill Unions, held in Three Rivers, Quebec, June 18-20, the undersigned were requested by the delegates from all CIP newsprint and pulp mills to give the Company the required 30-day notice for the holding of a conference to discuss an upward revision in wage rates.

The reason for this request is because the two divisions of the International Paper Company in the United States were recently granted wage increases for this year: the Southern Kraft Division — 7 cents and other substantial benefits, and the Book and Bond Division in the Northern States — 3½ per cent also with other social benefits.

In view of the above, we are writing to enquire if it is your desire for us to arrange a conference with your company under the 30-day clause as agreed to last year and which is incorporated in your Memo of Agreement.[48]

When the unions had approached CIP in July they continued to use the IP settlements as an argument for wage increases in Canada. In reply company spokesmen had stated that conditions in Canada had not improved to the same degree as they had in the United States and that the company's wage policies had to be based on Canadian rather than U.S. conditions.[49] They continued to push for the parent company pattern, particularly the one which was arrived at for the Southern Kraft Division and, not surprisingly, in the November negotiations agreed to by CIP, almost all of the discussion revolved around the U.S. parent company settlement and comparative Canadian and American economic conditions in the industry. On November 14 the company proposed a settlement which was almost identical in all respects (wage and fringe benefit increases) to the Southern Kraft pattern.[50] It provided for a 7 cent increase on November 1, 1959 and an 8 cent increase (in two 4 cent stages) in 1960. In addition, as had been the case in the Southern Kraft contract there was provision for one more paid holiday; 3 weeks' vacation after ten, instead of fifteen, years of service; 3 days' funeral leave in the event of death in the immediate family (not previously provided for in the Southern Kraft Division or at CIP); and special wage adjustments for some skilled jobs. This was

---

48. Correspondence from J. A. D'Aoust (Vice-President and Canadian Director, UPP) and William H. Burnell (First Vice-President, IBPSPMW), to Local Unions in mills of seven Ontario Companies, June 25, 1959 (in the files of the Department of Research and Education, IBPSPMW, Montreal, Quebec).

49. Memorandum of Information, Canadian International Paper, July 31, 1959 (in the files of the Department of Research and Education, IBPSPMW, Montreal, Quebec).

50. Other than different effective dates for the wage increases there was one other additional difference. The increases in the Southern Kraft Division were 3 per cent and 4 per cent. At CIP the increases in 1959 ranged from 7 cents, for base rates between $1.78 to $2.50, up to 11 cents for $4.01 to $4.50. In 1960 the range was from 8 cents to 16 cents. In percentage terms, therefore, the settlements were slightly different.

accepted by the unions and set the pattern for the ensuing 1960 negotiations for all the other companies whose contracts expired in that year.

Twenty-five one-year agreements were signed by mills east of British Columbia in 1960. All followed the wage and fringe benefits pattern established at CIP. With regard to the wage increases there was one difference. The November 14 CIP package provided for a 7 cent increase on November 1, 1959 and 4 cents on May 1, 1960 and November 1, 1960. The settlements reached in 1960 at the other Eastern Canadian companies called for 11 cents on May 1, 1960 and 4 cents on November 1, 1960.[51]

The settlement in British Columbia in June 1960 was also a one-year contract calling for a 4 per cent (8 cents) increase. This was exactly the same as the IP Southern Kraft provision in the second year of its 1959 contract. The U.S. West Coast employers had also signed a contract in May, 1960 which provided for a 3½ per cent (7½ cents) increase; and Great Northern, which had provided no increase in 1959, signed a one-year contract in 1960 which was identical to the 1960 agreements in Eastern Canada, i.e., 11 cents plus 4 cents.

In summation, therefore, the 1959 IP pattern for the Southern Kraft industry influenced all ensuing settlements in 1959 and 1960 on the North American continent.

1961 to 1962

In the final two years of the analysis period the relationship between Canadian and U.S. wage changes in the industry diminished to some extent. In 1961 the Canadian settlements, for the most part, came several months after the key settlements in the United States. The key settlement in Eastern Canada, however, was, for the first time, with the Eastern Canada Newsprint Group (comprised of three companies in Quebec and one in Nova Scotia — St. Lawrence Corporation, Anglo-Canadian, James MacLaren, and Bowaters

---

51. When consideration is given to the increases for jobs above the common labor rate level, the differences between the CIP settlement and others in Eastern Canada were somewhat greater than expressed above. A union analysis of the Canadian International Paper settlement compared with all the other settlements indicated that, while the workers in CIP mills received a wage increase six months ahead of the other mills amounting to approximately 70 dollars and up per employee, plus 3 cents adjustment for mechanics during the life of the agreement, all the other settlements provided a lower break-off point. All workers between $2.01 per hour and $2.50 per hour received an 18 cents general wage increase as against 15 cents in the CIP mills where the break-off point to receive 18 cents was $2.51 per hour.

Mersey). This agreement was arrived at on May 16, 1961, more than a month before any U.S. settlements. It established a 5 cent pattern on a one-year contract. Other companies in Eastern Canada followed the same pattern, some of them, however, going to conciliation beforehand. At CIP, negotiations which began in early April were recessed until mid-September. The company had requested the recess because of uncertain market conditions. The parties finally agreed to a two-year contract on October 8 which provided for a 5 cent increase in 1961 and an additional 5 cent increase in 1962. The latter increase provided the pattern for Eastern Canada mills when their contracts expired in 1962. They settled in that year before any agreements were signed in the U.S. industry. The settlements in British Columbia in 1961 and 1962 were not similar to either the eastern Canadian or U.S. settlements in those years. It should be noted, however, that over the two-year period total wage increases were the same at CIP, the Ontario mills, the U.S. West Coast, and IP's two divisions.

The major union emphasis in both 1961 and 1962 was on fringe benefits, particularly in the former year. The unions in Canada were especially concerned with changes in the health and welfare, sick leave, and pension plans.[52] One of the major issues which proved to be a stumbling-block in Eastern Canada negotiations, was the companies' request that continuous operations be accepted by the unions. The mills in Eastern Canada stressed that seven-day operations were necessary if they were to continue to compete on an equal basis with mills in British Columbia and the United States. The agreements at Eastern mills were influenced by the provision or lack of provision for continuous operations in the various settlements in 1961 and 1962.

While precise international pattern-bargaining in terms of wage increases was not in evidence in the final two years, there was some continental pattern-following in the fringe benefits area. In British Columbia, for example, there was provision in 1961 for four weeks vacation after twenty-three years of service (instead of twenty-five years). This had been part of the U.S. West Coast package three months earlier. The same change took place at Canadian International Paper and the Northern and Southern Divisions of International Paper. The latter also improved the health and welfare plans at both of its Divisions and this was generally true of all mills in Eastern Canada.

_____

52. In very few Canadian pulp and paper companies was the pension plan in the collective agreement at that time. One of the major demands of the unions was to include the company retirement plans in the collective agreement.

In 1961 what seemed to take place, therefore, was an emphasis on fringe benefit increases by the unions. The changes were somewhat similar from company to company. There were variations, however. For example, a higher wage increase was provided for in IP's Northern Division than in its Southern Division. In lieu of the larger increase negotiated at the Northern Division, the company assumed the full cost of the life insurance and weekly sickness and accident insurance programs for the employees and established a severance pay plan, in addition to similar fringe changes that were granted by the company at its Northern Division. This took place in Canada in 1961 with the various companies improving some aspects of their fringe benefits. Because of differences in individual company health and welfare plans the changes from company to company were not identical. In British Columbia there was no wage increase but an industry-wide health and welfare plan was established.

The same was true of the 1962 negotiations, as well. Wage increases were not uniform and various fringe benefit changes were included. Some degree of uniformity in contract provisions was achieved following the varied provisions of the previous year. For example, the situation at IP Southern and Northern Divisions was reversed. This time the Southern Division was granted a higher wage increase than the Northern Division. In the Northern Division, however, the company assumed the employee's contribution for the group life, sickness and accident insurance program in place of the larger wage increase negotiated at the Southern Kraft Division.

This was the case in Eastern Canada. Most mills which had not granted four weeks vacation after twenty-three years in 1961, made such a provision in 1962. Also, companies which had not fully followed the pattern in the health and welfare area in 1961 increased contributions the following year.

There was one other international pattern-following incident. On the U.S. West Coast the eligibility requirements for four weeks vacation had been reduced from twenty-three to twenty years, and this was also included in the B.C. agreement in 1962. In addition, a job evaluation program, based on the one on the U.S. West Coast, was agreed to by the British Columbia companies.

AN ASSESSMENT OF U.S. INFLUENCE AND UNION POLICY IN THE PULP AND PAPER INDUSTRY

The examination of negotiations over the ten-year period revealed a high degree of interrelatedness between U.S. and Canadian settlements in the industry. It merely supplied supporting evidence to the presentation for the period prior to 1953. During Canadian negotiations there was frequent reference by both parties to wage rates, fringe benefits, and economic conditions in the United States. There was participation by American officials and the presence of President Burke seemed to be especially important. At times he apparently dedicated more time to Canadian negotiations than to those in the United States, as the following statement indicates:

> As President of the International Union I gave more of my time to these negotiations than I did to the negotiations of any other companies. I did not go to Mobile, Alabama, for the negotiations with the Southern Kraft Company this year. I did not go to the West Coast for the negotiations, but I did go to Toronto three times to help in the negotiations with the Ontario companies.[53]

In the last two years of the analysis period Burke did not participate in Canadian negotiations but in years prior to that he was present and it is difficult to escape the conclusion that he was at least partially responsible for the international pattern-bargaining observed. To illustrate, his role in the 1959 reopening at CIP was most crucial. It was Burke who pushed for the reopening at CIP and who exerted pressure on the company to follow the IP Southern pattern. There is evidence which indicates that many of the local delegates actually opposed the contract reopening in November. The following excerpt indicates the conflict that existed with regard to the opening, and the fact that it was entirely Burke's idea.

> Vice-President L. H. Lorrain said that President Burke had been called at lunch time because we had to know what he really thought. This November conference has been the result of a suggestion of his. President Burke was putting his judgment at stake because he was confident that we could get as much as had been obtained in the U.S. settlements . . . .
> G. Trepanier of Local 163 pointed out that he had instructions from his local membership to negotiate wage increases. If the unions cannot go to the end of the procedure, as they would under normal conditions of bargaining, what can be gained, he asked, from the coming conference. He and his fellow delegates cannot go back empty hands [sic]. It is hard to negotiate under the present conditions. He had to sell to the local membership the idea of coming to Montreal for the conference. He had had to interpret President Burke's point of view, which can be easily misunderstood by the local membership.
> Chairman D'Aoust said that he felt he must say again that it was not a Burke and Company agreement. The idea of the coming conference had originated with President Burke. But it had been submitted to membership and accepted . . . .
> Pat O'Farrell of Local 142 said that if there is a vote on the motion, then the delegates from his local would have to be excused from voting.[54]

53. Correspondence from John T. Burke to the Secretary of Local 92, Fort Frances, Ontario, November 21, 1953 (in the files of the Department of Research and Education, IBPSPMW, Montreal, Quebec).

54. Minutes of Canadian International Paper Labour Conference, November 9, 1959 (in the files of the Department of Research and Education, IBPSPMW, Montreal, Quebec).

After the delegates finally agreed to the wage conference Burke successfully obtained a wage increase for the membership which, as noted previously, was similar to the spring settlement in the Southern Kraft industry.[55]

There was, therefore, no diminishing of U.S. influence over the ten-year period. This did have an impact on Canadian settlements although perhaps not on comparative wage levels in the long run. That is, the wage changes may have been "barometric" rather than "coercive". The exact uniformity witnessed, however, must have been due to the use of U.S. orbits of comparison by both parties.

The pressure exerted by the internationals was primarily a response to competition in the product market. The existence of competing unions, U.S. corporate ownership and geographical proximity did at times, however, have a bearing on negotiations and union approaches. Firstly, pressure on union leaders for settlements at least as high as prevailed at International Falls was continuously exerted by the local union in Fort Frances, as the following letter to President Burke indicates:

> At International Falls the CIO and other A.F. of L. Unions received and accepted five cents (.05) general increase . . . . A conciliation officer was sent from Toronto (Mr. Davis) immediately and made a settlement receiving four cents for hourly employees and seven dollars a month for the monthly.
>
> This sure makes the boys very much disappointed. They are of the opinion that we are slipping and falling by the wayside. They are all for getting tough.[56]

The existence of the Catholic Syndicate began to take on added significance in the mid 1950's and, while there is no evidence to suggest that this was responsible for attempts by the Internationals to follow U.S. patterns, it was unquestionably of concern to the union

---

55. There were two amusing incidents connected with Burke's suggestion to reopen the contract. In the minutes of the CIP negotiations Burke, even though he was responsible, was quoted as saying that "whoever was responsible for the timing of the conference could not have chosen a better time to do it."

Secondly, in reply to a telegram from one Ontario local which protested the action of Burke without prior consultation, he stated, "This is a reply to your telegram regarding negotiations with the CIP. Our locals in the CIP mills insisted upon negotiations because the wage rates in the Canadian mills had fallen behind the rates paid in the mills of the division in the U.S." Telegram from John Burke to the Secretary of Local 92, Fort William, Ontario, November 13, 1959 (in the files of the Department of Research and Education, IBPSPMW, Montreal, Quebec).

56. Correspondence from the Secretary of Local 92, Fort Frances, Ontario, to John P. Burke, August 24, 1953 (in the files of the Department of Research and Education, IBPSPMW, Montreal, Quebec).

leadership. An interview with a company official disclosed that the threat of the National Federation to the jurisdiction of the Internationals had a significant effect in 1965. The result was that the CIP settlement was higher than it would have been without that factor.[57] The company granted the additional amount primarily to place the Internationals in a more favorable position in their battle with the Federation.

The existence of U.S. ownership also seemed to be of some importance. In two of the cases where an American pattern was specifically followed in Canada it was the IP pattern settlement in the United States that was transmitted first to CIP, and then to other companies in Eastern Canada. It was made clear in both these cases that the union pressed for the U.S. pattern because CIP had fallen behind rates at the parent company. Union correspondence, in addition, indicates that it had some importance in other areas as well. It may have aided the union, for example, in keeping as much standardization as possible on a continental basis in the fringe benefits area. The Canadian research department of the IBPSPMW was able to evaluate the pension, and health and welfare plans of Canadian subsidiaries in the light of developments in those areas at the parent companies. There were numerous pieces of correspondence between the Canadian and U.S. research departments to facilitate such comparisons. The flow of information was by no means all in a Canada to U.S. direction. The U.S. research office often requested information from the Canadian department regarding the provisions of Canadian fringe benefits and wage rates, particularly in U.S. subsidiaries. One of the most important aspects of the existence of U.S. subsidiaries in Canada, then, was the fact that the union was probably more fully informed of developments and provisions in the United States.

There was, however, not as much direct impact because of this factor as might have been expected. International pattern-bargaining took place on occasion when U.S. subsidiaries were not the pattern setters in Canada. There were no cases of Canadian or American union officials attempting to broaden the scope of the bargaining unit to continental dimensions. Only one minor case approaching a consolidated approach came to the attention of the author. In 1960, when Kimberly-Clark (the parent company of Spruce Falls Paper) was considering changes in its group life insurance and pension plans, the U.S. officers of the IBPSPMW met with top management in Chicago to explore management proposals which were to be applicable to its U.S. and Canadian operations. This was the one instance of a union dealing with an international corporation on an

---

57. Anonymous interview at the Canadian International Paper Company, September 9, 1965.

international basis.[58] The major reason for this not being done more often seems to be that most U.S. subsidiaries in the Canadian pulp and paper industry are operated quite independently from their parent companies, at least in the industrial relations area. An official at CIP indicated that the company is operated independently from the parent firm adding, "you can't help in a big organization having some similarities because there is a common basic philosophy which trickles down".[59]

The existence of some proximity also probably influenced the Internationals as the above excerpt from the Fort Frances local indicated. As well, the job evaluation plan worked out in British Columbia was based on the industry plan to the south. This plan is not used in any other regions in Canada and the following state-
Paper Company, September 9, 1965.
ment suggests that the reason it is used in British Columbia is partially due to geographical proximity:

> The question of adopting a Job Evaluation plan for the industry is a subject which has been discussed during many Wage Conferences over the past ten years. Perhaps one of the main reasons why the mills in British Columbia, (both Union and Management) have been interested in coming to a formalized method of rate determination is because of their close association, geographical and otherwise, with the pulp and paper mills on the U.S. Pacific Coast, where a jointly administered Job Analysis plan was designed specifically for the pulp and paper industry . . . .
>
> During the 1959 Wage Conference with the three Paper Maker Local Unions which were party to the B.C. Labour Agreement, it was agreed that a joint rate study would be conducted throughout these Locals during the contract year using the Pacific Coast Association's Job Analysis method of rate determination.[60]

In the years prior to 1953, partially because of the proximity factor, the unions at Eastern Canada mills often exerted pressure

---

58. This is clear from the following — "A meeting with top management of Kimberly-Clark has been arranged by our International Union in Chicago, U.S.A. on the 24th and 25th of April at the Morrison Hotel to further explore management proposals.

"Because the Company's proposals affect the union members in both Canada and U.S.A. the issues are being investigated on an International basis.

"I will be in attendance at these meetings representing the interests of our Canadian locals along with representation from the Washington office as well as Vice-Presidents from our International Union." Correspondence from R. W. Ostling, Director, Canadian Department of Research and Education, to the Secretary of Local 933, St. Hyacinthe, Quebec, April 13, 1961 (in the files of the Department of Research and Education, IBPSPMW, Montreal, Quebec).

59. Anonymous interview with an official at the Canadian International

60. D. Gray, "Job Evaluation for Hourly-Rated Classifications" (Canadian Pulp and Paper Association, Industrial Relations Conference, 1965).

on the companies for wage changes and levels similar to those at Great Northern. This pressure diminished during the ten-year analysis period. As noted with wage controls in the United States in the early 1950's, rates in Eastern Canada moved ahead of those at Great Northern. The benchmark was naturally no longer appealing to the unions and hence comparions with Great Northern were used less frequently, and none of the settlements in Canada during the analysis period were based on agreements at that company. Instead, the opposite took place and settlements at Great Northern in 1953 and 1954 were based on Eastern Canada wage levels and, in 1955 and 1956, the Great Northern wage increases were based on the CIP pattern.

Union competition, U.S. ownership and geographical proximity, then, probably had some limited impact on union policy. By far the most important factor, however, was the product market. From the beginning, the unions showed an awareness of the possible impact of low-wage competition on the well-being of their membership. The first evidence of this was their position on free entry for Canadian imports. A large portion of the negotiations examined, involved a discussion of U.S. rates and conditions of work on the basis that the U.S. companies were competitor mills. One of the interesting aspects was that Eastern Canada companies, in 1953 and 1954 particularly, began to use the argument that consideration should be given to rates at competitor mills in the U.S. This was due to the fact that most companies in Eastern Canada were paying higher rates than in the U.S. Northeast and South immediately after wage controls were lifted in the United States. At the CIP negotiations in 1953 the President of the company presented the following argument:

> After listening to the remarks of the union delegates yesterday morning and afternoon, I came away with the impression that I had failed to get over the essential facts of the conditions facing our companies. I made reference to the fact that our competitors in the United States enjoy wage rates lower than ours . . . .
> Our pulp competitors in the southern part of the U.S. enjoy a base rate of $1.32 on a forty-hour week.
> Base rates vary in newsprint mills. At the Lufkin mill in Texas, the rate is $1.24 per hour. The Coosa River rate is $1.32. Further north, the base rates are at Bucksport (Maine) $1.36, St. Croix, $1.38, Mechanicville, $1.38, Great Northern $1.39. In the middle west, base rates are a bit higher, $1.42 at Fort Edward (Wisconsin), and $1.46 at both Kimberly and Niagara.[61]

As a further indication of the importance of the product market, key Canadian settlements played much the same role in the United

---

61. Minutes of Canadian International Paper Labour Conference, statement by V. E. Johnson, April 30, 1953, Montreal, Que. (in the files of the Department of Research and Education, IBPSPMW, Montreal, Quebec).

States. On the U.S. West Coast there was no direct influence from Canada but Canadian developments did affect the expectations of the parties. They were often used as a benchmark by both unions and the companies. In the 1953 negotiations, for example, with the Pacific Coast Association the following statement was made by a union delegate:

> During the past week there have been increases granted to paper industries on the east coast and in Canada; two and a half, three, three and a half percent. I see Mr. Heron smiling. I guess I know what he is smiling about. I think I do. But nevertheless, Mr. Heron, and the members on your side of the table, the trend is that they are not holding the line so to speak.[62]

The interesting aspect was that the union arguments for wage increases were similar to those used in Canada, with the arguments simply reversed. Vice-President Brown of the IBPM in 1955, for example, presented this argument to the West Coast manufacturers:

> Now here is what happened in I.P. in Eastern Canada. They received a 5 per cent general increase calculated to the nearest cent. They have $1.46 base rate there. They increased their shift differential from three and five to four and six which was a one cent increase. They changed their procedure of calculating overtime so that a tour worker will be paid at the rate of time and one-half for all work performed beyond their regular daily hours except with two exceptions. One is when the work is caused by change of shifts when one tour worker agrees with another tour worker for an exchange of shifts, or when a tour worker is held over for a two-hour period due to lateness of his relief. One other condition which they granted was that an hourly paid employee with at least six months of continuous service who could furnish proper evidence from a physician that he had been wholly unable to perform any of his duties for a period of ten days that the company would pay him sick leave to the tune of one normal work week earnings less income tax.
>
> This indicates to me that as this round of negotiations continues that you are going to see improvements . . . .[63]

Thus, the unions' desire for uniformity stemmed primarily from the necessity to "take wages out of competition". They consider wages and wage changes in all regions of the continent but with certain benchmarks being traditional, or more feasible for economic reasons. For example, the following excerpt illustrates union considerations in British Columbia:

---

62. Transcript of record of negotiations between the Pacific Coast Pulp and Paper Manufacturers' Association and the IBPSPMW and IBPM, April 30-May 11, 1953, Portland, Ore. (in the files of the Department of Research and Education, IBPSPMW, Montreal, Quebec), pp. 165, 166.

63. Transcript of record of negotiations between the Pacific Coast Pulp and Paper Manufacturers' Association and the IBPSPMW and IBPM, April 15-April 23, 1955, Portland, Ore. (in the files of the Department of Research and Education, IBPSPMW, Montreal, Quebec), pp. 282-283.

Saturday, June 17th, I received a telegram, as per enclosed copy, from President Burke regarding the Great Northern Paper Company settlement. The contents of this settlement were most interesting and enlightening. Many of our Members in the early 40's should recall that this Company set wage patterns for many of our Canadian Mills. Later, we in British Columbia, began to establish our own wage patterns and during this period we have enjoyed a 10¢ to 12¢ per hour differential over Eastern Canadian agreements. It is self-evident that the differential is now being eradicated. You were previously advised of the St. Lawrence Paper Co., Red Rock, and Newfoundland settlements and these, along with the Great Northern settlement, bear out my contention. I feel it is imperative that we endeavour to maintain our differential and narrow the gap between our B.C. Standards and the Uniform Labour Agreement.[64]

The telegram mentioned in the letter reveals much about union policy towards Canada. In essence, Canada is treated as just another region in the overall strategy of the unions. Any settlement in North America is an expectation for the unions in their other negotiations. In his telegram to Hansen, Burke, after conveying the terms of the agreement with Great Northern, stated: "This settlement with Great Northern will have a favorable impact upon all our negotiations both in the United States and Canada, I hope." In setting up expectations, however, any key settlement is considered within the context of regional factors. A key settlement on the U.S. West Coast, for example, was never precisely followed in Canada even though negotiations in many cases were proceeding at the same time. It was an expectation which undoubtedly influenced union policy in Canada, but was never a pressing issue in Eastern Canada negotiations and had only a limited influence in B.C. A key settlement in the U.S. South or North, on the other hand, often had a direct influence in Eastern Canada and vice-versa.

The policy of the unions, then, can best be viewed as a product of rank-and-file, company, and economic pressures. It is not simply a reflection of egalitarian philosophy. Firstly, union delegates are aware of wage levels and developments in other regions and these were used by delegates during negotiations. This undoubtedly puts pressures on the union executive. As an example, the Fort Frances local wrote to President Burke condemming international headquarters after a lower increase had been negotiated for their mill than at International Falls in 1953.

At our last regular meeting after the members heard the report of the wage conference in Toronto given by our two attending delegates, I was instructed by a motion to write you and advise you that the members of Local 92 are not satisfied with the agreement and the

64. Correspondence from H. L. Hansen, International Vice-President, IBPSPMW, to all Locals Party to the Standard Labour Contract, June 28, 1961 (in the files of the Department of Research and Education, IBPSPMW, Montreal, Quebec).

membership also felt that they did not get the same co-operation as they gave the International.[65]

Along the same lines, another basic consideration is the danger of inter-local competition. For example, the Kapuskasing local in 1963 expressed a great deal of concern over the below standard wage rates negotiated by the union at the Gaspesia Pulp and Paper Company in Quebec. The President of that local tried to have the local break away from the IBPSPMW over the issue. The Ontario local was particularly concerned because both mills shipped paper to the New York Times.

Secondly, high wage companies often confront the unions with the competitive threat of low wage firms. This puts pressure on the unions to pursue wage uniformity. Also, the unions cannot allow major deviations from an established pattern, at least in the important firms, because of the effect this would have on future negotiations. A below pattern settlement at a large company would weaken the unions' position at subsequent negotiations. Strategic considerations, therefore, are of vital concern.

Another factor which dictates a uniform outlook on the part of the unions is industry wage policy. Industry policy stems from price uniformity, the homogeneous nature of the product, the size of capital investment, and the fact that labor costs are high enough to merit their concern. The companies seek stability and are concerned with low wage competition. This has resulted, as another study points out, in the companies being industry oriented in the formulation of their wage policy. They are fully knowledgeable of wage changes and levels throughout the industry and the unions, in order to be on an equal footing, must also take a North American approach.

> Generally speaking, employers are industry oriented in the formulation of their wage policies. Because of the competitive nature of the industry, they tend to stress the wage position of competitors and the wage concessions granted in competing mills. Indeed, equalization of wage competition has played an important role in the development of multi-company bargaining; and similar interests have encouraged many companies to participate in studies and surveys of wages and working conditions within particular areas and regions and within particular competing groups.[66]

The pressures from these forces, which are both institutional and economic, have been reflected in the internationals' general strategy. This involves an interdependent wage policy for the

---

65. Correspondence from the Secretary of Local 92, IBPSPMW, Fort Frances, Ontario, to Mr. John P. Burke, November 21, 1953 (in the files of the Department of Research and Education, IBPSPMW, Montreal, Quebec).
66. MacDonald, *Pulp and Paper*, p. 108.

industry *throughout the continent* and a uniform policy within each major producing region, but with some deviations being necessary, between and within the various areas. The most interesting aspect is that union and industry policies complement each other. The outcome has been that settlements in Eastern Canada, the Lake, Northeastern, and Southern States all had some influence, in some cases a direct influence, on each other, while the influences between the U.S. West Coast and British Columbia and other regions were operative to a lesser extent. The latter is probably due to the fact that the unions in B.C. are also interested in keeping pace with IWA wage levels in the province.

With regard to economic pressures, it is important to note that the union leadership is realistic in that it considers what a firm is capable of paying, and generally becomes a moderating influence late in negotiations. John Burke, for example, when he pushed for the Southern pattern at CIP in November of 1959, was able to obtain most of the pattern and he was able to do so because of his ability to judge how far the company was willing to go. When it was apparent that the company had made its final offer, he urged the rank-and-file to accept what the company had offered. "He reminded the delegates that there was danger in overloading at this time."[67]

The union is also willing to settle for less than the regional standard at companies that do not have the ability to pay. This was clearly brought out in correspondence between International Vice-President L. H. Lorrain and John Burke, with the former reporting that a settlement had not been reached with a New Brunswick firm because of their refusal to follow the Eastern Canada pattern.

> Their action is based on the fact that we sign agreements with some of their competitors for lower wage rates, that is Gaspesia and Irving Pulp. As you know, Gaspesia has had hard times for several years, last year were in the red for nearly $200,000, and we had to give them relief. In the case of Irving Pulp, we have brought that from the lowest paid industry in 1946, 56 cents per hour and nothing else, even overtime rates to the highest paid in Saint John, $1.62 base rate, and you know we have had to go to Conciliation year after year to get it, almost to the point of going on strike. Irving has had construction going on all those years, bringing the Sulphite Pulp mill from 90 tons per day to over 200 tons per day, (not a large tonnage), and building the new Kraft mill which will be in production this fall. Irving has promised us that when he makes some money he will match industry rates. Frasers are not comparable to either of these two cases. If they were, we would consider their position.[68]

67. Minutes of Canadian International Paper Labour Conference, November 14, 1959 (in the files of the Department of Research and Education, IBPSPMW, Montreal, Quebec).

68. Correspondence from International Vice-President L. H. Lorrain, IBPSPMW, to John P. Burke, July 4, 1960 (in the files of the Department of Research and Education, IBPSPMW, Montreal, Quebec).

The stand of the international executive regarding the need for continuous operations at Eastern Canada companies, so that they could more effectively compete with United States and British Columbia mills, also demonstrated the flexibility of the unions when employment is threatened. The companies received more co-operation at the international level than at the local level. The following statement made by the President of CIP in the 1965 negotiations indicates this:

> Five years ago, we explained to you how necessary it was to have the right to operate our mills on a continuous basis. You agreed with us; and together we took the lead in introducing continuous operation in the pulp and paper industry in Quebec . . . .
> To their credit, the Pulp Workers and the Papermakers, at the international level, presented a strong case for continuous operation. But a major segment of organized labor in Quebec as well as one of the locals represented at this Conference strenuously opposed continuous operation before the Commission.[69]

The following, from the same statement as above, and many similar statements, indicates that most of the companies in Canada probably preferred the active participation of U.S. union officials in Canadian negotiations:

> The name of John P. Burke comes first to mind of those who have withdrawn recently from active participation in our relations. While he was in office John P. was always closely identified with what was best in the labor movement. His thinking was honest, far-sighted, and constructive. Both the companies and the employees in our industry have every reason to be grateful to him for his wisdom and restraint.[70]

One Canadian company official indicated that if he had a choice between the International unions and a purely Canadian union, excluding nationalistic feelings on the question, he would prefer to deal with the Internationals.[71] They serve as a coordinating force.

Burke summarized the position of the unions through a series of statements on July 12 and 13, 1949 when dealing with the companies represented in the Ontario Newsprint Group.

> July 12 — We are not getting anywhere here. The employers want to renew the agreements as is. Well, we can't do that. We

---

69. Remarks by Mr. E. B. Hinman, President, Canadian International Paper Company and New Brunswick International Paper Company at the Canadian International Paper Labour Conference, April 7, 1965, Montreal, Quebec (in the files of the Department of Research and Education, IBPSPMW, Montreal, Quebec).

70. *Ibid.*

71. Anonymous interview with an official of the Canadian International Paper Company, September 9, 1965.

have met other companies and got gains there. Great Northern didn't want to shift premiums but they did give them. There was hard bargaining there. Now we cannot permit any increase in the differentials between that mill and yours. You will have to give at least what we gained in other mills.

July 13 — I regret having to take this step. We have signed agreements after peaceful negotiations for many years, and we are proud of this record. But this year you have made it necessary for us to take this step. We went to B.C. and St. Croix and Great Northern and made settlements. We got something in each of those cases. But all you say is 'no' — 'no' to the two paid holidays, 'no' to the vacations, 'no' to everything . . . .

As unions we can't go to Great Northern and St. Croix and make one kind of deal with them, and then meet you, their competitors, and make a different deal. We wouldn't maintain our integrity if we did. We can't do it and we won't do it.[72]

This explains why U.S. union officials participate in key sets of Canadian negotiations and why there was a reverse pattern effect in 1955 and 1956. Union officials carry the pattern. The underlying determinants of the pattern contour, however, are the scope and structure of the product market. Put another way, union centralization was probably not the cause of international pattern-bargaining but a reaction to the underlying environment. The pre-1940 record tends to reinforce this.

---

72. Ontario Newsprint and Pulp Conference, Toronto, Ontario, July 12 and 13, 1949 (in the files of the Department of Research and Education, IBPSPMW, Montreal, Quebec).

CHAPTER 3

THE AUTOMOBILE INDUSTRY

INDUSTRIAL BACKGROUND

The characteristics of the auto industry are well known but some of them are particularly pertinent to this study and merit some attention. First, the Canadian industry reflects its counterpart in the United States. Indeed, one of the major features of the Canadian industry is its ownership by, and dependence on the U.S. parent or related firms. As in the U.S., the five major auto manufacturers over the analysis period were General Motors, Ford, Chrysler, American Motors, and Studebaker.[1] In a similar fashion output is concentrated in the subsidiaries of the U.S. "Big Three". As shown in Table 3-1 GM, Ford, and Chrysler have accounted for 94 to 97 per cent of the passenger cars produced in Canada. Similarly, these same firms produce the bulk of commercial vehicles.

It is of further importance to note that, in addition to U.S. ownership, technologies are similar and many components and parts for the Canadian industry are manufactured in the U.S., in many cases at plants owned by a parent firm.[2] The Canadian industry is clearly dependent, therefore, on the U.S. industry and this is manifested when there are labor stoppages in the U.S. They have an immediate effect on the Canadian industry. Employment in both countries is subject to sharp seasonal and cyclical fluctuations with the patterns in both countries following basically parallel courses. Oligopolistic pricing policies are conspicuous on both sides of the border and, together with the above relationships, suggest at least some overlap on the product-price side.

Plant location is concentrated and relatively stable. The Canadian industry is fixed in Southwestern Ontario (a high wage area) with two principle factors in mind — first, nearness to the biggest Canadian market and, second, nearness to the U.S. source of supply of parts.[3] General Motors has plants at Oshawa, Windsor, London, St. Catherines and Toronto; Ford at Windsor, Oakville, and Toronto;

---

1. In 1954, Nash and Hudson merged to form American Motors and in the same year Studebaker and Packard joined forces. In the early 1960's Studebaker shut down both their U.S. and Canadian operations.

2. *Report of the Royal Commission on the Automotive Industry* (Ottawa: Queen's Printer, 1960), p. 21.

3. *Ibid.*, p. 22.

Table 3-1

PRODUCTION OF PASSENGER CARS, BY MANUFACTURER, CANADA, 1947-60

	General Motors		Ford		Chrysler		Others	
Year	Thousands of Vehicles	% of Total	Thousands of Vehicles	% of Total	Thousands of Vehicles	% of Total	Thousands of Vehicles	% of Total
1947	58.8	35	35.4	38	43.5	26	1.5	1
1948	65.2	39	54.6	33	45.0	27	2.0	1
1949	62.6	32	72.9	38	46.6	24	11.5	6
1950	117.9	42	94.2	33	55.1	19	16.9	6
1951	133.0	47	79.4	28	52.9	19	17.4	6
1952	136.0	49	82.9	29	51.8	18	12.5	4
1953	162.9	45	124.2	34	61.8	17	16.1	4
1954	122.6	43	102.5	36	51.1	18	7.7	3
1955	128.6	34	137.6	37	97.4	26	10.9	3
1956	148.2	40	119.6	32	92.1	24	14.8	4
1957	153.4	46	109.9	32	69.4	20	7.7	2
1958	158.7	53	89.3	30	44.1	15	5.3	2
1959	150.2	50	99.7	33	42.6	14	8.3	3
1960	175.1	54	94.2	29	50.4	15	5.7	2

SOURCE: *Royal Commission on the Automotive Industry* (Ottawa: Queen's Printer, 1960).

Chrysler at Windsor; Studebaker at Hamilton; and American Motors at Brampton.[4]

Economies of mass production and specialization are extensive. Capital costs are high and the technology of the industry demands more and more expensive and specialized machinery. The size of the U.S. market enables at least the major producers to take full advantage of the optimum scales of production but, because output was traditionally only about one-twentieth of that in the U.S., no producer could do so in Canada. Prior to 1965, the primary reason given for higher costs in Canada was the frequent changes in "set-ups" for comparatively smaller runs. The optimum size in the

---

4. Until 1958, American Motors assembled passenger cars in Toronto. In that year they closed the Toronto plant and from 1958 to 1960 all their cars sold in Canada were imported from the company's Kenosha, Wisconsin, plant. Production in Canada was resumed in 1961 at a new plant in Brampton, Ontario.

industry, however, apparently varied with the type of work to be performed.[5] During the 1953 to 1962 period, the operations of the Canadian auto manufacturers reflected this. American motors and Studebaker were mainly assemblers. Chrysler was primarily an assembler of vehicles and engines but did some manufacturing, body building, and machining and assembly of engines. Ford was in a somewhat similar situation. GM and McKinnon Industries together constituted the most highly integrated operation in Canada.[6]

During the 1950's and early 60's the market for Canadian produced cars was, for all practical purposes, domestic. Canada was a net exporter of motor vehicles prior to World War II but, beginning in 1950, became a net importer (Table 3-2). The few motor vehicles that Canada did export went, almost entirely, to Commonwealth countries. The U.S. *ad valores* tariff of 6.5 per cent and higher Canadian costs accounted for the lack of exports to the U.S. On the import side, foreign competition in the late 1950's constituted a serious threat to the industry in both countries but this was alleviated somewhat by the introduction of the compact car.

Canada's export-import position was, of course, dramatically changed following the unilateral introduction of the Drury plan and then by the Canada-U.S. auto pact. The latter is the lineal descendant of the former. The standard Canadian automobile tariff had been 17.5 per cent. The Drury plan, introduced in 1963, was designed to enable the Canadian industry to specialize in the manufacture of automotive products and to increase production and employment. The Canadian Government offered auto manufacturers duty-free imports of parts and vehicles manufactured in the U.S. up to the amount that the firms increased their own exports of automotive products to the U.S. It was an export subsidy — one dollar increase in exported Canadian content was to earn the remission of duties on one dollar of dutiable imports. This was followed in January of 1965 with the Canada-U.S. auto pact which entailed the joint removal of duties on motor vehicles and parts by the two countries. It permitted Canadian manufacturers of motor vehicles to import similar vehicles as well as parts for assembly. In return, the manufacturers agree to maintain the same balance between the value of their production and the value of their sales in Canada which they had in the 1964 model year, and to maintain the same dollar volume of Canadian content which they had in 1964 models. While not a free trade pact, it did increase Canadian dependence on the U.S. market and has had some notable effects. Since 1965 Canada's

---

5. *Report of the Royal Commission on the Automotive Industry*, p. 23.
6. Though McKinnon is independent of General Motors of Canada it is a subsidiary and included in the master agreement covering GM's Canadian employees.

Table 3-2

EXPORTS AND IMPORTS OF MOTOR VEHICLES,
CANADA, 1925-38, 1946-60.

Year	Total Exports	Total Imports	Net Imports (—) Exports (+)
1925	74,151	14,632	+ 59,519
1926	74,324	28,544	+ 45,780
1927	57,414	36,630	+ 20,784
1928	79,388	47,408	+ 31,980
1929	101,711	44,724	+ 56,987
1930	44,553	23,233	+ 21,320
1931	13,813	8,736	+ 5,075
1932	12,534	1,444	+ 11,085
1933	20,403	1,781	+ 18,628
1934	43,368	2,926	+ 40,442
1935	64,330	4,125	+ 60,206
1936	55,570	9,974	+ 45,596
1937	65,867	20,250	+ 45,617
1938	57,768	15,360	+ 42,462
1946	68,111	22,242	+ 45,869
1947	83,765	42,663	+ 40,902
1948	48,178	20,612	+ 27,568
1949	29,616	38,697	- 9,081
1950	54,334	38,528	- 54,194
1951	60,489	48,334	+ 12,155
1952	79,934	38,993	+ 40,941
1953	60,250	58,475	+ 1,775
1954	29,955	43,482	- 13,517
1955	35,105	57,949	- 22,844
1956	32,961	89,232	- 56,271
1957	28,116	80,011	- 51,895
1958	23,192	113,377	- 90,185
1959	18,787	165,584	-146,777
1960	23,142	180,029	-156,887

SOURCE: *Report of the Royal Commission on The Automotive Industry* (Ottawa: Queen's Printer, 1960).

dollar share of automotive production in North America has risen to 5.5 per cent from 4 per cent. Automotive exports to the U.S. have grown from $199 million in 1964 to $845 million in 1966. Imports from the U.S. concurrently have increased. Employment in the

Canadian industry increased substantially — from approximately 69,000 in 1964 to 84,000 in 1967.[7]

The industry is totally unionized and labor costs are significant although not unduly high. The direct labor content in Canada was estimated to be only around 9 per cent of total costs in Canada.[8] The characteristics of the labor force are substantially the same in the two countries. The plant work force is almost entirely male. The occupational composition is heavily weighted with relatively unskilled or semi-skilled jobs. Approximately 80 per cent of the production workers could be characterized as such with very large numbers of employees engaged in highly repetitive assembly work.

To recapitulate, there is a certain amount of North American dependence in product and process with a natural tendency for some overlapping in business policies. The oligopolistic nature of the industry (reinforced by tariff protection and supplemented in the mid-60's by a tariff windfall) along with the fact that there is no non-union competition suggests an area of latitude for collective bargaining.

The existence of U.S. ownership alone has guaranteed a union argument of equal pay for equal work for Canadian and U.S. workers. Common ownership is clear cut and complete. Operations on both sides of the border are, if not identical, reasonably close to it. Job content and work practices are basically similar, although again not identical.

The centers of the two industries (Michigan and Southwestern Ontario) are contiguous. Further, the Detroit-Windsor area, separated only by the Detroit River, has been the historical core area. The labor markets, therefore, to some extent are geographically interdependent. Wages and working conditions in Windsor have been affected by those in Detroit. Taft[9] has noted that as Detroit developed into the leading center of production the high wages of the auto plants drew labor from Canada and, significantly, when Ford and Chrysler were located in Windsor they offered Detroit wage levels. There is little doubt, therefore, that the labor market aspect is an inducement to a coordinated union policy. The Canadian UAW leadership and membership have always been aware of the Canada-U.S. differential. The product market has been dealt with above and needs no further elaboration. The extension of the Canadian product

7. Canadian Department of Industry statistics cited in *Toronto Globe and Mail*, December 12, 1967, p. B1.
8. Royal Commission on Canada's Economic Prospects, *The Canadian Automotive Industry* (Ottawa: Queen's Printer, 1956), p. 77.
9. Philip Taft, *The Structure and Government of Labor Unions* (Cambridge: Harvard University Press, 1954), p. 215.

market now acts as a stimulus for the union to take wages out of competition.

While there was some organization of auto workers in the U.S. dating back to 1918, it was not widespread and was confined to craft workers.[10] Intensive organization awaited the Great Depression and the National Labor Relations Act. Under the aegis of the CIO, the United Automobile Workers (presently the International Union, United Automobile, Aerospace and Agricultural Implement Workers) made major organizing breakthroughs in the late 1930's but by 1939 was racked by internal strife. In 1940, the union split into two groups one going to the AFL and a larger group remaining with the CIO. The UAW-AFL, really only had strength in the small plants. There are other smaller groups as well but the UAW has approximately 90 per cent of the industry organized. While the factionalism was felt in Canada, the UAW-CIO was the only organizing force.

COLLECTIVE BARGAINING BACKGROUND, STRUCTURE, AND PROCESS

Organizing efforts in the Canadian auto industry were an integral part of the movement in the U.S. Once again it illustrates the fact that a movement in the U.S. tended to lead to a concomitant drive in Canada. After successes in the U.S. industry in 1936 and 1937, the union crossed into Canada in the latter part of 1937. It gained recognition at General Motors, although it took a lengthy strike to do so and the company refused to mention the international *per se* in the first agreement.[11] By 1942 they had gained recognition at all of the major firms. Today there are eighteen regions in the international, seventeen of them in the United States. All of Canada constitutes one region. Originally designated as Region 7, it is now simply referred to as the Canadian region. It included approximately 100,000 members in 1966, with locals spread across the country but concentrated in Southern Ontario.

The Canadian region does not differ from the rest of the international with respect to structure, policy, and other characteristics. A number of features have special meaning for this study. Firstly, the structure of the union affords ample opportunity to interrelate policy on both sides of the border. Secondly, inter-plant wage uniformity has been a traditional ingredient of union policy. Thirdly, the union is relatively decentralized and the locals fairly autonomous. Fourthly, the membership is militant, but, particularly in the 40's, divided by factionalism.

---

10. W. H. McPherson, *Labor Relations In the Automobile Industry* (Washington: The Brookings Institution, 1940), pp. 16-25.

11. Logan, *Trade Unions in Canada*, pp. 233-35.

The union remains fairly decentralized in structure with the local unions still possessing a substantial amount of autonomy, despite the fact that "purges" and the passage of time have reduced this somewhat. As is true for all the locals, Canadian locals are autonomous subject only to the restriction of the constitution. For example, no body or individual can commit a local to an agreement with an employer without ratification by the membership.[12] The mechanics are available, as well, for local determination of contract demands whether in Canada or the U.S. Prior to international conventions, a Canadian Economic Conference, which includes bargaining committee members from the locals, is held to determine broad Canadian demands. In addition, the Canadian UAW Council, made up of approximately 150 delegates from all locals in Canada meets frequently to recommend policy.

On the other hand, the 25-man International Executive Board is the highest authority between conventions. Convention delegates, elected by the membership of their local, elect their own regional director and, together with all the other delegates, vote for the other seven members of the I.E.B., viz., a president, a secretary, two vice-presidents, and three board members at large. The Canadian regional director, therefore, is the communicator of I.E.B. policy to the locals. The departments corresponding to the large companies, such as the General Motors Department, are another vital structural aspect. They are headed by officers at international headquarters and correspond to the intra-corporation councils set up to coordinate inter-plant negotiations at the big firms. The councils have delegates from all of the locals involved and Canadian delegates are included with a voice but no vote.

Contract demands, therefore, may be drawn up by the local union's negotiating committee but obviously a number of bodies, regional and international, impinge on policy formulation. Furthermore, the locals are assisted either by an international representative or the regional director, or both, and no agreement can be signed until approved by the regional director. A local, before it can take strike action, is required to call in the regional director and if no agreement is reached it must wait again for presidential approval of strike action.[13]

The UAW's long-run wage policy is quite clearly defined at this particular point in time. They have always emphasized inter-plant wage uniformity regardless of area.[14] Impinging upon that, however, is

---

12. UAW Constitution, 1962, Art. 19, sections 3, 4.
13. UAW Constitution, 1962, Art. 50, section 2.
14. Robert M. MacDonald, *Collective Bargaining in the Automobile Industry* (New Haven: Yale University Press, 1963), pp. 206-18.

the fact that locals are noted for their independence and strong feelings of autonomy. It has been pointed out that the union has changed its president four times, that political factions have been pervasive, and that members have been both individualistic and militant.[15] The factionalism came to a head at the 1947 convention a year after Reuther was elected president. Since that time opposition and factionalism rapidly declined. Although it was not completely eradicated, Reuther won over many of his former opponents.[16] This has been true in Canada where factionalism has existed and the characteristics of the auto worker have been much the same. In 1947, the right wing with Reuther's support made a determined bid to defeat the existing Canadian regional director, George Burt. Burt was re-elected by a narrow margin, has remained in office ever since and became a staunch Reuther supporter. The divisiveness, therefore, has been on the wane but individualist locals in the past frequently adopted policies opposed by the central organization.

Collective bargaining in the Canadian industry has been dictated by union tactics and the lack of inter-employer cooperation. Employer behaviour is a carry over from the United States.[17] It has been fostered by product market competition and the strategy of the UAW. The competitive aspects that characterize the industry have resulted in mutual distrust. Although changing somewhat, the outcome has been little in the way of cooperation among the firms in the face of union demands and a reluctance on the part of any company to take a strike particularly when sales are high. The UAW has consistently followed the policy of focusing their demands on one company at a time, effectively isolating the firms and following a well defined system of pattern bargaining.

The variations in company policy and approaches to labor relations problems constitute a final important dimension, particularly in the bi-national context. GM's approach is fairly centralized. Each division and plant has its own labor relations staff but they receive instructions from a central staff and all agreements are subject to approval by the latter before becoming operative.[18] Ford, after being more centralized than General Motors reorganized under Henry Ford II and developed a system more in line with its chief rival.[19] If anything, Chrysler has taken a more centralized approach

---

15. Taft, *The Structure and Government of Labor Unions*, pp. 213-17.

16. *Ibid.*, p. 223.

17. For an informative article dealing with this aspect of collective bargaining see, William H. McPherson, "Bargaining Co-operation Among Auto Managements," *Monthly Labor Review*, LXXXIII (June, 1960), pp. 592-95.

18. MacDonald, *Collective Bargaining in the Automobile Industry*, p. 10.

19. *Ibid.*, p. 33.

than either of the other two members of the Big Three.[20] American Motors has followed a policy of extreme decentralization.[21]

The outstanding feature of the industry is that a fairly rigorous form of international pattern bargaining has evolved. In light of this, attention is directed in the next section to comparative wage rates. Wage adjustments and the wage systems are the same in both countries. Wage changes have generally taken the form of — (1) "annual improvement factor" or "productivity factor" increases; (2) cost-of-living adjustments, based on an escalator formula; and (3) a periodic additional increase to workers in skilled classifications. There is a set of job classifications with related wage rates but no formal system of job evaluation. The UAW is unalterably opposed to incentive pay and the industry is strictly on an hourly rated system.

U.S.-CANADA WAGES

Over time the percentage differential in earnings between the two countries in the industry has declined and the absolute differential has increased (Table 3-3). The decrease in the percentage differential has been gradual, not unduly large, and more than half of it came in a six-year period spanning 1947 to 1952. Over the ten-year analysis period the relative differential was quite stable. In 1962 it was still fairly large (18 per cent). Using the U.S. industry as a benchmark, therefore, the earnings adjustments in the Canadian industry were not exceptional up to the end of the analysis period. Viewed in the light of the trends in the durable and non-durable goods sectors, a similar conclusion is apparent. The U.S.-Canada differential in those two sectors had behaved in a similar manner. Table 3-3 reinforces this. Canadian auto earnings advanced markedly over both sectors in absolute amount but, on a relative basis, very little. From 1953 to 1962 it is evident from these data that auto earnings moved up almost uniformly with those for the durable goods sector.

Turning to negotiated wage increases, the decrease in the relative U.S.-Canada differential from 1953 to 1962 in earnings was not supported by a comparable movement in wages. General negotiated wage changes, including cost-of-living adjustments, were approximately 13 cents higher in the U.S. industry (Table 3-4). Both the absolute and the relative differential for common labor were larger in 1962 than in 1952. This is attributable mainly to a more liberal U.S. escalator clause, particularly prior to 1958. While this was so

---

20. *Ibid.*, pp. 317-21.
21. See Edward L. Cushman, "Management Objectives in Collective Bargaining", *The Structure of Collective Bargaining*, esp. pp. 73-75.

for base rates in the lowest classification, Table 3-5 indicates it was also the case for the higher skilled classifications. The table compares base rate data for Ford and Chrysler in both countries for selected jobs over a similar period of time. The jobs are by no means comprehensive but are representative of the occupational scale and are ones which seemed most suitable for international comparison purposes. Skilled workers did no better vis-à-vis their U.S. counterpart than unskilled.

Table 3-3

AVERAGE HOURLY EARNINGS DIFFERENTIALS (PRODUCTION WORKERS) BETWEEN AUTO MANUFAC-TURING, MANUFACTURING, DURABLE GOODS, AND NON-DURABLE GOODS, CANADA; AND BETWEEN AUTO MANUFACTURING, U.S. AND CANADA, 1947-62.

Year	Absolute and Relative Differential							
	Autos and Manufacturing		Autos and Durable Goods		Autos and Non-durables		U.S-Canada Autos	
	¢	%	¢	%	¢	%	¢	%
1947	32	40	25	28	39	53	34	23
1948	33	36	26	26	40	47	36	22
1949	32	32	24	22	40	44	39	23
1950	34	33	25	22	42	44	40	23
1951	31	26	22	17	41	38	42	22
1952	34	26	23	16	46	39	41	20
1953	33	24	21	14	46	37	45	21
1954	30	21	19	12	41	32	40	22
1955	35	24	24	15	53	35	49	21
1956	36	24	24	15	49	35	47	20
1957	37	23	25	15	51	35	48	20
1958	39	24	25	14	52	34	50	20
1959	48	28	33	18	62	39	51	19
1960	46	27	32	17	62	38	55	20
1961	51	28	35	18	66	39	52	19
1962	59	31	43	21	74	43	52	18

SOURCE: Canada, Dominion Bureau of Statistics, *Review of Man-Hours and Hourly Earnings, 1945-62;* U.S., Department of Labor, Bureau of Labor Statistics, *Employment and Earnings Statistics for the United States, 1909-62* (Bulletin No. 1312-1).

Table 3-4

CHANGES IN COMMON LABOR RATES[a], SELECTED AUTOMOBILE COMPANIES, U.S. AND CANADA, 1952-62

Company	1952	1962	Increase	
			¢	%
General Motors (U.S.)	$1.65	$2.43	78	47
General Motors (Canada)	1.52	2.17	65	43
Ford (Canada)	1.53	2.17	64	43
Chrysler (Canada)	1.54	2.19	65	43
U.S. - Canada differential	11-13¢	24-26¢		
U.S. - Canada differential	7-8%	9-10%		

a. Includes cost-of-living adjustments.
SOURCE: UAW Canadian headquarters, Windsor.

Table 3-5

U.S.-CANADA BASE RATE DIFFERENTIALS[a], SELECTED JOBS, FORD AND CHRYSLER, 1952 AND 1962

Classification	Ford				Chrysler			
	1952		1962		1952		1962	
	¢	%	¢	%	¢	%	¢	%
Assembler-Major	21.5	12.8	41.5	18.7	21	12.7	36	16.3
Millwright	44.5	24.3	62.5	23.4	41	22.9	66	25.5
Electrician	36.5	18.9	61.5	22.1	41	22.3	67	24.8
Lath Operator	60.0	34.7	111.0	50.4	54	30.7	118	54.5
Die Maker	35.5	17.4	58.5	20.0	41	20.6	70	26.0

a. Includes cost-of-living adjustments.
SOURCE: UAW Research Department, Contracts Section, Detroit.

Negotiated fringe increases may have been relatively higher in Canada than in the U.S., although an unequivocal conclusion cannot be drawn because an estimate of the value of the benefits could not be obtained from the union or the companies. Taking General Motors for comparison purposes, however, it would seem that the Canadian region made considerable progress. The major reasons for so concluding are:

1. GM workers obtained all of the innovations which the UAW gained in the U.S. in 1955, 1958 and 1961. These included SUB, short workweek benefits, severance pay, moving allowances, and jury duty pay. In each case the provisions were identical to those in the U.S. agreement.

2. While a differential remained in pension benefits, it had been reduced in 1961 due to a large increase (from $.40 to $1.80 for each year of credited service) in the supplementary pension benefit.

3. GM of Canada by 1962 paid the entire costs of the hospital-medical plan. In the U.S. the company only made partial payment.

4. In 1952 an equal number of paid holidays were in effect but by 1962 the relationship had become 8 in Canada to 7 in the U.S.

5. Night shift premiums had been increased in Canada from 5 cents to 5 per cent or 10 per cent, depending on the shift. The latter had been in effect in the U.S. in 1952.

6. The relationship for paid vacations was the same in both 1952 and 1962.

Nevertheless, many of the fringe innovations either would not be reflected in earnings or the costs in Canada would be lower because they are related to wages. In total it is doubtful that the full wage-fringe differential declined, absolutely or relatively, over the ten-year period. That is, approximately the same relationships existed in 1962 as in 1952. This has changed, of course, with the 1967 agreements which were designed to equalize U.S. and Canadian wages in terms of domestic currency by 1970.

Other studies have emphasized the UAW's uncompromising position on inter-plant and inter-firm uniformity and the application of patterns in the U.S.[22] This has undoubtedly been the case but certain pieces of evidence suggest some flexibility in Canada. Firstly, from the mid-50's to the mid-60's they followed the American pattern, but in percentage rather than in absolute amount. Secondly, while wage parity was introduced as a demand, it was never pursued during the analysis period. Thirdly, the retroactive dates in Canada were later than in the U.S. — in some cases by as much as six months. Fourthly, wages at all five Canadian firms were quite similar but there were differences in 1962 at Studebaker and

_____

22. Both Levinson and MacDonald have indicated, however, that the UAW took a more flexible stance in the 1950's than in the late 40's. As far as Canada is concerned, the union practiced pattern deviation from 1946 to 1951.

American Motors in comparison with the Big Three, particularly for the skilled classifications (Table 3-6).[23]

Table 3-6

BASE RATES FOR SELECTED JOBS AT CANADIAN AUTO MANUFACTURERS, 1962

Classification	GM (Oshawa)	Ford (Oakville)	Chrysler (Windsor)	American Motors (Brantford)	Stubebaker (Hamilton)
Janitor	$2.11	$2.11	$2.13	$2.04	$2.07
Assembler	2.21	2.21	2.23	2.14	2.17
Painter and Glazier	2.51	2.65	2.47	2.37	2.40
Carpenter	2.61	2.55	2.57	2.47	2.50
Welder — production	2.585	2.32		2.23	2.21
Welder — maintenance	2.61	2.52	2.62	2.54	2.33
Toolmaker	2.77	2.80	2.78	2.62	2.65
Electrical Technician	2.77	2.80		2.62	2.65

SOURCE: UAW Canadian Headquarters, Windsor.

THE COLLECTIVE BARGAINING RECORD

Pre-1953 Experience

By the time the UAW had organized the Big Three and signed initial contracts in Canada the country was engaged in World War II. There were several developments of moment, however, prior to and during that period — historical precedents that would set the stage for later developments. Prior to the entrance of the UAW, it is clear that there had been some coordination between U.S. and Cana-

---

23. In 1958 the union itself pointed to wage rate differentials between Studebaker and Ford which amounted to 34 cents an hour (*Financial Post*, May 9, 1959, p. 16).

dian policy by the *companies*. The following statement by a UAW official at National War Labour Board hearings in 1944 is instructive:

> Being employed for the past ten years with Chrysler before going on the staff of the international union, I believe I can speak with some authority as far as wage rates paid are concerned and how they happened . . . previous to 1942 it was the desire of the company to follow closely the Chrysler Corporation and the workings of the American company . . . . I would like to point out that every time there was an agreement signed in the United States with the Chrysler Corporation for new rates, those rates were put into effect in Canada.[24]

During Board hearings a year later a GM spokesman made a similar observation. He testified that: "It is common knowledge that for many years past, wages and working conditions in Windsor have been directly affected by wages and working conditions in the Detroit area."[25] He later pointed out that, when Ford and Chrysler were established in Windsor "they brought with them the industrial wages paid in Detroit at that time".[26] Logan has confirmed the fact that hiring rates at Ford were the same in Detroit and Windsor prior to the war.[27]

It is difficult to say whether or not GM followed a similar procedure but they did set one precedent. In their first agreement with the union in Canada they had the contract run concurrently with the one between the union and the company in the U.S. In the postwar period, they were the first to agree to a coordination in timing and then a more formal tie-in between U.S. and Canadian contracts.

During the war years the same thing occurred in the auto industry as in others — a gradual drawing apart of U.S. and Canadian rates.[28] In addition, the union attempted to close inter-plant and inter-company differentials but with little success. When the controls were lifted the union made no immediate attempt to join Canadian and American negotiations. In retrospect, the circumstances were probably simply not propitious at that time, firstly, because of their failure to negotiate master agreements or eliminate inter-company differentials and, secondly, because of factionalism and the autonomy of the locals. Herlihy, in his analysis of collective bargaining by the UAW in Canada from 1946 to 1951, backs up this point in noting that the above two factors were par-

---

24. *Proceedings of the National War Labour Board* (Canada), February 1, 1944, p. 50.
25. *Ibid.*, April 21, 1945, p. 93.
26. *Ibid.*, p. 107.
27. Logan, *Trade Unions in Canada,* p. 244.
28. *Ibid.*

tially responsible for pattern deviation within Canada.[29] Walter Reuther, in an address to Ford of Canada workers in 1949, attributed the lack of international pattern bargaining to "the old row we used to have in our union."[30] Some locals made it doubly difficult by deviating from union policy. In 1950, for example, five-year agreements had been signed in the U.S. and these included a pension plan. Chrysler of Canada had offered a somewhat similar five-year contract. The Chrysler workers, however, rejected the pension plan and, in lieu of it, took 6 cents and a two-year contract.

The lack of bargaining symmetry nationally and internationally as late as 1953 is evident from a consideration of contract expiry dates. GM employees in Canada were covered by a five-year agreement negotiated in 1950. It was similar in substance to the U.S. agreement. Elsewhere in the industry, however, there were shorter term contracts which were to come up for renegotiation in 1953 and 1954. Chrysler had signed an agreement in 1952 to be in effect until June 1954. It provided that either party could reopen the agreement on wages only after June 17, 1953. Ford also had a two year agreement to expire in February 1954. It, too, was subject to opening at the request of either party. An agreement at Studebaker was scheduled to expire in the summer of 1953.

All of this changed in the 1953 to 1962 period. There were some indications even in the early postwar years, however, that a closer relationship between U.S. and Canadian contracts would evolve. U.S. corporate officials had started the practice of making their presence felt in Canadian disputes. Henry Ford II had visited Canada in 1946 to aid in the resolution of a dispute at Ford in Windsor over union security.[31] In 1948, Louis Seaton, GM's vice-president in charge of industrial relations, was asked by the Canadian regional director to help resolve a strike at McKinnon Industries. After a two week delay he did so and was a key factor in ending the strike.[32] Also, the union had been successful in meshing GM negotiations in Canada with those in the U.S. In 1950, approximately three weeks after the U.S. settlement, the Canadian agreement was signed and provided for basically the same wage adjustment system — an annual-improvement-factor and cost-of-living adjustments — and a similar expiration date in 1955.

29. H. M. Herlihy, "The Collective Bargaining Policies of the UAW-CIO In Canada" (Unpublished Ph.D. dissertation, Department of Economics, University of Chicago, 1954), p. 123.

30. *United Automobile Worker* (Detroit), February 1949, p. 1.

31. Logan, *Trade Unions in Canada*, p. 239.

32. *United Automobile Worker* (Detroit), November 1948, p. 4.

Collective Bargaining 1953 to 1962

The Canadian region over the period implemented a definite policy of following the U.S. pattern at the auto manufacturers. Tables 3-7 to 3-10 compare the U.S key bargain with the Canadian auto settlements for the 1953, 1955, 1958, and 1961 bargaining rounds. The figures make the comparison in terms of the dates the agreements were signed, their length, wages (including changes in the cost-of-living clause), and major fringe benefit changes and additions. They indicate the increasing degree to which the Canadian industry followed the U.S. pattern, beginning with the 1955 round, when to a limited extent the U.S. pattern spread into Canada, to the 1961 round when, in appearance, Canadian settlements closely conformed to the U.S. key bargain. This, along with material to be presented, indicates that an organic connection did exist between U.S. and Canadian settlements, particularly during the last two rounds, and that union and company policy evolved over time.

A perusal of Table 3-7 reveals no features common to all the agreements in 1953. The wage increase in absolute terms varied from firm to firm as did the minor provisions for fringe increases. This was true both among Canadian firms, and between the Canadian firms and the key agreement in the U.S. There was some basic similarity between the GM agreements in both countries but it was a similarity in form with the package in the U.S. being larger. The one common aspect of all the agreements was their modest size.

Table 3-8 reveals that, with the exception of the supplementary unemployment benefits plan, none of the other provisions were uniform for all the firms in the 1955 round. Other than the SUB provision, there was considerable variation with respect to the length of the contract, the timing of the signings, the increases to skilled workers, changes in shift premiums, the cost-of-living clauses, and all of the fringe benefits. There was comparability on some items between two companies but not on a Canada-wide or an international basis. The most common provision, along with SUB, in Canadian and U.S. settlements was a wage increase of 6 cents an hour for each of the three years. Chrysler and Ford, however, deviated from this with Chrysler providing a total of 14 cents and Ford 12 cents over two years. Also, the Ford agreement in the U.S. provided for three increases of 6 cents or 2½% of base rates whichever was greater, while in the Canadian settlements the percentage provision was not included. By providing for a percentage change, the increases in the U.S. actually ranged from 6 to 10 cents each year depending on the employees' base rate. In Canada, on the other hand, the wage increase was a flat, cents per hour, figure.

A COMPARISON OF CANADIAN AGREEMENTS WITH THE U.S. KEY BARGAIN, AUTOMOBILE INDUSTRY, 1953 ROUND

Terms	United States		Chrysler	Canada		American Motors
	General Motors	Ford		General Motors	Studebaker	
Date	May 22, 1953 (reopening) — existing agreement expires 1955	June 12, 1953 (reopening) — existing agreement expires 1954	June 29, 1953 (reopening) — existing agreement expires 1954	July 6, 1953 (reopening) — existing agreement expires 1955	August 24, 1953 One-year agreement. Expires Nov. 2, 1954	Existing agreement expires in 1954 (no 1953 reopening)
Length of Contract						
Wages	Increased annual-improvement-factor by 1¢ — from 4¢ to 5¢ an hr. Additional increase of 20¢ an hr. to pattern-makers and die sinkers and 10¢ an hr. to all other skilled workers. Incorporation of all but 5¢ of the cost-of-living allowance into base rates. Conversion to Consumer Price Index prevented a 2¢ an hr. wage cut.	Increased annual-improvement-factor by 1¢ — from 3¢ to 4¢ an hr. Across-the-board increase of 2¢ an hr. Same as GM (U.S.) 1¢ cost-of-living wage decrease ignored.	Across-the-board increase of 6¢ an hr.	Increased annual-improvement-factor by 1¢ — from 3¢ to 4¢ an hr. Additional increase of 10¢ an hr. to skilled workers. Same as GM (U.S.)	Across-the-board increase of 5½¢ an hr. Additional increase of 7½¢ to 10¢ an hr. to skilled workers.	
Fringe Benefits	Monthly pension benefits increased from $1.50 to $1.75 for each yr. of service up to 30 yrs.				Pension plan incorporated into contract; monthly benefits of $1.50 for each yr. of service up to 30. Life insurance increased to $2,500; sickness-accident benefits increased to $40 a wk.	

Table 3-8

A COMPARISON OF CANADIAN AGREEMENTS WITH THE U.S. KEY BARGAIN, AUTOMOBILE INDUSTRY, 1955-56 ROUND

Terms	United States Ford	Canada General Motors	Studebaker	American Motors	Ford	Chrysler
Date	June 6, 1955	February 13, 1956	March 22, 1956	May 10, 1956	July 27, 1956	December 17, 1956
Length of Contract	3 years	2½ years	3 years	3 years	2 years	20 months
Wages	Annual-improvement-factor of 6¢ or 2½% of base rates; total general increase — 18-30¢. Additional increase of 5-18¢ for skilled workers. Escalator clause changed: 1¢ adjustment for every 0.5 change in CPI.	Annual-improvement-factor of 6¢; total general increase — 18¢. 4¢ an hr. for wage inequities. Shift premiums increased from 5¢ to 5% (8¢ to 11¢) for the 2nd shift, and 10% (16¢ to 22¢) on 3rd shift.	Across-the-board increase of 6¢ each yr.; total general increase — 18¢. Additional increase of 9-20¢ for skilled workers.	Across-the-board increase of 6¢ each yr. plus 2¢ the 1st yr. for all workers except skilled trades; total general increase — 20¢. Additional increase of 7-15¢ for skilled workers.	Annual-improvement-factor of 6¢; total general increase — 12¢. Additional increase of 5¢ for skilled workers. Shift premiums increased; 2nd shift 7¢ to 10¢ and 3rd shift — 7¢ to 15¢. Cost-of-living bonus of 2¢ plus escalator clause to pay 1¢ for every 0.7-point change in CPI.	Across-the-board increase of 8¢ immediately and 6¢ in 1957; total general increase — 14¢. Night shift premiums increased from 5% to 10%. Obtained escalator clause: 1¢ adjustment for every 0.7-point change in CPI.
Fringe Benefits	SUB plan; 60-65% of take-home pay for up to 26 wks. Company contribution — 5¢ per hr.	Same as Ford (U.S.)	Same as Ford (U.S.)	Same as Ford (U.S.)	Same as Ford (U.S.)	Same as Ford (U.S.)

Table 3-8 (continued)

Terms	United States	Canada				
	Ford	General Motors	Studebaker	American Motors	Ford	Chrysler
Fringe Benefits (cont'd)	Added: 2½ weeks vacation pay for employees with 10 but less than 15 yrs. seniority.	Same as Ford (U.S.)	Added: 2 wks. vacation with more than 3 wks. pay (6¼% of annual earnings) after 10 years of service.			
	Normal retirement benefits increased to $2.25 a month. No restriction on the creditable years of service.	Same as Ford (U.S.)	Same as Ford (U.S.)		Same as Ford (U.S.)	Same as Ford (U.S.)
		Supplementary pension continues to be 40¢ a month for each year of service up to 25 yrs.	Supplementary pension continues to be 40¢ a month for each year of service up to 25 yrs.		Supplementary pension of $1.60 a month for each yr. of service (maximum $40) between 65 and 70.	Supplementary pension of $1.60 a month for each yr. of service (maximum $40) between 65 and 70.
	Scale of life insurance and accidental death and dismemberment benefits increased — $3200 to $6400 and $1600 to $3200 respectively.	Scale of life insurance and accidental death and dismemberment benefits increased — $2500 to $5000 and $1250 to $2500 respectively.				Paid up life insurance of $500-$1000 at age 65.
	Weekly sickness and accident benefits increased to $36-$76.80, for up to 26 weeks.	Weekly sickness and accident benefits increased to $28-$45.50, for up to 26 weeks.	Weekly sickness and accident benefits increased to $40 for 26 weeks. Company paid.		Weekly sickness and accident benefits increased to $40 for up to 26 weeks. Company paid.	Weekly sickness and accident benefits increased to $40 for up to 26 weeks. Company paid.

Table 3-9

A COMPARISON OF CANADIAN AGREEMENTS WITH THE U.S. KEY BARGAIN, AUTOMOBILE INDUSTRY, 1958–59 ROUND

Terms	United States Ford	Canada				
		General Motors	Ford	Chrysler	Studebaker	American Motors
Date	September 17, 1958	December 5, 1958	January 11, 1959	January 27, 1959	June 6, 1959	Canadian plant closed 1958-1961
Length of Contract	3 years	3 years	3 years	3 years	3 years	
Wages	Annual-improve-ment-factor of 6¢ or 2½%; total general increase — 18-30¢.	Annual-improve-ment-factor of 6¢ or 2½%; total general increase — 18¢.	Annual-improve-ment-factor of 6¢ or 2½%; total general increase — 18¢.	Annual-improve-ment-factor of 6¢ or 2½%; total general increase — 18¢.	Annual-improve-ment-factor of 6¢ or 2½%; total general increase — 18¢.	
	Additional increase of 8¢ for skilled workers.	Same as Ford (U.S.)	Same as Ford (U.S.)	Same as Ford (U.S.)	Same as Ford (U.S.)	
	Night shift premium increased: 10% from 7.5%.					
		Changed escalator clause: 1¢ for every 0.6-point change.	Changed escalator clause: 1¢ for every 0.6-point change.	Changed escalator clause: 1¢ for every 0.6-point change.	New escalator clause: 1¢ for every 0.6-point change. Plus a 5¢ cost-of-living allowance.	
Fringe Benefits	SUB changed to: an amount, which when added to unemploy-ment compensation, will equal 65% of take-home pay, or $30, whichever is smaller, up to 39 weeks.	Same as Ford (U.S.)	Same as Ford (U.S.)	Same as Ford (U.S.)	Same as Ford (U.S.)	
	Normal retirement benefits increased to — (1) $2.40 for each yr. of service prior to Jan. 1, 1958; (2) plus $2.43 for	Same as Ford (U.S.)	Same as Ford (U.S.)	Same as Ford (U.S.)	Same as Ford (U.S.)	

Table 3-9 (continued)

Terms	United States	Canada				
	Ford	General Motors	Ford	Chrysler	Studebaker	American Motors
Fringe Benefits (cont'd)	Added: Severance pay — 40 hrs. pay for employees with 2 yrs. seniority to 1200 hrs. pay for those with 30 or more yrs. seniority. Financed from SUB fund.	Same as Ford (U.S.)	Same as Ford (U.S.)	Same as Ford (U.S.)	Same as Ford (U.S.)	
	Jury duty pay of $5 a day, up to 14 days.	Same as Ford (U.S.)	Same as Ford (U.S.)	Same as Ford (U.S.)	Same as Ford (U.S.)	
	Scale of life insurance and accidental death and dismemberment benefits increased — $4000-$7600 and $2000-$3800 respectively.	Scale of life insurance and accidental death and dismemberment benefits increased — $4500-$7000 and $2250-$3500 respectively.	Scale of life insurance and accidental death and dismemberment benefits increased — $4200-$7200 and $2100-$3600 respectively.		Life insurance increased to $4000; additional $1500 for accidental death.	
	Weekly sickness and accident benefits increased — $48 to $91.20, depending on base rates, for up to 26 weeks.	Weekly sickness and accident benefits increased — $43 to $70, depending on base rates, for up to 26 weeks.				

Table 3-10

A COMPARISON OF CANADIAN AGREEMENTS WITH THE U.S. KEY BARGAIN, AUTOMOBILE INDUSTRY, 1961-62 ROUND

Terms	United States General Motors	Canada General Motors	Ford	Studebaker	Chrysler	American Motors
Date	September 20, 1961	December 13, 1961	January 14, 1962	February 10, 1962	April 18, 1962	July 1, 1962
Length of Contract	3 years	3 years	3 years	3 years	3 years	3 years
Wages	Annual-improvement-factor of 6¢ or 2½% (minus 2¢ the first year); total general increase — 16-34¢.	Annual-improvement-factor of 6¢ or 2½% (minus 2¢ the first year); total general increase — 16-19¢.	Annual-improvement-factor of 6¢ or 2½%; total general increase — 18-21¢.	Annual-improvement-factor of 6¢ or 2½%; total general increase — 18-21¢.	Annual-improvement-factor of 6¢ or 2½% (minus 1¢ the first year); total general increase — 17-20¢.	Annual-improvement-factor of 6¢ or 2½% (minus 2¢ the first year); total general increase — 16-19¢.
			Additional increase of 5-10¢ for skilled workers.	Additional increase of 4¢ for skilled workers.		
						Shift premiums increased from 10¢ to 12-18¢.
Fringe Benefits	SUB changed to: an amount which when added to unemployment compensation would equal 62% of straight-time weekly earnings for a 40-hour wk, plus $1.50 per dependent up to 4, for up to 52 weeks. Max. benefit — $40.	Same as GM (U.S.)	Same as GM (U.S.)	Same as GM (U.S.)	Same as GM (U.S.)	Same as GM (U.S.) but deferred 1 yr.
	Added: short work-week provision — 50% of regular hourly rate paid for each hour under 40 during unscheduled short workweeks and	Same as GM (U.S.)	Same as GM (U.S.)	Same as GM (U.S.)	Same as GM (U.S.)	Same as GM (U.S.) but deferred 1 yr.

Table 3-10 (continued)

Terms	United States General Motors	General Motors	Ford	Canada Studebaker	Chrysler	American Motors
Fringe Benefits (cont'd)	Severance pay liberalized — 50 hrs. pay for employees with less than 3 yrs. service to 1500 hrs. pay for those with 30 yrs. seniority.	Same as GM (U.S.)	Same as GM (U.S.)	Same as GM (U.S.)	Same as GM (U.S.)	Same as GM (U.S.) but deferred 1 yr. Also, only provides for 40-1200 hrs. pay.
	Added: moving allowance — provides for $55 to $215 for single employees and $180 to $580 for married employees, depending on the distance between plants.	Same as GM (U.S.)	Same as GM (U.S.)	Same as GM (U.S.)	Same as GM (U.S.)	Same as GM (U.S.) but deferred 1 yr.
	Jury duty pay changed to: greater of $10 or daily fee paid by court but, when added to court fee, not more than employee's straight-time daily earnings, up to 60 days.	Same as GM (U.S.)	Same as GM (U.S.)	Same as GM (U.S.)	Same as GM (U.S.)	Same as GM (U.S.)
	Increased normal retirement benefit to $2.80 a mo. for each yr. of service.	Same as GM (U.S.)	Same as GM (U.S.)	Same as GM (U.S.)	Same as GM (U.S.)	To be negotiated in 1963.
		Plus supp. pension of $1.80 a mo. per yr. of service, paid from 65 to 70 (max. of $55).	Plus supp. pension of $1.80 a mo. per yr. of service, paid from 65 to 70 (max. of $55).	Plus supp. pension of $1.80 a mo. per yr. of service, paid from 65 to 70 (max. of $55).	Plus supp. pension of $1.80 a mo. per yr. of service, paid from 65 to 70 (max. of $55).	

Table 3-10 (continued)

Terms	United States	Canada				
	General Motors	General Motors	Ford	Studebaker	Chrysler	American Motors
Fringe Benefits (cont'd)	Scale of life insurance and accidental death and dismemberment benefits increased — $5500 - $10500 and $2750-$5250 respectively. After age 65 Company-paid insurance of $825-$3150 depending on base rate and yrs. in the plan.	Scale of life insurance and accidental death and dismemberment benefits increased — $5000-$7500 and $2500-$3750 respectively. After age 65 Company-paid insurance of $750-$2250 depending on base rate and yrs. in the plan.	Scale of life insurance and accidental death and dismemberment benefits increased — $6000-$8400 and $3000-$4200 respectively.	Life insurance and accidental death and dismemberment benefits increased — $4500 and $2000 respectively.	Scale of life insurance and accidental death and dismemberment benefits increased — $6000-$8400 and $3000-$4200 respectively.	Life insurance and accidental death and dismemberment benefits of $5000 and $2500 respectively.
	Sickness and accident benefits increased — $55 to $110 a wk., depending on base rates, for up to 26 weeks.	Sickness and accident benefits increased — $45 to $80 a wk., depending on base rates, for up to 26 weeks. Company-paid.	Sickness and accident benefits increased to $55 a wk., for up to 26 weeks. Company-paid.	Sickness and accident benefits increased to $45 a wk., for up to 26 weeks. Company-paid.	Sickness and accident benefits increased to $50 a wk., for up to 26 weeks. Company-paid.	Sickness and accident benefits of $45 a wk., for up to 26 weeks. Company-paid.
	Hospital, surgical, and medical benefits for employees and their dependents to be Company-paid. Formerly the Company and employees paid 50% each. Company also agreed to pay 50% of the cost of hospital and medical coverage for retirees and their dependents.	Same as GM (U.S.)	Company continued to pay the full cost of hospital and medical coverage and agreed to pay 50% of the cost of such coverage for retirees and their dependents.	Company continued to pay the full cost of hospital and medical coverage and agreed to pay 50% of the cost of such coverage for retirees and their dependents.	Company continued to pay the full cost of hospital and medical coverage and agreed to pay 50% of the cost of such coverage for retirees and their dependents.	Same as GM (U.S.)
						Provided for 3 wks. vacation after 15 yrs.; no provision

In 1958, the pattern contour became more extensive and definitive. The broad similarity in 1958 is indicated in Table 3-9. All of the agreements provided for an annual-improvement-factor of 6 cents or 2½ per cent, plus an additional 8 cents for skilled workers. The absolute wage increase was still larger in the U.S., however, because of the higher base rates that existed there. The annual U.S. increase continued to range from 6 to 10 cents. In Canada, with only minor exceptions, base rates were still less than $2.40 so that the 6 cents or 2½ per cent provision amounted to a flat 6 cents an hour increase. In the area of fringe benefits there was little variation within Canada and on an international basis.

The same can be said of the 1961 round. The five Canadian agreements, taken as a whole, were closer to the U.S. pattern than at any previous time. All were three-year contracts. They provided for the same basic wage increases and similar, in many cases identical, liberalization of fringes. In the U.S., however, the wage increase now amounted to 6 to 12 cents with the exception of the first year when it amounted to 4 to 10 cents. Over the three years, therefore, they totalled 16 to 34 cents. On the other hand, in Canada they amounted to 6 to 7 cents and in the first year 2 cents of the increase at GM and American Motors were defrayed to help pay for increased welfare costs. At Chrysler, one cent was defrayed. This resulted in three-year general increases of 18 to 21 cents at Ford and Studebaker, 17 to 20 cents at Chrysler, and 16 to 19 cents at GM and American Motors. Only Ford and Studebaker provided special increases to skilled workers and there were minor variations in such areas as life insurance and sickness and accident benefits. Despite these variations, each of the Canadian agreements displayed a marked similarity to the U.S. key bargain. The lack of a pension plan at American Motors was a major deviation from the industry pattern. In 1963 the contract was opened and a pension plan was agreed upon.

Actually, Tables 3-7 to 3-10 do not completely reflect the evolution of policy. From 1953 to 1962 there were four bargaining rounds in the U.S. industry. Chronologically these occurred in 1953, 1955, 1958, and 1961, as shown. In the Canadian industry, during the same period, there were four rounds which directly followed those in the U.S., although in three instances the negotiations extended into the following year. Thus, the four Canadian rounds, which are shown in the tables, took place in 1953, 1955-56, 1958-59, and 1961-62. In the context of time, each of the Canadian settlements followed the U.S. key bargain. In addition, however, there was a fifth Canadian round in 1954-55 with all of the firms participating with the exception of General Motors. There were no wage increases at American Motors and Studebaker but wages at Ford and Chrysler were increased by 4 cents. It is essential to indicate that, while there were two bargaining rounds in the Canadian industry from 1954 to 1956, the second one (1955-56) was influenced by and, in a sense, was an integral part of the first (1954-55). For analysis purposes, therefore, it is necessary to examine them as a continuous round rather than as abstract and independent of each other. Immediately following the 1954-55 round an orderly form of international pattern bargaining prevailed.

1953 Reopenings

A step toward amending the five-year agreements in the U.S. was taken in September of 1952 when the union's GM Council adopted resolutions calling for incorporation of all but 5 cents of the cost-of-living allowance into base rates, an increase in the annual-improvement-factor from 4 to 5 cents, increases in pension payments, and a wage increase for skilled workers. The union based its reopening request on the claim that the contract should be "a living document". In late February 1953, GM agreed to part of what the union had requested. After the negotiations at GM were completed similar terms were agreed to at Ford and Chrysler on May 25 and 27, respectively. These agreements, however, also liberalized pensions and provided a 20-cent increase for patternmakers and die-sinkers. The union then went back to GM seeking these additional gains. The company, effectively "whipsawed", signed a supplementary agreement to come into line with Ford and Chrysler.

Developments in Canada were, to some extent, parallel. The GM agreement did not include a reopening provision but the company, following the course set in the U.S., agreed to open it in order to work out a formula for switching to the Consumer Price Index which was taking the place of the Cost-of-Living Index in Canada. The two-year agreements at Ford and Chrysler did provide for a reopening in June 1953 and the Studebaker agreement was due to expire.

After the UAW in the U.S. signed agreements with GM, Ford, and Chrysler, the union in Canada did not commence by approaching GM as they had in the U.S. Since officials of the UAW stated that they wanted to study the company's U.S. agreement first.[33] Instead, they began negotiating with Ford and by June 12 had settled.

The agreement reflected some of the features of the U.S. changes. Within a month, and without incident, there were settlements at GM and Chrysler and, in August, at Studebaker. Chrysler

---

33. *Financial Post,* May 30, 1953, p. 2.

employees settled for 6 cents shortly after the company had offered the same general increase as the parent company had granted in the U.S. (5 cents). At Studebaker the settlement called for a 5½ cent increase. Quite clearly the U.S. pattern had defined the Canadian increases. Duplication was most evident at GM. In June, the union asked the company to increase the improvement factor to 5 cents and for a master agreement covering GM locals at Oshawa, Windsor, St. Catherines, London, and Toronto.[34] The company refused but on July 6 a master agreement was signed which was quite similar in form, but not amount, to the U.S. pattern.

The GM agreement, of course, had to be ratified by the membership and it apparently came as a surprise when a group of young dissidents twice persuaded the rank-and-file at the Oshawa local to defeat ratification of the agreement. It was reported that this unexpected turn of events was the result of a building up of dissension since World War II. The schism was between a group called the "old guard" — veteran unionists, many of whom helped organize the union at the Oshawa plant in 1937 — and the "young turks" — a group of younger men who resented the control of the union's affairs by the older workers. They were described as an anti-Reuther, anti-international headquarters, left-wing group who felt they could get along without the help of the UAW parent.[35]

The situation came to a head with the signing of the master agreement in 1953. Largely on the grounds that the "old guard" supported the contract and that it was executive approved, the "young turks" opposed it. The issue split the membership between the two camps but the dissidents were able to dissuade enough workers to prevent ratification. It was reported that international headquarters had taken a "hands-off" attitude but Canadian director Burt, at a union meeting of Oshawa workers, told them that they were making a mistake in rejecting the contract.[36] Talks resumed at GM in the late summer but bogged down when it became evident that the left-wing group controlled the Oshawa local. Negotiations ran into 1954 without compromise and the Oshawa employees continued to work under the terms of the 1950 agreement. The seriousness of the rift became evident in June 1954 when the "young turks" won a majority in union elections at the GM Oshawa local.[37] A somewhat similar movement was in evidence at the Ford locals.[38] Little of a definitive nature was reported concerning this faction but

34. *Ibid.*, June 20, 1953, p. 1.
35. *Ibid.*, August 1, 1953, p. 8.
36. *Ibid.*
37. *Ibid.*, June 19, 1954, p. 10.
38. *Ibid.*, February 20, 1954, p. 1.

presumably they were similar to other factions which have been so much a part of the UAW. Interestingly, it was felt that, although they opposed international headquarters, they were more intransigent and more dedicated to obtaining wage parity with the U.S. industry.

1954 to 1956

The major innovative demand of the UAW in U.S. bargaining in 1955 was the guaranteed annual wage. GM's agreement expired on May 29 and Ford's on June 1, but the UAW concentrated on the latter firm. Ford had made an intensive study of the feasibility and cost of the guaranteed wage idea and had developed some variations of it. On June 6, Ford and the UAW signed a three-year contract, the major addition was the supplementary unemployment benefits plan — a palatable compromise for the guaranteed wage.

Labor-management relations in the Canadian industry were marked by a high degree of disorder and conflict during the 1954-56 period. Negotiations were protracted and the industry experienced two long strikes, one the longest in Canadian history. This was in sharp contrast to the peaceful settlements in the U.S. industry.

The first round began in 1954 when the Ford, Chrysler, American Motors, and Studebaker contracts were due to expire. In December 1953, Ford, whose contract expired on February 18, 1954, was presented a set of demands by the Windsor local. The same demands were later presented at Oakville and Toronto. By the time negotiations had culminated two factors of importance had emerged. First, the company agreed to a master agreement. Second, the conciliation process was a hindrance to settlement and, hence, this was the last time the UAW would take it seriously.

The original demands presented by the locals were extremely high and unrealistic in a year of recession. They were in the neighborhood of 57 cents on a one-year contract and included a demand for a master agreement.[39] Negotiations proceeded in a desultory fashion throughout the spring as the parties went through the first step of the conciliation process without modifying their positions. A separate conciliation board was set up for each Ford plant which resulted in further delays. Board hearings began in early June for the Windsor employees, in July for Oakville, and in mid-August for Toronto. To complicate things further, the board recommendations varied somewhat.[40] By late September strike votes had been taken at both Windsor and Oakville and, finally, on October 13 after more than nine months of negotiations between the company and

---

39. *Ibid.*, February 6, 1954, p. 1.
40. *Labour Gazette,* LIV (September, 1954), p. 1215.

local 200, the Windsor workers went on strike. They were followed a few days later by the workers at Oakville. On November 15, after the release of the conciliation board report, the Toronto employees joined the strike. The main deterrent to settlement at this point was a demand for a province-wide master agreement. On January 27, 1955, after a 109 day strike, and more than a year's negotiations, the parties settled. The package was estimated to be worth approximately 11 cents[41] (including a 4 cent wage increase) but contained two key features from the union point of view — (1) the company agreed to pay the entire cost of hospital and medical benefits, and (2) a master agreement.

Negotiations had also been in progress at Chrysler since the spring of 1954. Conciliation had been completed by the fall and thereafter the parties marked time waiting for a settlement at Ford. After the Ford settlement, negotiations continued to lag because of disagreements over non-monetary issues. On February 22, however, Chrysler settled for a package similar to that at Ford. In mid-April, Studebaker signed a one-year contract calling for no wage increase but the company agreed to pay the full cost of the hospital-medical plan. The union had also signed a 15 months' extension of the existing contract with American Motors in December of 1954 when the Ford workers were on strike. It provided for no wage increase and only minor improvements in fringe benefits.

There being no key bargain in the U.S. auto industry to follow, it is clear that the settlements during this round were the result of independent bargaining by the UAW in Canada. None of the terms were of a U.S. to Canada pattern following variety.[42] All the barriers to settlement were issues indigenous to collective bargaining in the Canadian industry. The Ford strike appeared to be the result of the following factors which together accounted for the protracted collective bargaining:

1. A very large set of union demands were presented. They originated not from the international but from the local level. The left-wing uprising may have had some influence in this regard and with regard to the uncompromising attitude of union negotiators.

2. Three sets of negotiations (Windsor, Oakville, and Toronto) were going on at the same time, all dealing with the same issues and all having to go through the two-step conciliation procedure before

---

41. *Financial Post*, February 6, 1954, p. 20.

42. This may not be quite accurate. There may have been some influence on negotiations at Studebaker and American Motors by way of developments taking place in the U.S. Both companies faced serious difficulties in the U.S. and were attempting to reduce labor costs during the 1954-55 period. (See MacDonald, *Collective Bargaining in the Automobile Industry,* Chapter 6.) The below pattern settlements at the Canadian subsidiaries may have been a reflection of this.

any strike action could be taken. As a result neither party bargained seriously until the last couple of weeks before the strike and by this time both sides were committed to inflexible positions.[43]

3. Ford was intransient because of the 1954 recession and the feeling that they had a role to play in holding down labor costs.[44]

The interjection of a U.S. official in the negotiations was a final interesting feature, but a positive one.

By Christmas, talks were being conducted in Toronto between the union, headed by its international secretary-treasurer, Mr. Mazey, and the company, headed by its executive vice-president. It was these talks which led to the final settlement in late January, 1955.[45]

The way had now been cleared to push for the guaranteed annual wage at General Motors in Canada. In April the Canadian region presented the same demand on General Motors as the international had at GM and Ford in the U.S. When the negotiations at those two firms were completed in June, the Canadian negotiations had just begun the first step in the conciliation process. At that time the complete set of UAW demands were made public. They had asked for the SUB plan won in the U.S., a pay increase that would close the U.S. - Canada wage differential, the all company-paid feature of the hospital-medical plan won at Ford earlier in the year, and a liberalization of other fringes. The parties did not settle until February 13, 1956, after a 149-day strike. The agreement included the SUB plan, which was identical to the one in the U.S., and a similar general wage increase. GM continued to pay only 50 per cent of the cost for hospital-medical benefits, however.

In March and May, 1956, Studebaker and American Motors, respectively, signed three-year contracts which included the SUB plan and similar wage increases. Ford, whose contract expired on June 1, 1956, settled in late July on the same basis for a two-year period. Chrysler and the UAW began negotiating in June, two months before the August 1 expiration date. It took until late December before a 20-month contract was signed which contained the essentials of the GM of Canada pattern. This final settlement, then, came 10 months after the GM of Canada settlement and 30 months after the Ford agreement in the U.S.

From the beginning of the GM negotiations to the end of the strike almost one year had elapsed. *A posteriori,* the following

43. The adverse effect that conciliation had on the 1954 Ford negotiations is contained in William C. Phillips, "Government Conciliation in Labour Disputes: Some Recent Experience in Ontario", *Readings In Canadian Labour Economics,* A. E. Kovacs, ed. (Toronto: McGraw-Hill, 1961), pp. 218-31.

44. *Financial Post,* October 2, 1954, p. 1.

45. Phillips, "Government Conciliation in Labour Disputes", p. 224.

factors interacting with each other, seemed to be the major reasons for the situation:

1. For the first few weeks there was a period of mutual stalling while the UAW bargained with GM and Ford in the U.S.

2. The conciliation process again failed, while at the same time it delayed serious negotiating by the parties.

3. There had been no sweeping revision of GM contracts for five years. This resulted in an abundance of issues to be resolved.

4. In essence, the union asked GM to set a pattern, based on the U.S. agreements, and to duplicate some of the gains won at Ford and Chrysler earlier in the year.

5. The union was split concerning some objectives. The Oshawa wing was opposed to a long-term contract and unwilling to compromise.[46] As a result union negotiators had to move cautiously.

By itself, the preliminary marking of time would not have been an important factor in delaying the settlement. Indeed, it was felt early in negotiations that, if Canadian union negotiators waited for the guaranteed wage issue to be settled in the U.S., and if local people did not force the issue, there would be an inclination on the part of GM to follow the U.S. pattern with a minimum amount of resistance.[47] This was unquestionably the case. When time was running out before the September 18 strike deadline, negotiators who had participated in the GM-UAW agreement in the U.S. moved to the bargaining table in Canada. The union had assistance from two representatives of its U.S. team and GM had the help of two top labor relations officials of the parent firm. Their function was to help the parties reach agreement on SUB. The U.S. negotiators were able to achieve such an agreement and the company offered this in a package, only slightly below the final settlement, before the strike began. Major disagreement came on demands originating in Canada, viz., the hospital medical plan and a one-year contract that was being pushed by the "autonomists".

The highlight of the negotiations came during conciliation board hearings when the Canadian director, followed by his fellow negotiators, twice walked out of board meetings. The union requested that the board immediately report failure to resolve the issues. Burt stated that real bargaining does not begin until a union is in a legal position to strike and that his action was intended to hasten the day when the union was in that position.[48] The chairman of the board rejected the union's advice and it was at this point that union

46. *Financial Post,* September 17, 1955, p. 1.
47. *Ibid.,* June 4, 1955, p. 1.
48. *Labour Gazette,* LVI (March, 1956), p. 278.

negotiators walked out.[49] This policy was followed by the union in the ensuing rounds.

By the end of the 1955-56 round it was evident that the opportunity and likelihood of international pattern bargaining on a more formalized basis had opened. The most noticeable dimension of the Canadian contracts was their length. With Ford signing for two years and Chrysler for 20 months, the Canadian Big Three agreements expired within a month of each other in 1958, and within three months of those for the U.S. Big Three. The companies had indicated a willingness (and perhaps a preference) to follow at least elements of the U.S. pattern. The union had achieved master agreements at GM and Ford, and instituted a policy to shorten conciliation proceedings. Finally the position of the "autonomists" had not been upheld and in the future their strength declined.

1958 to 1959

The key 1958 agreement in the U.S. was signed at Ford on September 17, after workers at the Big Three had worked without a contract throughout the summer. The three-year package was judged to be the least costly for the Big Three since World War II.[50] It involved a retention of the improvement factor and cost-of-living clause, a liberalization of jury duty and severance pay, plus 8 cents for skilled workers.

Bargaining in Canada began while negotiations were still in progress in the U.S. The GM contract expired on August 1, Chrysler's on August 15 and Ford's on August 31. The contract at Studebaker expired in November of the same year and American Motors had closed their Toronto plant. The most significant feature of the UAW demands in Canada was in the form of a request to close the differential between U.S. and Canadian wages.

When the U.S. pattern was established the union used it as a criterion and, later on, so did the company. Negotiations had bogged down in September and October when the Big Three disputes went through conciliation. During board hearings the union gave a statement of their demands, nothing more. The General Motors board reported in November and made no recommendations. By this time the union had dropped their wage parity demand and in

---

49. In early September the conciliation board reported its "findings". The board admitted that, because the union had not submitted a case, no suggestions for settlement could be made. Instead, it condemned Burt for his defiance, and it warned the UAW that it could not ignore labor laws without leaving itself open to sweeping changes. The majority report made unprecedented recommendations for changes in Canada's conciliation procedures.

50. *New York Times*, September 19, 1958, p. 16.

late November General Motors offered an almost identical settlement to the one at the parent firm. The union had again asked the company to pay the full cost of the hospital-medical plan and this was a major barrier to settlement.[51] No strike deadline was set, however, and the parties signed a three-year agreement on December 5 which contained all of the major provisions of the U.S. key bargain. It still left the Canada - U.S. differential unchanged and the financing of the hospital-medical plan remained on the same basis (50-50) as prevailed at U.S. plants.

Negotiations at Ford and Chrysler continued another month into 1959. The remaining issues were non-monetary and/or local in origin — production standards, rest periods, the right of the company to retire employees at age 60, etc.[52] At Chrysler, there reportedly was a left of center faction who pushed for a two-year contract in contrast to the position taken by the union executive.[53] The union settled at Ford on January 11, and at Chrysler on January 27, after a one-week strike. Both were three-year contracts and both followed the GM pattern.

At Studebaker the major issue was wage parity with other Canadian firms. Bargaining had started in January and the company had offered the industry pattern. The union, however, asked the company to bring base rates up to the Ford level. Local negotiators obtained strike authority in May after the dispute had gone through conciliation. At this point an assistant to the Canadian director arrived.[54] He claimed that Studebaker was 8 cents below base rates in the industry. The company replied that the rate for assemblers was actually one-cent higher than at Ford.[55] Negotiations broke off at this point and a strike began on May 13. It ended on June 6 and the agreement paralleled those of the Big Three but, in addition, included a cost-of-living clause and an immediate 5 cent cost-of-living bonus.[56]

At all four companies the notable fact was that the companies were willing to follow the U.S. pattern.

---

51. *Toronto Globe and Mail,* December 2, 1958, p. 1.
52. *Ibid.,* January 5, 1959, p. 1.
53. *Ibid.,* January 21, 1959, p. 1.
54. This may also have been a carry-over from the U.S. situation. MacDonald (*Collective Bargaining In The Automobile Industry,* p. 11) has observed — "Up to the mid-1950's, the international union was not an active participant (at Studebaker) . . . . The crisis of the mid-1950's when intensified competition threatened to engulf the small firms, brought the international union more actively into negotiations — partly to relieve the pressure on local union officials . . . ."
55. *Toronto Globe and Mail,* May 14, 1959, p. 10.
56. The union had negotiated out of the escalator clause with Studebaker in 1955.

1961 to 1962

The UAW began negotiations on June 28 with the U.S. Big Three whose contracts expired simultaneously on August 31. American Motors, however, whose agreement expired on September 6, made their surprising "progress-sharing" offer in late July. On August 26, they signed an agreement which set the pattern for the rest of the industry. On September 26, the UAW and GM signed a three-year contract providing benefits identical to those in the American Motors pattern. The only major difference was in the means of financing some of the increased fringe benefits. At American Motors they were to be financed from the "progress-sharing" fund into which the company agreed to pay 10 per cent of its profits before taxes, calculated on the amount left after setting aside 10 per cent for stockholders' equity. At GM, 2 cents of the first annual-improvement-factor adjustment were defrayed to help pay part of the company's cost of assuming the employees share of hospital-medical insurance for active employees and their dependents. Also, the 1 cent increase in the cost-of-living adjustment due in September 1961 was waived to help pay part of the increased company costs resulting from improved pensions.

Bargaining in Canada began in September at GM, whose contract expired on October 31. By this time the U.S. key bargain at American Motors had been signed and provided a standard for union negotiators. "Progress-sharing" never did carry-over into Canadian negotiations, however, even though American Motors was again producing cars in Canada. Instead, when the Canadian pattern at GM was set on December 13, the parent company formula of financing was followed. Almost the entire U.S. pattern was transferred to Canada.

The major demands of the union were similar to those contained in the U.S. pattern with two exceptions. Once again, the union asked for a wage increase which would narrow the Canada-U.S. differential. This was dropped fairly early in negotiations. Secondly, the union demanded increases in monthly pension benefits to close the pension gap which existed between the Canadian and U.S. industry. The UAW asserted that, considering contributions toward social security, companies in the U.S. made pension payments that were the equivalent of $3 a month more, per employee, than in Canada. All of the Canadian firms (with the exception of American Motors) already paid supplementary pensions in deference to these differences. At GM it amounted to 40 cents a month for each year of service to a maximum of 25 years, while Ford and Chrysler paid $1.60 a month for each year of service up to a maximum of $40.

By 1961 negotiations had a fixed pattern. As in 1955 and 1958 conciliation was a mere formality. At board hearings the company submitted only a short brief and the union only a terse outline of its demands before walking out during the hearings.[57] On November 28, the board released a one-sentence report. It stated that board recommendations on the issues in dispute would not be of assistance to the parties.[58] At this point a December 11 strike deadline was set. On December 7, GM offered a three-year contract almost identical to the U.S. pattern. Union negotiators rejected the offer because of disagreement on retroactivity and supplementary pensions. On December 8, as the strike deadline approached, officials from the U.S. were brought in by both parties. As in previous rounds their purpose was to help resolve the dispute.[59] Further negotiations failed to produce a settlement by the strike deadline and GM workers went on strike for two days.

The December 13 settlement provided gains slightly above those of the company's pre-strike offer and, in appearance, almost identical to the U.S. pattern. There were two significant departures from the U.S. contract. In addition to increasing monthly retirement benefits to $2.80 for each year of service, G.M. agreed to provide a supplementary pension, between the ages of 65 and 70, of $1.80 a month, up to a maximum of $55. This was 20 cents above the supplementary pensions that Ford and Chrysler had agreed to in 1956. In effect, GM had increased the maximum $10 supplement, previously paid in recognition of differences in social security legislation, to a maximum of $55 a month. After age 70, the pension payments reverted to $2.80 a month. Secondly, the company agreed to pay the full cost of the hospital-medical plan beginning in January 1962. This was not obtained in the U.S. until 1964. Offsetting these company concessions, however, was the fact that the improvement factor increases were retroactive only to November. In the U.S. the three annual increases were retroactive to the beginning of September in each year.

The GM pattern was followed at Studebaker and American Motors, and at Ford after a two-day strike. Ultimately Chrysler followed after an eight-week strike over production standards. At no time had the Canadian industry, in its entirety, followed the U.S. pattern so closely. But, again, the significant fact is that the Canadian industry followed it so readily.

---

57. *Toronto Globe and Mail,* November 27, 1961, p. 1.
58. *Ibid.,* November 30, 1961, p. 34.
59. *Ibid.,* December 9, 1961, p. 1.

AN ASSESSMENT OF U.S. INFLUENCE AND UAW POLICY

From 1937 to 1962 U.S.-Canada collective bargaining relationships had gone through several permutations. The period can be divided into three stages, each stage contained developments which eventually led to the ultimate evolution of current policy. Stage 1 (1937-46) included union recognition by the major producers, the first participation of U.S. corporate officials in Canadian negotiations and the initial occurrence (at GM in 1937) of concurrent U.S. and Canadian collective agreements. The war years, however, prevented coordination with U.S. bargaining. Stage 2 (1946-55) included more explicit and concrete developments. The position of the union leadership had begun to solidify by 1947, the Canadian region had won master agreements at GM and Ford, participation by U.S. corporate and union officials had become an accepted practice, and limited international pattern-following had occurred. But, the desires of individual locals had, to that point in time, contributed to an imperfectly defined system of pattern-bargaining within Canada. The third stage (1956-62), accompanied by a decline in factionalism and the elimination of the conciliation process as a hindrance, saw the formalization of U.S. to Canada pattern transference — limited, however, to below pattern equivalence in absolute amount.

Once established, international pattern bargaining continued with one added dimension in the ensuing rounds of 1964 and 1967. In both rounds there were pattern plus settlements in Canada. An additional general wage increase was obtained in 1964 to start eliminating the U.S.-Canada differential. On top of this, 19 cents for skilled workers in Canada was not applicable in the U.S.[60] In 1967, the Canadian pattern was again larger and, according to reports, wiped out the international differential by September 1970. International pattern bargaining, and now wage parity, is in part an extension of a union policy that stresses uniformity. From the analysis it is plain that the Canadian region, not the Detroit office, paved the way for the former. Government policy (the Canada-U.S. auto pact) made the latter viable.

Union policy springs ostensibly from coercive comparisons. But this is only a partial explanation and, moreover, it is not at all clear whence the pressure for conformity originated. The following correspondence to the author offers one interpretation:

---

60. The approaches to pension changes were entirely different in Canada. According to the Canadian Director — "I would like to point out that our approach in Canada to the Pension Plan negotiations did not follow the American pattern because of our difference in the manner in which Social Security is available at age 65 in the U.S. and age 70 in Canada." (Correspondence to the author, November 25, 1965.)

> The attempt to have contract terms match those in the U.S. has been an ambition of myself and my colleagues of the International Union for many years because we believe that it would be the first step toward the achievement of wage parity. Our difficulty has been with the local unions in Canada who have compared their non-economic contract terms with those of the U.S. and have stoutly defended their own contracts even though they were, in a number of instances not as good as those in the U.S.[61]

Alternatively, other material suggests local agitation and pressures. In an interview with a UAW official it was stressed that, for many years, at least segments of the rank-and-file were pressing for action on the international differential and that the Canadian region was building support for it.[62] Newspaper accounts have emphasized the pressures from the locals for wage parity. Also, as early as 1939, the closest local to Detroit, local 195 representing Chrysler workers in Windsor, demanded wage parity and, even during the war years, the locals were cognizant of Detroit wages. In the example below the local negotiator for Oshawa workers was contending that local rates should not control GM's wage level:

> The place and basis for comparison is the area or areas in which the bulk of the industry is located, and we have referred to Windsor, not because it is some convenient yard-stick, but because that is where, with the exception of General Motors plant at Oshawa the automobile industry of Canada is located.[63]

Later they broadened their comparison.

> Look at the wage rate prevailing in the United States plants at this same company, where they have both day workers and production workers — I do not urge that we must adopt the United States rates, but each does the same work.[64]

Local pressures for parity, though not necessarily international pattern-bargaining, heightened in 1953 with the left-wing upsurge. A credible interpretation, therefore, is that the union was split on strategy, but most elements supported the equal pay for equal work principle.

What is clear is that the goal never received U.S. support until the auto pact threatened U.S. jobs. Prior to 1965 U.S. officials felt that wage parity for Canadian workers was an unrealistic object-ive.[65] An alternative interpretation is that wage parity would mean larger Canadian settlements than American and this would be un-

---

61. Correspondence to the author from the UAW Canadian Director, November 25, 1965.

62. Anonymous interview at UAW Canadian headquarters, June 23, 1964.

63. *Proceedings of the National War Labour Board* (Canada), April 21, 1945, pp. 23-24.

64. *Ibid.*, p. 61.

65. Oral testimony at Research Department, Contracts Section, UAW headquarters, Detroit.

palatable to U.S. officials.[66] The ramifications of the auto pact, however, changed this position and the wage parity issue was fought and resolved at Chrysler negotiations in the U.S.

While some of the conformity must be attributed to union comparisons, an examination of the unfolding of, or development toward, bi-national patterns is more enlightening and informative. The surprising thing is that an interrelated system was not introduced earlier. At least two companies, Ford and Chrysler, had followed a system of interrelated increases (and presumably decreases) at times before the entrance of the union. The labor market had dictated closely conforming wage levels in Detroit and Windsor prior to World War II. After the war two companies, GM and Chrysler, gave tacit support to a closely corresponding policy in both countries — firstly, by sending U.S. negotiators to Canada and, secondly, by following parent company proposals particularly on contract length. In 1948, 1950 and thereafter, GM signed agreements that ran concurrently with the master agreement in the U.S. and made initial proposals that ran parallel to the parent's most recent settlement. They voluntarily agreed to a reopening of the agreement in 1953 after this was done in the U.S. Chrysler in 1950 proposed a five-year agreement similar to its U.S. parent but this was rejected by the union. Similarly, in 1956 it desired a contract of the same length as the Chrysler agreement in the U.S. These elements, then, were readily observable. Others may have been under the surface.

The significant feature about both of the latter firms is that they have been the two most centralized in their attitude toward Canadian operations. They are the only two who consistently send U.S. representatives to Canadian negotiations. With this in mind a telling point is that international pattern-bargaining was first applied at General Motors. More currently, the union by-passed Ford in the U.S. in their quest for wage parity even though that company set the pattern, and focused the parity demand on Chrysler. They clearly received a more favorable response.

The message is clear — the evolution of union policy did not take place in a vacuum. Both union and company policy (at GM and Chrysler) was integrated to some extent with the policy of their respective parent organizations. The structure of the union provides for a coordination of policy along company lines and complements, or is a response to, individual corporate attitudes. In contrast to GM and Chrysler, for example, U.S. union officials participated less frequently at Ford and never at all at American Motors and Studebaker. It follows that the projection of the U.S. pattern contour into Canada was the joint product of union and company approaches.

---

66. Crispo, *International Unionism*, p. 200-201.

The major reasons for the GM and Chrysler tendencies are probably contained in the following statement by an industry spokesman:

> While it is desirable to resolve each problem on its own merits at the appropriate level, obviously this principle cannot be applied without reference to the interest of the total establishment. The settlement of collective bargaining problems is but one (albeit an important one) of many considerations involved in running a business . . . . The decision-making authority at lower levels must be curtailed, most usually by appeals to higher levels within the company, if the alternative is a stoppage of production.
>
> As another illustration, there is a tendency in collective bargaining for a decision in one situation within a company to become a precedent for other settlements in the company. The freedom of the parties to resolve problems at lower levels must be subject to the additional restriction of over-all policy guidance from above.[67]

Besides institutional influences the external environment had an obvious impact. It limited the relationship essentially to wage change conformity prior to 1964. In turn, the union is indebted to government policy for their wage parity achievement. Let the union speak for itself:

> We have in our hands for the first time in our history, and with the courtesy of the governments of the United States and Canada, if you please, the key to perhaps the oldest and greatest collective bargaining objective of our union: the right to equal pay for equal work with our American brothers.[68]

A number of important developments flowed from the auto pact. The Canadian auto companies received a windfall in the form of tariff rebates. The Canadian industry is now more dependent on the U.S. market, and, individual firms, on their U.S. parent. The pact also has generated a sizeable increase in employment in the Canadian industry. The 1967 Chrysler agreement, therefore, evolved at a time when the economic climate dictated a very large settlement and closely conforming corporate policies on both sides of the border.[69]

The structural and procedural aspects survive because they have satisfied the requirements of the parties. From the union standpoint the broadened negotiating unit takes into account the effective decision-making levels and is administratively and strategically sound.

---

67. Cushman, "Management Objectives in Collective Bargaining," p. 62.

68. Statement by the UAW Canadian Director cited in W. List, "Canadian UAW Wins Parent Backing for Wage Parity with U.S.," *Toronto Globe and Mail*, October 6, 1965.

69. It should be stressed that the settlement provided for wage parity in Canadian dollars only and not until 1970. How many job rates have been, or will be, equalized has not been released.

> The reasons for the appearance of our American negotiators is because we have established collective bargaining departments in Detroit and we are anxious to make sure that all of the gains which were made in negotiations just prior to the opening of our contracts in Canada are going to be on the table before the company. As we do not participate in U.S. negotiations, it is necessary to have our negotiators from the U.S. participate.[70]

Canadian autonomy is concurrently preserved. From the same source:

> We allow our Intra-Corporation Councils and local unions to make the kind of demands on management they wish to make. The International Officers in Detroit do not interfere with this at all. They are not even present when my staff members and I help the Master Negotiating Committee to formulate these demands . . . . All strike authorizations for Canadian local unions of the UAW have a typewritten line which says "at the discretion of the Regional Director" . . . . There is no doubt our Constitution gives the International Executive Board the final say in these matters but it has not been exercised and my judgment has always been accepted . . . . There has been no strike authorization without the approval of the Canadian Director and only after the approval of two-thirds of the membership who attend the strike vote meeting.[71]

As far as the companies are concerned, oral testimony from Canadian officials at Ford and Chrysler prior to the parity agreement revealed that the companies agreed to an extension of U.S. contract terms to Canada because the costs were lower and because "we knew what we were getting into".[72] The participation of U.S. union officials was welcomed. Their responses complement each other.

> It is better to deal with a person who is high enough up to be statesman-like. The international arrangement brings this about. They help to reduce the issues.
> Generally they play a moderating role by saying, "Look you've got a good settlement grab it".

For both parties U.S. auto settlements probably appeared reasonable and were acceptable to the various constituent groups. Collective bargaining was simplified and took at least some account of differences, including appropriate adjustments for the institutional environment.

---

70. Correspondence to the author from UAW Canadian director, November 25, 1965.

71. *Ibid.*

72. Another benefit is that it minimizes divide-and-conquer tactics. This was illustrated at GM. By following the U.S. pattern they avoided paying the full costs of the hospital-medical plan until 1962, six years after Ford of Canada agreed to the provision.

CHAPTER 4

THE MEAT PACKING INDUSTRY

INSTITUTIONAL AND ENVIRONMENTAL BACKGROUND

The major elements of the meat packing industry can be summarized briefly. The industry in Canada, which parallels its counterpart in the U.S., is characterized by large variations in scale. On the one hand, there are three major national packers (Canada Packers, Swift Canadian and Burns) with plants whose operations extend more or less across country. At the other extreme are local slaughtering establishments which operate on a very small scale, serving in the main, rural areas and small centres of population and supplying a small part of the total market. It is in this area that the union has been least successful in its organization attempts. Between the extremes there are a relatively small number of operations of medium size which are in competition with the national packers in the principal markets. On the periphery, potential competition is high — something that the major packers are constantly aware of and which has, along with intense price and product competition from a large number of small firms (some of whom are non-union), placed constraints on collective bargaining. Because of the dominant position of the Big Three, attention will be focused on that group. The pattern for the industry is set within these firms and then spreads to many of the smaller packers.

The industry in the U.S. is similar to Canada's in terms of industrial structure, but on a much larger scale. It has been dominated by a "Big Four" — Swift, Armour, Wilson and Cudahy. This has become less true today, however, in the sense that it is more accurate to speak of a major eight or ten packers. It is the four large firms, nevertheless, and particularly Swift and Armour, upon which the union first concentrates its efforts during negotiations. As in Canada, there are a substantial number of independents and a multitude of small slaughtering and processing plants.

The meat packing industry is one of the few major industries in which a large share is not owned or controlled by U.S. interests. With the exception of one firm — Swift Canadian — the industry is owned and operated by Canadians. Statistical information available in Canada allows no precise measurement of the position of an individual firm or of a class of firms in the slaughtering and meat packing industry. It would seem safe to say, however, that Swift Canadian has less than 16 per cent, and probably less than 13 per

—111—

cent of the market for fresh and processed meat.[1] Of more importance, Canada Packers is the largest firm, and invariably signs the key agreement in the Canadian industry.

In relation to Canadian production, and more particularly U.S. domestic output, Canadian exports of meat products to the United States are not large. The reasons for this situation are quite obvious, the dominant ones being transportation costs and U.S. tariff rates. The tariff on dressed and processed meat varies depending on the product. Tariffs, on the majority of such products, however, when converted from a cents-per-pound to a percentage figure range from approximately 4 per cent to 15 per cent. There are some exports of pork to the U.S. but these take the form of specialty cuts and are not numerically significant.

The United Packinghouse, Food and Allied Workers (UPWA) has, for all practical purposes, sole jurisdiction in the Canadian sector of the industry.[2] The Canadian region (District 8) is only one of nine districts which make up the union. Bargaining structure and process in Canada resemble practices in the U.S. industry. The union has bargaining rights for all production workers in a plant. Master agreements are in effect in all multi-plant firms and individual negotiations are carried out with each firm.

Negotiations are not highly centralized and there is no overlap between the countries. Preliminary bargaining is conducted by the international officers in the U.S. and by the National officers in Canada. After preliminary negotiations, however, delegates from each of the locals involved are called into the bargaining sessions. Observers from the locals are also included. The numbers of the bargaining table, therefore, are substantial. The National Policy Committee, as it is referred to in Canada, is comprised of over twenty-five delegates plus the national officers. In the United States the committee is many times this size. The National Policy Committee votes on whether to accept or reject an offer. If it is accepted it is then submitted to the local membership for ratification.

Within the National Policy Committee are chain committees which meet separately with the individual companies. Each chain committee has a chairman — one of the assistant district directors — with the district director acting as an overall chairman of the committee. Constant union communication is maintained between the

---

1. This is based on various estimates of the relative size of Canada Packers, Swift Canadian and Burns given in the Restrictive Trade Practices Commission, *Report Concerning the Meat Packing Industry* (Ottawa: Queen's Printer, 1961), Chapter V.
2. After this study was completed the union merged with the Amalgamated Meat Cutters and Butcher Workmen.

various chains and the companies also exchange information. In the Canadian situation this has not been difficult due to the fact that negotiations with each of the Big Three have, more often than not, been carried on in Toronto in the same hotel.

Within and between the members of the Big Three and the larger independents, comparatively limited variations are to be found between plants in wage rates, fringe benefits, hours, and many other conditions of employment. There are two major influences which account in large part for this — (1) corporate structure, and (2) the extent of union organization. The Big Three employ about two-thirds of the production workers in the industry. While they operate establishments across the country, the union has negotiated single collective agreements at each multi-plant company and these, aside from limited variations, provide for similar working conditions. Such uniformity is found not only among the various plants of the Big Three but it also extends to the medium sized independents. It is mainly in the smaller establishments and unorganized plants that marked variations in working conditions are to be found.

U.S.-CANADA WAGES

There has consistently been a substantial wage differential between the major packers in the two countries. This is true both of average hourly earnings and of wage rates. The differential in comparative average hourly earnings was 17 cents, or 10.9 per cent in 1952 and 50 cents or 20.6 per cent in 1962.[3] These figures are stated in terms of domestic currency. Table 4-1 contains male common labor rates for the major packers in both countries for the years 1939-1963. The U.S.-Canada differential fluctuated somewhat in both absolute and percentage amount but without exception was positive throughout. In 1953 it stood at 10 cents or 6.9 per cent; in 1963 it had increased to 49.5 cents or 19.7 per cent. The same has been true for female common labor rates (Table 4-2). Over the 1952-63 period, the international differential in female rates widened by about the same amount as for males. It increased by 40.5 cents and stood at 25 per cent in 1963 compared to 15.7 per cent in 1952.

As far as special increases to workers above the common labor rate level are concerned, in both countries these have taken the form of wage inequity adjustments and increases in the spread between labor grades. The bracket system has been in effect in the U.S.

---

3. See Canada, Dominion Bureau of Statistics, *Review of Man-Hours and Hourly Earnings, 1945-62;* U.S., Department of Labor, Bureau of Labor Statistics, *Employment and Earnings Statistics for the United States, 1909-62* (Bulletin No. 1312-1).

industry since 1945 but was not attained in Canada until the 1954 round. Prior to 1954 it was not possible to make an international comparison of the differential existing for various jobs. There is every reason to believe that workers in the higher classifications in Canada did less well than their American counterparts. There were no special increases for these workers in Canada, while in the U.S. industry the increment between labor grades had been increased by

Table 4-1

COMMON LABOR BASE RATES,ᵃ MAJOR MEAT PACKING COMPANIES, CANADA AND UNITED STATES, 1939-63

Year	U.S.	Canada	Differential	
			¢	%
1939	$ .625	$ .485	14	22.4
1940	.625	.485	14	22.4
1941	.675	.485	19	28.2
1942	.725	.485	24	33.1
1943	.725	.535	19	26.2
1944	.725	.625	10	13.8
1945	.725	.675	5	6.9
1946	.885	.775	11	12.4
1947	1.02	.875	14.5	14.2
1948	1.15	.96	19	16.5
1949	1.15	1.02	13	11.3
1950	1.26	1.095	16.5	13.1
1951	1.41	1.285	12.5	8.8
1952	1.45	1.35	10	6.9
1953	1.50	1.40	10	6.7
1954	1.55	1.43	12	7.7
1955	1.69	1.46	23	13.6
1956	1.79	1.55	24	13.4
1957	1.865	1.61	25.5	13.8
1958	1.94	1.70	24	12.4
1959	2.165	1.75	41.5	19.2
1960	2.23	1.84	39	17.5
1961	2.35	1.90	45	18.1
1962	2.43	1.96	47	19.3
1963	2.51	2.015	49.5	19.7

a. Including cost-of-living allowance adjustments.

SOURCES: The files of the National Office, UPWA, Toronto; U.S., Bureau of Labor Statistics, *Wage Chronology — Swift & Co., 1942-63* (Report No. 260).

Table 4-2

FEMALE BASE RATES,[a] SWIFT & CO., CANADA AND UNITED STATES, 1941-63

Year	U.S.	Canada	Differential	
			¢	%
1941	$ .56	$ .375	18.5	33.0
1942	.62	.375	24.5	39.5
1943	.62	.425	19.5	31.5
1944	.62	.505	11.5	18.5
1945	.62	.54	12	19.4
1946	.78	.64	14	17.9
1947	.915	.74	17.5	19.1
1948	1.045	.81	23.5	22.5
1949	1.045	.87	17.5	16.7
1950	1.155	.935	22	19
1951	1.32	1.125	19.5	14.8
1952	1.40	1.18	22	15.7
1953	1.45	1.22	23	22.8
1954	1.515	1.25	26.5	17.5
1955	1.155	1.28	37.5	22.7
1956	1.765	1.37	39.5	22.4
1957	1.85	1.43	42	22.7
1958	1.94	1.57	37	19
1959	2.165	1.62	54.5	25.2
1960	1.230	1.71	52	23.3
1961	2.350	1.77	58	24.7
1962	2.43	1.83	60	24.7
1963	2.51	1.885	62.5	25.0

a. Including cost-of-living allowance adjustments.

SOURCES: The files of the National Office, UPWA, Toronto; U.S., Bureau of Labor Statistics, *Wage Chronology — Swift & Co., 1942-63* (Report No. 260).

1 cent between 1945 and 1952. With the establishment of the bracket system in Canada in 1954 it is possible to make international comparisons. Table 4-3 presents comparative base rate data for selected jobs at Swift in both countries over the period 1954 to 1963. The jobs are ones which are representative of the occupational scale and ones which seemed most suitable for international comparison purposes. Jobs in the pork dressing department were selected because the technology in this department has been quite

Table 4-3

WAGE DIFFERENTIAL COMPARISONS — SELECTED JOBS, CANADA AND UNITED STATES, 1954 AND 1963

Job Classification	1954		1963	
	¢	%	¢	%
Unskilled				
Common labor rate	15	9.7	45.5	18.4
Semi-skilled (Pork Dressing)				
Pull toe nails	17	10.5	47.5	18.6
Hang off on rail	18	10.9	48.5	18.6
Shaving hog carcasses	20	11.6	50.5	18.7
Open hogs (bellies)	23	12.6	53.5	18.9
Cut and disjoint head	22.5	11.8	52	17.8
Sticking	21	10.9	53	17.9
Skilled				
1st class millwright	26	12.3	54.5	17.0
1st class machinist	33	15.1	63.5	19.4
Bricklayer (masonry)	49.5	21.3	85	24.6

SOURCE: The files of the National Office, UPWA, Toronto.

stable over time. Since 1954, there have been inequity adjustments and increases in labor grade increments in both countries. The table indicates, however, that the international differential between similar jobs widened in both absolute and percentage amounts — not to the same extent as for the common labor rate, but, nevertheless, a significant widening in each case.

In addition to the widening of base rate differentials there is the question of incentive earnings but incentive pay was substantially higher in the U.S. and there were no major changes over the period.[4]

---

4. In one minor area of related wage practices the Canadian District did make some relative progress. They achieved shift premium parity with the U.S. Over the period, shift premiums had been raised in Canada from 7 cents, or 5.3 per cent of the common labor rate, to 12 cents or 6 per cent. In the U.S. industry they had been increased from 9 cents to 12 cents or a decrease from 6.2 per cent to 4.9 per cent.

A premium of 5 per cent and 10 per cent of base rates was included in the U.S. settlement of 1956 for Saturday and Sunday work on continuous operations. A similar provision was achieved in Canada in 1958. It provided for 10 cents on Saturday and 15 cents on Sunday. By 1962 these premiums were still much higher in the U.S., however, standing at 25 per cent and 50 per cent for Saturday and Sunday respectively, compared with 20 cents and 30 cents in the Canadian industry.

Tables 4-1 and 4-2 do reveal that the international differential in the common labor rate for both males and females was lower in 1962, in relative terms, than at the inception of the union. The reduction has not been a particularly significant one, however. In 1939 the male differential was 22.4 per cent compared with 19.7 per cent in 1963. Female rates were only available since 1941 when the differential stood at 33 per cent. In 1963 the differential was still substantial — 25 per cent. During the same period, there was a huge increase in the absolute differential for both males and females. There has, however, been some variability in the differential. It declined during the war years until 1945, then expanded in 1946 to 1948, contracted again during the next four years and then steadily increased. The narrowing from 1949 to 1952 was a phenomenon common to most Canadian sectors.

THE COLLECTIVE BARGAINING RECORD

Pre-1953 Experience

Fortunately, there is some information available which allows a resumé of the early experience of the Canadian District and in doing so sets the stage for the period under more intensive analysis.[5]

The most conspicuous fact concerning the early activity of the UPWA in Canada was the extent to which collective bargaining was shaped by government intervention and third-party dicta. It is not surprising, therefore, that an analysis of events and settlements reveals little in the way of international pattern-bargaining. Until 1948 the Canadian District was busy consolidating its gains and placed major emphasis on organizing the industry and obtaining company-wide agreements with each of the national packers. Its actions and strategy were enveloped by wartime emergency measures, its settlements by government fiat. The year 1947 saw the rescinding of the War Measures Act. In that year, however, arbitration played a large role in the Big Three negotiations. Not only did government intervention shape settlements during this period but it modified bargaining structure and encouraged inter-company cooperation in the industry.

---

5. There were two main sources used in this regard, one an investigation of unionism in the Canadian meat packing industry, the other the proceedings of arbitration hearings in a dispute arising in 1947. See J. T. Montague, "Trade Unionism In The Canadian Meat Packing Industry" (unpublished Ph.D. dissertation, University of Toronto, 1948) and *Proceedings of Arbitration between Burns & Co., Ltd. and Canada Packers Ltd. and United Packinghouse Workers of America*, November 4, 1947 (in the files of the National Office, UPWA, Toronto).

During the 1944-46 period, negotiations with all three national packers were closely associated, due to the appointment of a common commissioner to deal with the three companies. This encouraged inter-company cooperation. In 1947 a similar institutional factor reinforced this practice at Canada Packers and Burns. After several months of negotiations in that year the parties became deadlocked and a strike resulted at all of the companies. The union asked the Federal Government to aid in settling the dispute, but the War Measures Act had been repealed and authority over such disputes had returned to the provinces. The union, Canada Packers and Burns agreed to an arbitration of the outstanding issues. Burns associated itself with Canada Packers in the companies' presentation to arbitration. Swift Canadian had refused to submit their dispute and the union continued to negotiate with the company, with the result that Swift Canadian signed the pattern-setting agreement. It was the first and last time that this occurred.

The most interesting aspect of this period is that it set precedents with Swift Canadian in three key areas. In the first place, the company established the principle that it would not cooperate with the union with regard to third-party intervention. Secondly, the company made it clear that it was unwilling to have its Canadian plants brought under the U.S. master-agreement. The third feature was the use made by the union of a pressure tactic arising from the company's international character — the threat to negotiate to have the company's Canadian plants included in the U.S. master agreement.

The last two points arose for the first time during the 1946 negotiations. In that year it was decided at a meeting of the International Executive Board that, when the union's demands were presented to Swift in the United States, a request would be made to have the Canadian locals included in the U.S. contract.[6] This was to be used as a strategic weapon. When negotiations opened in Canada, Swift Canadian refused to bargain with the other two members of the Big Three and threatened to negotiate on a plant basis. In retaliation the union informed the company that it would exert pressure on the parent firm to be included in the latter's negotiations. The parent firm, however, took the position that its Canadian subsidiary was a separate operation and came under different labor laws making any inclusion of the Canadian plants impossible. When this impasse could not be resolved the Canadian locals took a strike vote and at the same time the U.S. section of the union filed notice with the U.S. Department of Labor under the provision of the Smith-

---

6. Minutes of UPWA Executive Board Meeting, Mount Royal Hotel, Montreal, Canada, May 25-27, 1946, p. 75 (in the files of the National Office, UPWA, Toronto).

Connally Act that it intended to strike in sympathy with its membership at Swift Canadian. Under this pressure the company agreed to
commence negotiations for a Canadian master agreement.

The precedent of non-support of third-party intervention on the
part of Swift Canadian commenced in 1947. The company had
refused to send the outstanding issues of their dispute to arbitration.
With Canada Packers and Burns agreeing to this arrangement, the
Ontario Minister of Labour went to Chicago to try to persuade
head-office management to decide otherwise. The company, however,
refused to accept the intervention of a third party into the dispute.
This policy is still maintained to the extent possible.

An investigation of the proceedings of the Constitutional Convention, the minutes of executive board meetings and of the files of
the Canadian District for the 1943 to 1952 period, revealed nothing
that would indicate that the Canadian District was attempting to
obtain U.S. wage standards. Union officials came up to Canada to
help the Canadian District during the 1945 and 1947 negotiations.
This was at the invitation of the Canadian District and their role
was minor.[7] Such participation was probably the result of the Canadian District being in a weak and precarious position at that time
and without a substantial number of experienced leaders. In this
regard, one company executive told of an occasion when his firm
requested the international to send up an official from the U.S. in
1943 to deal with a Canadian union representative, with whom the
company could not negotiate. The president of the union visited
Canada, and with the aid of one other international official straightened out the situation.[8]

Even with the removal of governmental controls in Canada,
collective bargaining in the industry in no way paralleled that in the
United States from 1948-53. In 1948 the pattern settlement in
Canada was for 8.5 cents or 9.6 per cent. In the U.S. there were
two settlements — one in May for 9 cents and one in October for 4
cents, for a total percentage increase of 12.7 per cent. There was a
settlement in the U.S. Big Four in 1949 but no settlement in the

---

7. One interesting feature was that the Canadian District won 8 paid holidays in 1945. The U.S. union officials went back to the U.S. and achieved
this in their 1946 settlements. This case of international pattern bargaining in
reverse, however, was an isolated one in the meat packing industry. The fact
that Canadian union membership, in practically every industry, is a small
proportion of total union membership and that Canadian wages and fringe
benefits are lower than in the U.S., makes the likelihood of such occurrences
seem small indeed. As indicated previously, it has, however, occurred in the
pulp and paper industry.

8. Interview with Mr. H. Hill, Director of Industrial Relations, Canada
Packers Ltd., November 20, 1964.

Canadian Big Three. Separate agreements were signed in the U.S. in August 1950 and February 1951 for 11 cents and 9 cents, respectively. The Canadian agreements were also signed in August 1950 but provided for two wage increases — one in 1950 for 7.4 per cent, or 7.5 cents, and one in 1951 for 3 cents. An additional supplemental contract was signed in the U.S. for 6 cents or 4.4 per cent in February 1952 retroactive to December 1951, followed by a two year contract in October of that year for 4 cents. The pattern agreement in Canada was also for two years but was signed approximately three months before the October 1952 agreements in the U.S. and provided for an increase of 5 per cent, or 6.5 cents.

This conclusion holds equally for all particulars of the bargaining process including any attempts to close the U.S.-Canada wage differential.[9]

Collective Bargaining 1953 to 1962

Table 4-4 exhibits the timing of the UPWA settlements in both countries over the period 1952-62. When there were negotiations in the U.S. and Canada in the same year, only in 1954 was the U.S. pattern set first.

Table 4-5 compares the U.S. key bargain and Canadian agreements of the Big Three and two representative independent packers over the 1953-63 period in terms of yearly negotiated absolute wage increases (excluding cost-of-living adjustments). The two independents have plants in Alberta and Saskatchewan. Although the wage changes for these two firms are negotiated substantially later than for the Big Three, the effective dates are the same, or very nearly the same, as for the national packers. The wage changes for the two independents are, therefore, placed in the years they became effective. The table reveals two things. Firstly, that the Canada Packers pattern for wage changes is followed exactly in the central segment of the industry.[10] Secondly, that with the exception of 1953 and 1962, the Canadian increases varied in absolute amount

9. This overall impression was confirmed in interviews with officials of two members of the Canadian Big Three and one of the assistant directors of the Canadian District.

10. There is a small amount of data available which strongly suggests that the general wage changes in the central segment of Canadian industry were similar even before the UPWA organized in Canada. In 1936, for example, each of the national packers increased wages by 11 per cent. In March of 1937 Swift Canadian increased wages by 23 per cent while Burns and Canada Packers made increases of 22 per cent during the same month. Industrial and Development Council of Canadian Meat Packers, *Summary of Wage Rates, Hours and Earnings in Canadian Packing Plants, 1941* (in the files of the National Office, UPWA, Toronto).

Table 4-4

DATES OF UPWA KEY SETTLEMENTS, CANADA AND UNITED STATES, 1952-62

Year	United States	Year	Canada
1952	Oct. 26 (2 yr. contract)	1952	Aug. 1 (2 yr. contract)
1953	Sept. 30 (reopening)	1953	Aug. 19 (reopening)
1954	Sept. 23 (2 yr. contract)	1954	Oct. 29 (2 yr. contract)
1955	July 29 (reopening)	1955	
1956	Sept. 25 (3 yr. contract)	1956	Aug. 15 (2 yr. contract)
1957		1957	
1958		1958	Aug. 11 (2 yr. contract)
1959	Aug. 31 (2 yr. contract)	1959	
1960		1960	April 3 (2 yr. contract)
1961	Sept. 10 (3 yr. contract)	1961	
1962		1962	April 19 (2 yr. contract)

SOURCE: The files of the National Office, UPWA, Toronto.

Table 4-5

NEGOTIATED GENERAL WAGE INCREASES[a] IN THE MEAT PACKING INDUSTRY, CANADA AND UNITED STATES, 1953-63
(cents per hour)

	1953	1954	1955	1956	1957	1958	1959	1960	1961	1962	1963
.S. Key Bargain	5	5	14	10	7.5	7.5	8.5	6.5	7	6	6
anada Packers	5	3	3	9	6	9	5	6	6	6	5.5
vift Canadian	5	3	3	9	6	9	5	6	6	6	5.5
urns	5	3	3	9	6	9	5	6	6	6	5.5
tercontinental	5	3	3	9	6	9	5	6	6	6	5.5
ainers	5	3	3	9	6	9	5	6	6	6	5.5

a. Excluding cost-of-living allowance adjustments.

SOURCES: The files of the National Office, UPWA, Toronto; U.S., Bureau of Labor Statistics, *Wage Chronology — Swift & Co., 1942-63* (Report No. 260) and *Wage Chronology — Amour & Co., 1941-63* (Report No. 187; Revised 1963).

Table 4-6

NEGOTIATED GENERAL WAGE INCREASES[a] (AS A
PERCENTAGE OF THE COMMON LABOR RATE) IN THE
MEAT PACKING INDUSTRY, CANADA AND
UNITED STATES, 1953-63

	1953	1954	1955	1956	1957	1958	1959	1960	1961	1962	1963
U.S. Key Bargain	3.4	3.3	9.0	5.9	4.2	4.0	4.4	3.0	3.1	2.6	2.5
Canada Packers	3.7	2.1	2.1	6.4	3.9	5.6	2.9	3.4	3.3	3.2	2.8
Swift Canadian	3.7	2.1	2.1	6.4	3.9	5.6	2.9	3.4	3.3	3.2	2.8
Burns	3.7	2.1	2.1	6.4	3.9	5.6	2.9	3.4	3.3	3.2	2.8
Intercontinental	3.7	2.1	2.1	6.4	3.9	5.6	2.9	3.4	3.3	3.2	2.8
Gainers Ltd.	3.7	2.1	2.1	6.4	3.9	5.6	2.9	3.4	3.3	3.2	2.8

a. Excluding cost-of-living allowance adjustments.

SOURCES: The files of the National Office, UPWA, Toronto; U.S., Bureau
of Labor Statistics, *Wage Chronology — Swift & Co., 1942-63*
(Report No. 260; Revised 1964) and *Wage Chronology —
Armour & Co., 1941-63* (Report No. 187; Revised 1963).

from the U.S. key bargain, although in 1963 the Canadian increase
was only a half cent below the increase in the U.S. Table 4-6 makes
a similar comparison in percentage terms.[11] While percentage increases in both countries were quite close in 1953, 1957, 1960, and
1963 in no case were the increases between the countries identical.

The increases for females were not always identical to those
for males. In 1953 the Canadian agreements called for a wage
increase of only 4 cents for females compared with 5 cents for
males. The only occasion when they received a higher increase was
in 1958. Female rates were increased by 5 cents in addition to the
general wage increase of 9 cents. This was in sharp contrast to the
experience in the United States where special increases, over and
above the general wage increase, had been added to female rates in
each bargaining round since 1952, until the female differential was
eliminated in 1958.

---

11. The common labor rate in Toronto and the Metropolitan or "Chicago"
rate (i.e., the rate which prevails in packing plants in the large cities) were
used for Canada and the U.S., respectively, in converting the absolute wage
changes to relative changes. The same rates have been used when comparing
wage levels over time.

In trying to determine the interrelatedness of U.S. and Canadian wage changes, Table 4-7 demonstrates more clearly the lack of similarity and relatedness between American and Canadian wage settlements. The table considers the total wage package (excluding increases in labor grade increments and cost-of-living adjustments) in each country for each bargaining round. In only one instance was the Canadian wage package identical, in either absolute or relative amount, to its counterpart in the U.S. This was the 1953 round when the absolute increase was 5 cents in both countries. Pattern-following in this case cannot be inferred because the Canadian pattern preceded that in the United States by about 5 weeks.

The dissimilarity in the length of the contracts beginning in 1956, while eliminating the possibility of international pattern-bargaining in the same year, opened up such a possibility on a lagged basis. In one case this may have occurred. A U.S. pattern of 14 cents in 1955 was followed by a Canadian pattern of 15 cents in 1956.

There was only one instance where the same fringe benefit was provided in both countries in the same year (see Table 4-8). This was in 1956 when the agreements with the major packers reduced the requirement for two weeks vacation to three years. Again, however, the Canadian pattern was set first. The only area where there perhaps was some lagged pattern bargaining was vacations. In 1960 the Canadian requirement for 3 weeks vacation had been reduced to 12 years service. This had been provided for in the 1959 U.S. key bargain. In 1962, the requirement for 4 weeks vacation was reduced to 20 years of service in Canada. This had been called for in the U.S. key bargain the previous year.

On the surface, at least, it would appear that if there were influences from the U.S. they were minor. At the same time, an analysis of negotiations revealed modest U.S. influences at Swift Canadian.

1953

The two-year agreements signed in the industry in both countries in 1952 provided for a reopening in 1953. Negotiations with the Canadian Big Three paralleled those in the U.S. with respect to time. They began on June 24 when the union presented demands, based on policy adopted by the District 8 conference, to Swift Canadian in Toronto. Similar demands were presented to Burns and Canada Packers early in July. The Canadian officers of the union met twice with each of the Big Three but no offer was made on

Table 4-7

TOTAL NEGOTIATED WAGE INCREASES EACH BARGAINING ROUND IN THE MEAT PACKING INDUSTRY, CANADA AND UNITED STATES, 1953-63

United States			Year	Canada		
Length of Contract	Total Package			Length of Contract	Total Package	
	¢	%			¢	%
1 year	5[a]	3.4[a]	1953	1 year	5[a]	3.7[a]
2 years	5	3.3	1954	2 years	6	4.3
	14[a]	9.0[a]	1955			
3 years	25	16.1	1956	2 years	15	10.3
			1957			
			1958	2 years	14	8.7
2 years	15	7.7	1959			
			1960	2 years	12	6.9
3 years	19	8.5	1961			
			1962	2 years	11.5	6.5
			1963			

a. Reopened the agreement.

Table 4-8

A COMPARISON OF FRINGE BENEFIT CHANGES — U.S. KEY BARGAIN, CANADA PACKERS AND SWIFT CANADIAN — 1953-63

Provision	U.S. Key Bargain	Canada	
		Canada Packers	Swift Canadian
Welfare Plan	1953: All company-paid hospitalization, surgical, medical plan for employees with 6 mos. continuous service and their dependents.	1953: Nil	1953: Nil
Paid Vacations	1954-55: 4 wks. after 25 or more yrs. service.	1954-55: Nil	1954-55: Nil
Welfare Plan	Minor improvements in existing plan.		
Paid Vacations	1956-58: Length of service requirement for 2 wks. vacation reduced to 3 yrs.	1956-57: Same as U.S. Key Bargain.	1956-57: Same as U.S. Key Bargain.
Sick Pay Plan	Increased to: 55% of employees' weekly pay for 2nd compensable wk. of disability, 60% for 3rd and 4th wk., and 65% for 5th and subsequent wks. Maximum yearly benefit payment increased to 13 wks. for employees with less than 7 yrs. service.	Increased: males — from $24 to $33; females — from $18 to $26 weekly.	Nil, but sick pay goes up with wages automatically.
Separation Allowance	Benefits extended to employees permanently separated because of technological changes.	Nil	Nil

Table 4-8 (continued)

Provision	U.S. Key Bargain	Canada	
		Canada Packers	Swift Canadian
Welfare Plan	Minor improve-ments in hospitaliza-tion benefits.	Inprovements within existing contributory plan. Surgical benefit increased from $200 to $300 plus improvements in medical coverage.	Established a contributory (50-50) hospitalization plan.
Jury Duty Pay		Same as U.S. industry achieved in 1952.	Same as Canada Packers.
Pension Plan	Increased: normal retirement benefits and total and permanent disability benefits; added: early retirement benefits at age 60 and deferred vesting rights.	Pension Plan not covered by collective bargaining.	
Paid Holidays		1958-59: One additional paid holiday for a total of 9.	1958-59: Same as Canada Packers.
Welfare Plan		1.2¢ devoted to improving the existing contributory plan: .5¢ for improved life insurance.	1.2¢ devoted to im-proving the existing contributory plan; .5¢ to improve the benefits under the sickness and accident plan. The changes paralleled those at the parent firm in 1956.
Paid Vacations	1959-61: Requirement for 3 wks. vacation reduced to 12 yrs. of service.		
Separation Allowance	Added: benefits for all employees having one or more yrs. service losing seniority by reason of layoff exceeding 2 yrs.		

Table 4-8 (continued)

Provision	U.S. Key Bargain	Canada	
		Canada Packers	Swift Canadian
Automation Fund	Company-financed fund, maximum $500,000 to be used to finance study and solutions for problems resulting from modernization programs. Company contribution to be 1¢ per cwt. shipped from slaughtering and meat packing plants covered by agreements.		
Insurance Plan	Added: Diagnostic laboratory and X-ray benefits — maximum $50 for all sickness during 6 consecutive mos. and for each accident.		
Pension Plan	Increased: Normal retirement benefits, total and permanent disability benefits and deferred vesting rights. Added: Disability benefits, early retirement benefits extended to women at age 55.		
Bereavement Pay		1960-61: One days pay at regular rate to attend funeral of a member of the immediate family.	1960-61: Same as Canada Packers.
Paid Vacations		Requirement for 3 wks. vacation reduced to 12 yrs. of service. (This is the same as U.S. Key Bargain in 1959.)	Same as Canada Packers.

Table 4-8 (continued)

Provision	U.S. Key Bargain	Canada	
		Canada Packers	Swift Canadian
Sick Pay Plan		Increased: males to $40 per wk., females to $32 per wk.	Sick pay benefits go up with wages.
Clothing Allowance		One-half of the cost of work clothing to be provided by the company. (This was provided for in the U.S. industry as early as 1945.)	Nil
Paid Vacations	1961-63: Requirement reduced to 10 yrs. service for 3 wks. vacation and to 20 yrs. for 4 wks.		
Bereavement Pay	Established up to 3 days paid leave at regular wage rate for arranging or attending funeral of member of immediate family.		
Notice of Closing	Established: Company to give 90 day advance notice of closing plant. Employee permanently separated before expiration of such 90-day notice to receive 8 hrs. pay at regular rate for each workday before expiration of the 90 days.		
Separation Allowance	Increased: 1 wks. pay for each year of continuous service through 10, plus 1¾ wks. for each year from 11 through 20, plus 2 wks. pay for each year over 20.		

Table 4-8 (continued)

| Provision | U.S. Key Bargain | Canada | |
		Canada Packers	Swift Canadian
Automation Fund	Company contributions to fund discontinued with remainder of fund to be available for employee relocation and retraining costs.		
Technological Adjustment Plan	Established: Company-financed plan to provide immediate benefits for employees permanently separated from service by closing of plant, division, or major department. Benefits available to employees under age 60 with 5 yrs. of service or more.		
Welfare Plan	Added: hospital room and board; X-ray, radium, or radioactive isotope therapy.		
Pension Plan	Increased: normal retirement benefits; Added: survivorship option and optional early retirement.		
Work Clothing		1962-63: Outer clothing specified by the company as required for work will be supplied to employeees by the company.	1962-63: Added: Company to supply required clothing at one-half the cost to the company of such clothing.

(Provisions for work clothing similar to the above had been in effect in the U.S. industry since the mid-1940's.)

Table 4-8 (continued)

| Provision | U.S. Key Bargain | Canada | |
		Canada Packers	Swift Canadian
Bereavement Pay		Increased: to 2 days paid leave at regular wage rate for death in immediate family.	Same as Canada Packers.
Paid Vacations		Eligibility for 4 wks. vacation reduced to 20 yrs. service. (This had been provided for in the 1961 U.S. key bargain.)	Same as Canada Packers.
Welfare Plan		Minor improvements in the hospital-medical plan but it remained on a contributory basis.	Same as Canada Packers.

SOURCES: The files of the National Office, UPWA, Toronto; U.S., Bureau of Labor Statistics, *Wage Chronology — Swift & Co., 1942-63* (Report No. 260; Revised 1964) and *Wage Chronology — Armour & Co., 1941-63* (Report No. 187; Revised 1963).

wages or any other matter during the following month.[12]   The firms quickly disposed of a union argument for changes in the various incentive systems and the area of argument narrowed down to the union demands for a substantial wage increase and the bracket system.   The national officers bargained until mid-August with the three companies and then called in the National Policy Committee. Round-the-clock negotiations with each member of the Big Three resulted in a settlement with Canada Packers and Burns on August 19 and with Swift the following day.   This was six weeks before the key bargain was signed with Armour in the U.S.

At no time did demands originating in the U.S. or the negotiations to the south affect those of the Canadian industry.   The em-

---

12. Correspondence of Fred Dowling, Canadian District Director, to all Big Three locals, delegates to the policy committee, and staff, dated July 31, 1953 (in the files of the National Office, UPWA, Toronto).

phasis in the two countries was entirely different. The negotiations in the Canadian industry were relatively short and were in no way prolonged in anticipation of the U.S. settlement. All of the Canadian bargaining was done by the Canadian officers and the National Policy Committee without any assistance from international headquarters.

1954

The Canadian and U.S. agreements expired just a month apart in 1954. The Canadian agreements expired first on July 31, the Armour and Swift agreements in the U.S. on September 1.

The most notable demand in Canada was one for an all company-paid welfare plan won by the union in the United States at Swift, in 1953.[13] The existing agreements with Canada Packers and Burns called for the company to pay half the cost of hospital and medical insurance, while at Swift Canadian a sick pay plan was provided at company cost but with no hospitalization plan. In the 1953 U.S. negotiations, Swift and other U.S. packers accepted the union request to pay the full cost of providing hospital, surgical and medical insurance. The strategy of the union in District 8 was to obtain the U.S. pattern at Swift Canadian and after doing so, exert pressure on the other Canadian packers to "come into line".[14]

This demand was the outcome of the policy of the national office of going over the union's contract with the parent firm and comparing it with the Canadian agreement in an effort to "upgrade" the latter contract. This was enunciated clearly by the research department in Canada in a bulletin to the Swift chain which stated:

> These clauses were set down in this comparison only when their inclusion in the contract was a loss, rather than a gain for the Canadian members as compared to the American, since the purpose of this comparison is to show ways in which the Canadian contract can be improved . . . . It will be noticed that certain clauses have been marked with a star. These clauses are the ones that it seemed most obviously could be improved by being made more like the American clauses dealing with the same subject.[15]

Negotiations in Canada began June 8, slightly before those in the U.S. By mid-July the union had dropped most of their demands

---

13. Another interesting feature was that the "Swift chain decided against a suggestion to put their chain under negotiations in the U.S. . . ." (*Canadian Packinghouse Worker* (Toronto), May 1954, p. 10). A different decision was made in later negotiations.
14. *Canadian Packinghouse Worker* (Toronto), May 1954, p. 14.
15. "Comparison Between American and Canadian Swift Contracts," prepared for UPWA Convention, May 1954, by District 8 research department, p. 1 (in the files of the National Office, UPWA, Toronto).

(such as increased premium pay, payment of 100 per cent instead of 75 per cent of bonus, inclusion of the pension plan in the agreement, increased vacations with pay, etc.) but had reached agreement on only a few minor items.[16] No official counter proposal on wages, the bracket system or welfare was forthcoming from any of the three firms by July 28 with the result that the union decided to break off negotiations as of that day and proceed to conciliation. At that point the union had not even presented their case for the U.S. hospitalization plan.

The delegates on the National Policy Committee returned home and the national officers continued negotiating with the companies. They were now faced with the prospect of securing the cooperation of the companies regarding a system of national conciliation. In addition they had to persuade the Minister of Labour in each province to recognize the decision of the conciliation board established in Ontario, or at least to nominate the same people as were appointed to that board. Both Canada Packers and Burns agreed to cooperate with the union in this regard. Swift, on the other hand, refused to cooperate, or to take any action that would help resolve the difficulties encountered under provincial conciliation. By September a conciliation board had been established for Burns and Canada Packers in Ontario. Saskatchewan, Alberta, and Prince Edward Island had indicated that they would accept the board established in Ontario as complying with the provisions of their labor acts, and British Columbia had accepted the same people on its board as had been nominated in Ontario. Only Manitoba and Quebec refused to follow either of these procedures. Conciliation proceeded on this basis.

The union had re-opened negotiations with Swift Canadian on August 18. At this meeting the union maintained that the time was appropriate for Swift Canadian to take the lead in negotiations instead of waiting for Canada Packers to set the pattern. The company would not make any move, however, and suggested in effect that the union should proceed to conciliation with the other two companies and then resume negotiations with Swift.[17] No agreement was reached and the union told the company that they would continue to negotiate but if nothing came of the negotiations they would proceed to conciliation, if necessary establishing separate boards in each province. Further meetings were held with Swift Canadian in August and September with the union threatening to start concilia-

---

16. "Report on Swift Negotiations," 1954 (in the files of the National Office, UPWA, Toronto).

17. UPWA-Swift Negotiations, Notes of Mr. S. Hughes, Assistant Canadian Director, August 18, 1954 (in the files of the National Office, UPWA, Toronto).

tion procedures if the company would not cooperate in setting up conciliation boards on the same basis as Burns and Canada Packers.[18]

The same Ontario conciliation board was appointed to hear both the Burns and Canada Packers disputes. The issues referred to the board by the parties were those items upon which agreement could not be reached — wages, job rating, and health and welfare. The lengthy conciliation process resulted in the Canadian negotiations extending past the date on which the U.S. key bargain was signed (September 23). On September 24 the board heard the briefs presented by the two companies and the union. On September 25 an attempt was made to conciliate the issues. On October 1 the chairman held a meeting with the parties, and the companies and the union then presented their rebuttals. The three-man board unanimously recommended a settlement to the Ontario Minister of Labour on October 13 after a number of mediation efforts.[19]

During conciliation hearings it had become apparent that Swift Canadian would not set the pattern so the union, as in the past, placed major emphasis on obtaining a pattern-setting agreement with Canada Packers which could then be applied to the other two national packers. In the union submission for Canada Packers they concluded by stating: "It must be obvious that an agreement must be reached with this company before we can expect to get anywhere with the others."[20]

In the union's argument for an increase in welfare coverage it revealed to the board that one of the reasons for its failure to make more progress was "due to the fact that the Swift company has refused to make contributions toward hospital, medical or surgical coverage for employees or dependents, maintaining that the cost of its sick pay plan was higher than that for the benefits provided at Canada Packers".[21] It then made reference to the 1953 agreement in the U.S. industry, making particular mention of Swift, which provided employees and dependents with Blue Cross semiprivate hospital coverage and Blue Shield surgical and medical coverage. The brief then went on to state: "In view of this agreement by the parent company in the U.S., the union expects that the

18. Correspondence of F. Dowling, Canadian District Director, to all Big Three locals, September 10, 1954 (in the files of the National Office, UPWA, Toronto).
19. Correspondence from the conciliation board to the Ontario Minister of Labor, October 13, 1954 (in the files of the National Office, UPWA, Toronto).
20. Submission of the United Packinghouse Workers of America, "In the Matter of Proceedings before a Conciliation Board Dealing with a Dispute between Canada Packers, Limited and the United Packinghouse Workers of America," 1954, p. 44 (in the files of the National Office, UPWA, Toronto).
21. *Ibid.*, p. 37.

Canadian subsidiary will now be prepared to liberalize its position in Canada."[22]

This is the only area in its presentation where there was any mention of the U.S. industry; and, the argument that the U.S. industry had provided welfare increases was not used by the union to obtain identical changes in Canada, but was presented as an additional reason for an increase in the welfare plan at Canada Packers.

The recommendations of the conciliation board, however, determined the industry settlement. The board chairman decided to try to work out a formula that would give the union the bracket system but, because of its complexity, dropped any possibility of working out a compromise solution in the welfare area. As a substitute, he decided upon a general wage increase.[23] As finally enunciated by the board, the settlement took the form of a 3 cent per hour increase retroactive to August 1, 1954, and an additional 3.25 to 3.5 cents on December 1, 1954 for the establishment of the bracket system, and another 3 cents per hour on August 1, 1955. The contract ran to August 1, 1956. The increase in 1955 was also to be earmarked, if needed, for the establishment of the bracket system, or in any manner agreed upon between the union and the companies. This was in addition to the minor provisions which had been worked out by the parties outside of conciliation.

Following receipt of the board's recommendations the Canadian officers of the union met, and agreed that if the companies accepted the report, they would recommend acceptance to the National Policy Committee.[24] On October 29 agreement was reached with Burns and Canada Packers on this basis. Several meetings were held between Swift Canadian and the Canadian officers and an agreement was worked out which was essentially the same in all respects to the agreements with the other two members of the Big Three.

1955 and 1956

The agreements signed in the U.S. industry in 1954 were to run for two years. A similar situation prevailed in Canada. Unlike the Canadian settlements, however, there was provision in the U.S. for three reopenings for possible adjustments in wage rates. U.S. negotiations began in May of 1955 and were consummated on July 29, with Armour agreeing to an increase of 14 cents per hour. The decision in Canada for spending the 3 cents provided for in the

22. *Ibid.*, p. 38.
23. *Canadian Packinghouse Worker* (Toronto), October 1954, p. 13.
24. *Ibid.*

1954 agreements was made at the Canadian conference held in Vancouver in June and was agreed to by the Big Three in July.

In 1956, the two-year contracts expired on July 31. The Canadian District held a conference in Toronto at the end of April, six weeks prior to the International Convention which was held in Cincinnati. The U.S. contracts were due to expire a month after those in Canada. Preliminary meetings between the Canadian Big Three and the national officers were held on June 4. Negotiations in the U.S. began a month later when the UPWA and the Amalgamated Meat Cutters jointly notified the major meat packing companies that they intended to terminate their master contracts on September 1.

After three meetings with each of the national packers had been held, the National Policy Committee was called to Toronto on July 15. When the bargaining sessions opened on Monday, July 16, no counter proposal on wages had been received by the union. Both Swift Canadian and Burns, according to the union, "sat back and stated flatly they would not make an offer on wages, but would wait and pay whatever Canada Packers was willing to pay".[25] Canada Packers did make an offer on money matters but this offer was unanimously rejected by the Policy Committee.

On August 10 the Canadian officers received a second offer of settlement from Canada Packers and the National Policy Committee met in Winnipeg five days later. At that time the Committee endorsed the proposed basis of settlement and the agreement with Canada Packers was quickly ratified. Agreement in the U.S. industry was not to come until the end of September. When it was reached the settlements had no resemblance to those in Canada and, additionally, were for three years rather than 20 months as had been agreed upon in Canada. The Canadian pattern of 9 cents in 1956 and 6 cents in 1957 was only a cent higher than the U.S. pattern in 1955. There is no evidence to indicate that the union was attempting to follow the U.S. pattern of the previous year, however. Therefore, any such conclusion would be highly tenuous.

While Swift Canadian accepted the pattern set by Canada Packers, an interesting side issue developed which delayed formal settlement until October. The principal reason for the disagreement was the policy of Swift of centralizing policy in Chicago and unilaterally passing on to their Canadian labor force some of the benefits they provide their U.S. employees. The result of the latter is that the Swift Canadian contract contains certain fringes which are distinctly different from those in the contracts of Canada Packers

---

25. *Canadian Packinghouse Worker* (Toronto), August 1956, p. 8.

or Burns. In bargaining with the UPWA in Canada, the general procedure followed by Swift has been to offer the union the Canada Packers' pattern, in terms of cents per hour rather than in terms of identical benefits. This means that, if the pattern settlement in Canada includes "x" number of cents per hour for welfare, Swift Canadian will improve their welfare plan in a manner which will cost the company the same amount. Such a situation arose in 1956. Without making any judgment on the merit of either the union's or the firm's position in the dispute, the following excerpts from union correspondence do divulge the union's reaction to what it considered to be the lack of decision-making power of Swift Canadian officials.

Sam Hughes, Assistant Canadian Director and chairman of the Swift negotiating committee, informing one of the union's local presidents of the prevailing situation with Swift Canadian stated:

> While we were still in Winnipeg (August 15), I phoned Mr. Wylie, Superintendent, Swift Canadian Company and told him of the agreement reached with Canada Packers. I stressed how much the cost would be to Packers and that the Swift people [union] were willing to go along with this program if Swift would meet these costs. This, in effect, meant that the only negotiations that would be necessary would be in connection with a proposed Surgical and Medical Plan . . . . Mr. Wylie replied that he understood my position and that he could go along with it . . . .
>
> Today, on my return to the office from my vacation, I got in touch with Mr. Wylie and asked him what progress he had made with respect to the plan. He said he was sorry but he had got simply nowhere. At this time, I told him that I had lost my patience and was thoroughly disgusted with the manner in which Swift's had carried on negotiations this year. I said that the committee were completely frustrated during negotiations and felt that he and Mr. Summerall were acting as mere stooges and were sent into negotiations by the company with their hands tied behind their backs . . . .
>
> I hope we will be able to get some results on a Surgical and Medical Plan within the next week or two. However, I must stress that Mr. Wylie stated that he will still have to talk to the powers that be in Chicago before he can actually make a definite offer on a plan.[26]

Canadian District Director Dowling re-iterated the union's belief of lack of Swift Canadian authority[27] as did Hughes[28] in later correspondence. The company no doubt reaps some benefits by cen-

---

26. Correspondence from S. S. Hughes, Assistant Canadian Director, to Mr. J. McKnight, President Local 180, UPWA, September 4, 1956 (in the files of the National Office, UPWA, Toronto).

27. Correspondence of Mr. F. Dowling, Canadian Director, to Mr. R. Hamilton, Chairman, Sub-District 104, UPWA, September 25, 1956 (in the files of the National Office, UPWA, Toronto).

28. Correspondence of S. S. Hughes to the Swift locals and Staff Representatives, September 26, 1956 (in the files of the National Office, UPWA, Toronto).

tralizing certain labor relations policies in Chicago; but it also encourages the Canadian District to use a lever they possess as a result of Swift's international holdings. This was disclosed in a letter from the Canadian District Director to the superintendent at Swift Canadian in dealing with the same issue.

> The officers of this union are now in the position where they can do two things. Get an agreement from the company which must be on the basis agreed to by the packing companies in the industry or call in the representatives from all the plants to reconsider the whole matter.
>
> If the committee is called it will result in opening up the whole agreement as arrived at and we will consider the advisability of demanding the settlements which your company has agreed to with our union in the United States which you can realize has had an impact on our locals here in Canada. We will also have to consider including a demand for the settlement of the dispute in the Vigoro plant here in Toronto and for the inclusion of the plants which you call branch plants in Montreal and Toronto.
>
> I want to emphasize again that it is our desire to settle this matter before proceeding to any such drastic action but we have no intention of accepting any agreement which in our opinion will jeopardize the future of our organization in the Swift plants.[29]

While such remarks could be construed as an attempt on the part of the Canadian District to obtain the U.S. pattern, it is clear, when the context of the remarks and the situation eliciting them is considered, that such was not the case. They were a response by the union to the feeling that the Chicago office was not allowing its subsidiary to bargain independently. Threatening to attempt to obtain the U.S. pattern was simply a lever the union had, along with the others Dowling mentioned in his letter, to pressure Swift Canadian to consummate the 1956 bargaining. It is difficult to judge how much effect this had, but it was shortly after the Dowling letter that the impasse was broken and the agreement was signed.

1958

It has been maintained to this point that the length and character of negotiations, and the timing of settlements in the Canadian meat packing industry were the outcome of autonomous bargaining and the institutional factor of conciliation. The validity of this conclusion was reinforced by the 1958 negotiations in the Canadian industry. Paradoxically, at the same time that the Canadian negotiations were displaying even less similarity in length and timing to those in the U.S., the Canadian District was attempting to have Swift

---

29. Correspondence of Mr. F. Dowling, Canadian Director, to Mr. S. Wylie, Superintendent, Swift Canadian Company Limited, October 5, 1956 (in the files of the National Office, UPWA, Toronto).

Canadian plants included in the Swift master agreement in the United States.

The Canadian agreements signed in 1956 were to run for 20 months, expiring on March 31, 1958, to allow the parties to conclude an agreement before summer vacations. The provision had exactly the opposite effect. The Big Three negotiations extended throughout the summer of 1958. There were, of course, no U.S. negotiations until 1959.

A noteworthy factor concerning the 1958 round, was again, the role played by the conciliation board in forming the final settlement. When the board convened on August 8 they learned that only certain non-cost items had been resolved by the parties. The board chairman expressed disappointment that so few items had been settled. He then asked the union to draw up a list of cost items that would represent their minimum demands and asked the company to make some financial offer.[30] On August 9 Canada Packers offered a two-year 12 cent package which the union's policy committee rejected. The UPWA's list of cost items came to about 41 cents per hour. When the board chairman received this figure he asked to speak to the union delegates and urged them to reduce their demands. The union complied with a 31 cent per hour package, which the board chairman used in his discussions with the company. The union's representative on the board appeared before the National Policy Committee on August 11 with a new 21 cent package which he believed the company would agree to if accepted by the union. The Canada Packers committee voted to accept the package as did the Swift Canadian and Burns delegates and it, therefore, became union policy.

The 21 cent offer merely provided for 13 cents on August 1, 1958 and 8 cents on August 1, 1959. How the money was to be spent was to be negotiated between the parties. If agreement on the details could not be reached the board was to come back later in the week and make specific recommendations on any outstanding issues. The union and each of the three companies were able, however, or so they thought, to agree independently on how the money would be spent. One of the provisions in each of the three agreements was to spend 1.7 cents to improve the welfare plan. The improvements were to be effective April 1, 1959. This minor provision led to a bitter dispute with Swift Canadian and consummated the Canadian District's decision to formally ask to be included in the master agreement of the parent firm.

Just prior to the 1958 negotiations, the union chairman for the Swift Canadian committee proposed, before the Ontario Select Com-

---

30. *Canadian Packinghouse Worker* (Toronto), August 1959, p. 8.

mittee on Labour Legislation, that U.S. corporations be forced to give their Canadian management full autonomy or deal with their Canadian employees themselves.[31]   In an editorial in the *Canadian Packinghouse Worker* he commented:

> Our union is not opposed to bargaining with either the office in Chicago or the one in Toronto, but we are opposed to Swifts using policy in the Toronto head office as the final authority when it suits their purpose of trying to give less to their Canadian workers, or denying benefits gained by our union from the other packers in Canada by saying they cannot go against the policy as dictated in the U.S.[32]

During the negotiations Swift Canadian again took the stand that they would prefer to negotiate rather than conciliate and refused to cooperate with the union when the latter had decided to request conciliation.[33] This simply added fuel to the fire.

Because the 1958 settlement provided for 1.7 cents to be spent on welfare in 1959, discussions on this feature began with the company in December and further meetings were held on February 11, February 24, March 11 and April 2. Parallel negotiations were going on between the union and the other two national packers. The National Policy Committee was called to a meeting in Toronto on April 6, at a time when it was clear that there was a major difference of opinion between the parties. The union's position was that the total 1.7 cents set aside should be spent on improvements in the existing welfare plans with no further cost to the employees. The companies felt that any money spent on welfare by the companies should be matched by the employees since the plans were contributory.[34] On April 10 Burns and Canada Packers reached an agreement with the union. It called for no increase in the employees' contribution.[35] Agreement on the same basis could not be reached

31. *Canadian Packinghouse Worker* (Toronto), January 1958, p. 2.

32. *Ibid.*

33. In a letter to Swift Committee delegates and all Canadian staff representatives, July 23, 1958, Hughes stated — "Please be advised that we have not been able to reach an understanding with the Swift Canadian Co. Limited as to setting up conciliation boards across the country.
"It is quite evident that the company is not going to go out of their way to co-operate with us in setting up a board with the co-operation or blessings of the various provincial governments affected to deal with our dispute on a national basis." (In the files of the National Office, UPWA, Toronto.)

34. *Canadian Packinghouse Worker* (Toronto), March 1959, p. 16.

35. Canada Packers agreed to use 1.2 cents to improve the welfare plan and .5 cents to increase life insurance. At Burns 1.2 cents was used to improve welfare and .5 cents for a clothing allowance.

with Swift. The union saw this as more indecision and lack of authority on the part of Swift Canadian officers.[36]

In fairness to the company a strong argument could be made that any contributions should be on a 50-50 basis and they had made a proposal for improving the welfare plan on such a basis on February 24.[37] At any rate, when no further progress had been made at two meetings in May the union threatened that it was going to take the dispute to arbitration. Also, it was at this point that the Canadian District decided to request the international office to attempt to have Swift Canadian locals included in the United States master agreement which was due to expire on August 31, 1959. Their request was agreed to by the union's international officers.[38] Such action was clearly a reaction arising from their feeling that Swift officials in Canada were not bargaining in good faith. It is also clear that the action was not taken at the instigation of international headquarters but was simply a device used by the Canadian District to put pressure on Swift.

When the International presented its demands to Swift in the U.S., the first one was the demand to bring under the U.S. master contract all locals represented by the UPWA in the United States and Canada.[39] Nothing further was heard of the demand and any such broadening of bargaining structure was not part of the 1959 settlement with the company in the United States. What effect the action had on the Canadian situation is difficult to ascertain. Swift Canadian and the Canadian District finally did resolve their dispute in the middle of November 1959. The settlement called for use of 1.2 cents for the welfare plan and .5 cents to improve the benefits under the company's sickness and accident plan. A compromise was agreed to in regard to the contributory aspect. There was an increase in the employees' contributions but it was stipulated that such increases would be paid out of the accumulated funds built up by the 1.7 cent contribution from April to November.

---

36. Correspondence of S. S. Hughes, Assistant Canadian Director and Chairman of the Swift Canadian chain to members of the Swift committee and staff representatives April 13, 1959 (in the files of the National Office, UPWA, Toronto). A letter to the same parties April 20, 1959, reiterated these sentiments as did an editorial by Hughes in *Canadian Packinghouse Worker* (Toronto), May 1959, pp. 2, 14.

37. Report of meeting, Seaway Hotel, Toronto, May 1, 1959, UPWA, p. 2 (in the files of the National Office, UPWA, Toronto).

38. Evidence of the autonomy of Canadian locals is given in the following telegram, dated May 27, sent by Dowling to the presidents of Swift Canadian locals — "Our experience dealing with Swifts on welfare plan and their recent merger with Alberta Packing indicate it is impossible to negotiate a settlement with officials appointed here in Canada. Request your local give us the authority to demand all Canadian plants be included in the master agreement covering plants in the States."

39. *Canadian Packinghouse Worker* (Toronto), August 1959, p. 3.

One benefit for the Canadian District was that the parent firm gave top management at Swift Canadian the final authority to deal with grievances that develop in Canada.[40] This would seem to have improved relations between the parties in Canada. Certainly the ensuing two bargaining rounds appeared to reflect a situation in which the air had been cleared.[41]

1960 and 1962

Negotiations leading to the 1960 key bargain in Canada were refreshingly short and resulted in the signing of a two-year contract. This brevity was repeated in 1962.

The fact that the United States industry had settled in the latter part of 1959,[42] and that the agreements were to run to 1961, opened up the possibility of the Canadian District attempting to follow the U.S. pattern in 1960 and 1962 but with a lag of at least six months. If such was the union's strategy it certainly was not manifested at either of the Canadian conferences held in Edmonton and Montreal in November of 1959 and 1961, respectively, nor in their negotiations.

There was a resolution adopted at the 1959 conference which granted a Swift chain request to take the lead in negotiations. This was not requested in order to tie the Canadian contracts closer to those in the U.S. but to allow the Swift chain to deal with major issues at that company, rather than having the Swift Canadian officials marking time for the Canada Packers' key bargain.

> In the past, the Company has never considered amendments to the body of the contract, but stalled until the money package is arrived at with Canada Packers, then put the Union in the position of having to accept it. The Swift delegates want to put themselves in a stronger bargaining position by opening negotiations prior to the other two chains, which will get them through the preliminaries and conciliation, and in a position to take whatever action is necessary to force adequate discussion with Swifts on non-monetary contract points.[43]

---

40. *Canadian Packinghouse Worker* (Toronto), November 1959, p. 3. This was also confirmed in an interview with Mr. S. Hughes, Assistant Director and Chairman of the Swift committee.

41. For an interesting case where improved grievance machinery has dramatically altered labor-management relations see Robert B. McKersie, "Structural Factors and Negotiations in the International Harvester Company," *In The Structure of Collective Bargaining* (ed. Weber), pp. 279-303.

42. The key bargain in the U.S. was signed on August 31, 1959, with Armour.

43. Policy Committee Meeting (Edmonton), UPWA, November 10, 1959, p. 2 (in the files of the National Office, UPWA, Toronto).

The Swift chain's success in taking the lead would appear to have been minimal. Negotiations began in February and the pattern agreement of April 3 was again signed with Canada Packers, without conciliation services. The Swift Canadian settlement was not signed immediately but the negotiations were not extended as they had been in 1959.

The 1962 negotiations were a duplicate of those in 1960. The pattern-setting Big Four agreements had been signed seven months before those in Canada. Negotiations in the U.S. had started in the summer of 1961, with the key bargain for the UPWA being signed on September 10, once again with Armour. The policy of the Canadian District was not affected either by the policy pronouncements of the International or by the Big Four settlements.

As far as negotiations were concerned they commenced with preliminary meetings between the national officers and Canada Packers in early February. Official negotiations between the company and the union delegates began on March 21. The Swift Canadian and Burns delegates met with their respective companies a few days later. The key bargain with Canada Packers was reached on April 17. While the negotiations were routine they were marked by one development of note. The union's relations with Swift Canadian during negotiations continued to improve from the 1959 low point. The change in Swift Canadian did not go unheeded by the union. Reporting on the Swift negotiations the *Canadian Packinghouse Worker* stated:

> The interesting thing here is the obvious fact that Swift Canadian was willing and able to bargain collectively with a sincere objective of reaching an amicable settlement. The new element in the Swift Canadian Company's approach to the union is this determination to speak with a more positive voice for management of the Swift Company here in Canada.[44]

AN ASSESSMENT OF U.S. INFLUENCE AND UNION POLICY

Throughout the 1953 to 1962 period the policy adopted by the union in Canada did not display any great change in emphasis from one wage round to the next. In each round there was a demand for a nondescript "substantial wage increase"; to increase the bracket spread; to eliminate geographical differentials within Canada; to liberalize paid vacations and the number of paid holidays; and so on. There was little in the way of new provisions such as the automation fund adopted in 1959 in the United States; rather, the Canadian District seemed content to build on the existing provisions in their own contracts with little reference to U.S. settlements. Further-

---

44. *Canadian Packinghouse Worker* (Toronto), April 1962, p. 16.

more, UPWA wage policy was not influenced to any meaningful extent by wage comparisons with the U.S. industry. While the Canadian District was concerned about the U.S.-Canada wage differential there were no demands to reduce or eliminate it.[45] Consequently, there was little perceptible influence on negotiations from the United States. This continued to be the case in ensuing wage rounds.

Paradoxically, within this framework of essential independence, there were union chain demands on Swift Canadian which clearly arose from scrutinizing the U.S. master contract, plus the request of the Canadian District in 1959 to have Swift's plants covered by the U.S. master contract. This ambivalence arose from diverse union and corporate factors.

While it would be incorrect to assume that there is no desire for wage parity at the local union level, it is certain that there is very little pressure for it.[46] An examination of local union resolutions to Canadian policy conferences indicated almost exclusive concern with geographical differentials within Canada in the meat packing industry, those with other Canadian industries, and local and domestic issues. The local unions have an effective degree of autonomy, are well represented at Big Three negotiations, and the national offices are responsive to their desires. It is also clear that there is no pressure of any kind from UPWA officials in the U.S. A speculative reason is the absence of a Canadian competitive threat to U.S. industry wage standards. At any rate, there is no pressure throughout the union hierarchy for wage parity or international pattern-bargaining.

The UPWA's negotiations with Swift Canadian must be viewed against this background of Canadian oriented policy formulation. It is then evident that Canadian District attempts to upgrade the Swift Canadian agreement through use of the U.S. master contract must lie elsewhere. An historical perspective leaves little doubt that such actions were induced by U.S. influence on the corporate side.

The problems the Canadian District have in negotiating with Swift Canadian have already been indicated. The decision of the Canadian officers to request that Swift Canadian employees be included in the U.S. master agreement was clearly a final response to Swift's centralized policy which had entailed serious problems for the union as far back as the 1940's. A brief on the subject to President Helstein in 1959 stated:

---

45. This was confirmed through interviews with Canada Packers and Swift Canadian officials.

46. Interview with Mr. J. Lenglet, Assistant Canadian Director, UPWA, Toronto, October 25, 1964.

> One of the most frustrating things we go through here is having to deal with "office boys" whose hands are tied by decisions and policies arrived at and dictated in Chicago . . . . [If] there is something agreed to by the other packers in Canada that is against the Swift U.S. policy, then we get into serious trouble.[47]

Swift, throughout its entire history, has adopted the practice of centralizing policy at its head office in Chicago and in pre-union days gave its Canadian labor force some of the benefits instituted by the company in the U.S. As examples, in 1929 the company established a 40-hour guaranteed week and extended this to Canadian plants shortly thereafter; pension and sick leave plans were provided for before the existence of the union in both countries; the 40-hour week and 8-hour day were unilaterally granted in Canada shortly after their inception at Swift plants in the U.S.; and, in pre-union days, any changes in vacations at the parent firm were soon passed on to Swift Canadian employees.

The effect that this can have on Canadian bargaining was illustrated in 1962. In the previous round in the United States the union had won 4 weeks vacation after 20 years of service. Swift Canadian then unilaterally granted this to their foremen. This set a standard for the Canadian round and presented the union with a fulcrum in negotiations. While Canada Packers, in setting the pattern, did not want to concede on the issue, the established Swift Canadian policy was used successfully by the union in winning the benefit.

The unilateral transmission of U.S. provisions by the parent firm is now an extremely rare occurrence. It was, however, the formative cause of and instrument for any U.S. oriented policy by the UPWA. Similarities in Swift's U.S. and Canadian contracts, originally at company initiative, presents the formalized framework for a clause by clause comparison by the Canadian office of the union. The union's policy toward Swift Canadian, although largely unsuccessful,[48] does indicate the importance of centralized corporate policy as a transmission agent of American collective agreement provisions. Although the transmissions were minor, the repercussions could have been more significant, and it was clearly corporate policy that was the paramount cause of union actions which at a distance appeared to be a groundless effort to effect a closer tie-in with Swift bargaining in the U.S. If the long history of paternalism had not existed it seems certain, in retrospect, that union policy would have demonstrated an even greater degree of independence. The inter-

---

47. In the files of the National Office, UPWA, Toronto (Mimeographed).
48. Interview with Mr. S. Hughes, Assistant Canadian Director, UPWA, Toronto, November 1, 1964.

esting phenomenon was that U.S. oriented demands played little or no role at Canada Packers or Burns and were of little significance in Big Three negotiations. The reasons are dichotomous, although interrelated.

Firstly, the delegates for the Swift committee must bargain within the context of over-all union policy. In formulating demands, although the benchmark used by Swift Canadian delegates was occasionally the parent firm,[49] the orbit for delegates from Canada Packers and Burns only encompassed other Canadian industries when external comparisons were made. The Canada Packers' committee constitutes the largest portion of the National Policy Committee and they, along with the Burns' delegates, effectively control Big Three wage policy formulation. Therefore, only on occasion has Canadian policy towards the Big Three included a specific demand which had its origin in a U.S. meat packing agreement.[50] In most cases where U.S. oriented demands are introduced, the Canada Packers' committee asks the company for a provision in the Swift Canadian contract which, in turn, had its rudiments in the agreement of the parent firm.

Secondly, the important position of the Canada Packers' committee carries over to negotiations. The union's contract ratification procedures call for acceptance of the key settlement by the National Policy Committee before it is submitted to the membership for ratification. Therefore, not only are the Swift committee demands immersed in over-all union policy, but the Canada Packers' committee because of its size has a determining influence on tactical and strategic decisions during negotiations.[51] This, plus Canada Packers' pre-eminent position in the industry, has meant that Swift Canadian negotiations have a diminished function in total union strategy and

---

49. An example is the following — "Whereas Swift & Co. has had a medical, surgical and hospital plan in American plants for the past three years, therefore be it resolved that we demand a medical, surgical and hospital plan compared to the American plan." Proposed amendments to the Swift Contract, April 1956, p. 20 (in the files of the National Office, UPWA, Toronto).

50. There is also the possibility that American patterns could first be transmitted through another international union, for example the UAW, which in turn then spread to the Canadian meat packing industry. While the UPWA does express interest in the major pattern settlements in Canada, there was no evidence to support this proposition.

51. That the Canada Packers' Committee has the balance of power was revealed in the following union correspondence — "One of the dangers of 'breaking rank' . . . is the possibility of the Packers Plants [Canada Packers Committee] taking to block voting . . . . They now have the controlling votes and you know what difficulties this could cause us in the future." Correspondence of Mr. J. Lenglet, Assistant to Mr. N. Riches, Assistant Canadian Director, September 5, 1968 (in the files of the National Office, UPWA, Toronto).

ensures Canada Packers perennial position as the pattern-setter. Although the canonization of Canada Packers as the key company was reinforced prior to 1964 by the refusal of Swift Canadian to set the industry pattern, there can be little doubt that this was also by UPWA choice. Swift actually tried to set the pattern in 1964 but the National Policy Committee, after receiving a substantial offer from the company, shelved it and exerted pressure on Canada Packers to exceed the offer.[52]

The invariable determination of the industry monetary package at Canada Packers left little latitude in Swift Canadian negotiations and consequently diminished the likelihood of international pattern-following. Thus, while the U.S. parentage of Swift Canadian in conjunction with the firm's centralized and paternalistic policies has fostered and accommodated sporadic and limited union overtures to expand the area of impact of parent firm contractual provisions to North American dimensions, these were reduced to the meaningless.

There was one supporting institutional factor which made any tie-in with U.S. bargaining difficult. The conciliation process was an important element in shaping agreements, determining the length of negotiations and the timing of settlements.[53] The Canadian District has demonstrated little propensity or desire to circumvent the process; yet, conciliation boards have shown little inclination to accept U.S. patterns or wages as a standard for Canadian settlements.

It is impossible to ascertain definitively whether there was a cause and effect relationship between the independence of the Canadian District and the nature of the institutional variables. These aspects were probably important but there are grounds for believing that economic factors were equally significant. The lack of serious union attempts to effect a closer tie-in with U.S. bargaining may have primarily been due to the realization that such efforts would be unrealistic. Canada Packers has shown no inclination to follow a U.S. pattern. Competitive wage differentials between the large com-

---

52. Interview with Mr. H. Hill, Director of Industrial Relations, Canada Packers Ltd., Nov. 20, 1964. The 1964 negotiations were completely free from any type of U.S. influence. The U.S. Big Four agreements in 1961 expired August 31, 1964, the two-year agreements in Canada on March 31, 1964. While Canadian negotiations were longer than their counterpart in the U.S., agreement was reached at Canada Packers by July 22, over a month before the U.S. key bargain was signed.

53. The conciliation process also influenced the union decision to change the Big Three expiration dates from the summer to the spring. The summer expiration dates often resulted in conciliation conflicts with other major industries such as steel and autos. The change makes it almost inevitable that the Canadian pattern will be set first when there are meat packing negotiations in the same year in both countries.

panies and the small, specialized, and in some cases unorganized, local packers also restricts the collective bargaining stance of the union. A Canada Packers official stated: "While most of these competitors are not major in a national sense, the point is they are very major in the local or provincial sense."[54] Consequently, Canada Packers strongly oppose any increase in the differential between themselves and the smaller packers and this undoubtedly inhibits the union in Big Three negotiations. Therefore, rather than simply saying the UPWA has little desire for either international pattern bargaining or wage parity, it is probably more accurate to say they do not have the power or the desire, with the former being a partial determinant of the latter.

---

54. Correspondence to the author from Mr. R. Joyce, General Employee Relations Manager, Canada Packers Ltd., June 5, 1967.

CHAPTER 5

THE BASIC STEEL INDUSTRY

INDUSTRIAL BACKGROUND

Of the four large basic steel producers in Canada, Stelco, Algoma, and Dosco[1] are unionized. Dofasco, in spite of union efforts, remains non-union. The United Steelworkers of America (USWA) is the bargaining agent at the three organized companies. This chapter deals mainly with the above three fully integrated producers. The analysis, however, will include some reference to other firms for specific reasons in particular parts of the study.

The manufacture of steel in both Canada and the United States is centered in areas contiguous to the Great Lakes. While steel is produced in many areas of the U.S., the states of Pennsylvania, Ohio, New York, Illinois, and Indiana still account for the bulk of U.S. production. In Canada, the center is Hamilton, on Lake Ontario, where Stelco and Dofasco have their mills. The Algoma works, likewise, are located on the Great Lakes (Lake Superior) but at a considerable distance north and west of the industrial heart of Ontario. As well, they have a subsidiary — Canadian Furnace — on Lake Ontario. The fourth producer, Dosco, is the exception. It is located on the Atlantic Coast in Sydney, Nova Scotia.

The steel industry is an extremely important part of the Canadian economy but is small by U.S. and world standards. In 1960, Canada ranked twelfth in steel production and on an individual firm basis none of the four major companies in Canada were larger than the largest ten American producers.

There is little in the way of U.S. ownership of the Canadian industry. A study for the Royal Commission on Canada's Economic Prospects reported: "Among the major Canadian manufacturing industries, primary iron and steel is an outstanding example of Canadian ownership and control."[2] A study by the Dominion Bureau of Statistics estimated that 83 per cent of the Canadian industry was owned in Canada. The comparison on the basis of control was even more striking, the percentage of Canadian control being approximately 96 per cent. Only one notable firm — Union Drawn — is

---

1. Before the completion of this study Dosco was sold to the Nova Scotia government.
2. Royal Commission on Canada's Economic Prospects, *The Primary Iron and Steel Industry* (Ottawa: Queen's Printer, 1956), p. 37.

owned by U.S. interests (Republic Steel). It is a very small non-integrated rolling mill.

Canadian steel makers, in the main, find their market in Canada. Steel exports to the U.S. are normally only a fairly small percentage of their total business. While important to the individual companies they constitute no threat to the United States industry. The opposite is true of imports entering Canada. Because the Canadian industry has never been able to supply all the domestic needs of the Canadian economy, steel imports have been relatively large. Those from the United States constitute by far the largest portion — roughly four-fifths as against one-fifth from overseas. This has been the case despite tariff protection.

COLLECTIVE BARGAINING BACKGROUND, STRUCTURE, AND PROCESS

For administrative purposes and the implementation of policy the United Steelworkers is made up of 29 districts. The Canadian region comprises three of those districts — 2, 5 and 6.[3] Districts 2 and 5 embrace the Maritime provinces and Quebec, respectively, while District 6 takes in Ontario and all of western Canada. The latter is, therefore, by far the largest of the three in terms of both members and area covered. Because the Stelco and Algoma locals (1005 and 2251, respectively) are contained in this district it is also the most important in terms of collective bargaining in Canadian basic steel.

Historically, the union has been highly centralized in the United States with respect to its internal administration, bargaining objectives within basic steel, and its attitude towards strikes. Livernash has pointed out that centralization has been a dominant characteristic of union structure since the inception of the Steelworkers Organizing Committee which later became the USWA.

> To understand the early structure of the SWOC, the dichotomy between the top leadership and the membership should be explained. The SWOC was not an autonomous, member controlled union. Its affairs were shepherded by the United Mineworkers of America who furnished the greater part of its finances and staff and the imprint of the miners was discernible in its early leadership, attitudes and tactics. There was tight control from the top which took the form of a benevolent autocracy . . . . No formal, representative convention was held until 1942. (As a matter of fact it was in 1946 — 11 years after SWOC was first established and 10 years after its first contract

3. Originally there were only 2 districts in Canada with District 5 encompassing the Maritime provinces and Quebec, and district 6, Ontario and the Western provinces. The present organizational framework was provided for at the 1962 International Convention.

with U.S. Steel — that a steelworker was first elected as an international officer.)[4]

Livernash goes on to state that a review of the eight conventions chaired by Philip Murray between 1937 and 1952 reveals a struggle between the international officers and the delegates from the locals.

While some of the centralization is of a *de facto* nature it is also provided for the international constitution. Under the constitution the international, in the form of the International Executive Board (made up of the international president, secretary-treasurer, vice-president, district directors, and the national director of Canada), can exert a considerable amount of leverage on local unions. The constitution provides that the International Executive Board "shall enforce the constitution and carry out the instructions of the International Conventions, and between the International Conventions, shall have the power to direct the affairs of the international union."[5] Disciplinary powers lie in the hands of the president. Additionally, the constitution provides that no strike can be called without the approval of the president and the International union is to be the contracting party in all collective agreements. All contracts must be signed by the International officers.[6]

Canadian locals are subject to these same provisions and disciplinary powers and pay the same dues as the U.S. locals. At the same time it should be pointed out that Canadian officers are elected by Canadian members only. Canadian staff men report to and take orders from the Canadian executive. In addition, the international union established a constitutional third officer to be elected by Canadians known as the National Director for Canada with an office located in Toronto. The Canadian office includes specialists who dispatch data for collective bargaining purposes to the locals. While there is some exchange of information between the U.S. and Canadian departments, the latter is an independent unit. National headquarters coordinate collective bargaining in industries and corporations which spread across district lines within Canada.

With regard to collective bargaining in Canada, the basic steel companies have been very successful in limiting bargaining to single company dimensions. While there is pattern-bargaining in the industry the pattern is less rigidly followed in Canada than was the

4. E. Robert Livernash, *Collective Bargaining in the Basic Steel Industry: A Study of the Public Interest and the Role of Government* (Washington: U.S. Government Printing Office, 1961), p. 78.

5. Constitution of the International Union, United Steelworkers of America, p. 15.

6. *Ibid.*, pp. 75, 76. In all cases the relevant local union membership must ratify an agreement also.

case in the United States before the emergence of industry-wide bargaining. Even the expirative dates of the contracts for the major three producers have, on many occasions, been significantly different and there has been little in the way of inter-company cooperation. Stelco, the leader in the product market, has generally been the pattern setter in collective bargaining.

Also in contrast with the situation in the U.S., is the relatively less strategic role during negotiations, of the national director, who is comparable in Canada to the international president. The district directors in Canada play a significant part during negotiations and the relevant local union officers participate in more than a *pro forma* manner throughout bargaining. The practice generally followed has been for the director of District 6 to head up the important Stelco negotiations, the national director those at Algoma. The director of District 2 leads the negotiations at Dosco.

Other than a few minor similarities, there appear to be few parallels in Canadian wage policy formulation, bargaining structure, or the mode of bargaining in the basic steel industry vis-à-vis practices in the U.S. industry.

U.S.-Canada Wages

With the exception of 1951 and 1952 Canadian minimum plant rates have been well below those in the United States (see Table 5-1). It is interesting to note, however, that in 1952 the USWA in Canada attained an announced objective of eliminating the U.S.-Canada differential. This was achieved only at the job class 1 level. Parity, even at this level, was short-lived.

During the central analysis period negotiated wage and fringe increases in the U.S. industry outstripped those in Canada by a significant degree. Negotiated wage increases totalled 79 cents per hour or an increase of 55.1 per cent over 1952 base rates in the U.S., while the Canadian region at Stelco had won general wage increases of 63.5 cents per hour or 44.3 per cent over 1952 base rates. The major reason for the higher U.S. increases was the inclusion of a cost-of-living escalator clause in U.S. basic steel contracts negotiated in 1956.[7] By 1962 the allowance had amounted to 18.5 cents per hour. The differential between Stelco and U.S. Steel increased from 0 in 1952 to 28.5 cents or 12.5 per cent by 1962. While there was some relative progress by the Canadian region for the higher classifi-

---

7. The cost-of-living clause called for 1-cent adjustments in straight-time hourly earnings for alternating 0.4 and 0.5-point changes in the Consumer Price Index, and with downward adjustments occurring only when the index declined sufficiently to warrant a 2-cent decrease.

cations (the increment at Stelco was increased from 4 cents to 6.5 cents in contrast to U.S. Steel where it increased from 5.5 cents to 7 cents), Table 5-2 reveals that the international differential for the majority of the workers above job class 1 was positive and increased over the ten-year period. From 1953 to 1962 workers at Stelco up to job class 13 actually suffered a decline in their position relative to those in the same classifications at U.S. Steel. The reason was that the cost-of-living allowance in the U.S. contracts outweighed the

Table 5-1

MINIMUM PLANT RATES,[a] U.S. STEEL AND
THE STEEL COMPANY OF CANADA, 1935-62[b]

Year	U.S.	Canada	Differential	
			¢	%
1935	$ .47	$ .375	9.5	20.2
1936	.525	.375	15	28.6
1937	.625	.375	25	40.0
1938	.625	.415	21	33.6
1939	.625	.465	16	25.6
1940	.625	.465	16	25.6
1947	1.09	.775	31.5	28.9
1948	1.185	.94	24.5	20.7
1949	1.185	1.04	14.5	12.2
1950	1.31	1.17	14	10.7
1951	1.31	1.27	4	3.1
1952	1.435	1.435	0	0
1953	1.52	1.435	8.5	5.6
1954	1.57	1.485	8.5	5.4
1955	1.685	1.555	13	7.7
1956	1.82	1.655	16.5	9.1
1957	1.96	1.735	22.5	11.5
1958	2.12	1.785	33.5	15.8
1959	2.13	1.855	27.5	12.9
1960	2.20	1.955	24.5	11.1
1961	2.285	2.00	28.5	12.5
1962	2.285	2.00	28.5	12.5

a. Common Labor Rate up to 1947 in the United States and up to 1950 in Canada.

b. Including cost-of-living allowance adjustments.

SOURCES: The files of the National Office, USWA, Toronto; U.S., Bureau of Labor Statistics, *Wage Chronology — United States Steel Corporation, 1937-60* (Report No. 186).

STANDARD HOURLY WAGE RATE COMPARISONS,[a] SELECTED JOBS, U.S. AND CANADA,[b] 1953-62

Job Class	Typical Job Within the Respective Job Classes	1 9 5 3				1 9 6 2			
		U.S.	Canada	Differential ¢	%	U.S.	Canada	Differential ¢	%
1	Janitors	$1.435	$1.435	0	0	$2.285	$2.00	28.5	12.5
5	Machinist's Helpers	1.655	1.595	6	3.6	2.495	2.26	23.5	9.4
6	Pipefitter's Helpers	1.71	1.635	7.5	4.4	2.565	2.325	24	9.4
8	Craneman	1.82	1.715	10.5	5.7	2.705	2.455	25	9.2
11	Engineer (limited area)	1.985	1.835	15	7.6	2.915	2.65	26.5	9.1
13	Pipefitter	2.095	1.915	18	8.6	3.055	2.78	27.5	9.0
14	Millwright	2.15	1.955	19.5	9.1	3.125	2.845	28	9.0
15	Roll Turner	2.205	1.995	21	9.5	3.195	2.91	28.5	8.9
16	Machinist	2.26	2.035	22.5	10.0	3.265	2.975	29	8.9
18	Toolmaker	2.37	2.115	25.5	10.8	3.405	3.105	30	8.8
25	First Helper O.H.	2.755	2.395	36	13.1	3.895	3.56	33.5	8.6

a. Including cost-of-living allowance adjustments.
b. The rates used for Canada were those at the Steel Company of Canada; in the United States those that were in effect at the major steel mill operations.

SOURCES: The files of the National Office, USWA, Toronto; U.S., Bureau of Labor Statistics, *Wage Chronology — United States Steel Corporation, 1937-60* (Report No. 186).

increment gains in Canada up to job class 13. Those above job class 14, on the other hand, made relative gains on their American counterparts.

It is more difficult to evaluate the changes in fringe benefit levels than it is for wage levels because of the considerable variation in benefit provisions on both sides of the border. Fortunately, the costs of the individual packages (including both wage and fringe benefit changes) were widely publicized for each bargaining round in each country. They appear to be quite accurate and by deflating them by the amount of the negotiated general wage increases an indication of the total cost of the changes and additions to fringe benefits in each country can be obtained. Table 5-3 presents such a comparison. It substantiates a conclusion that the increase in U.S. wages and benefits was vastly higher than in Canada. After reducing the sum of the total packages negotiated in each bargaining round by the amount of the negotiated general wage increases, the value of the remaining benefits amounted to approximately 48 cents in the United States compared to only 28.5 cents in Canada. Ideally, the cost of providing increases in the increment between job classes should have also been deducted from the totals. A breakdown of the cost (in cents per hour) of such changes was not available. Any such adjustments, however, would result in greater decreases from the total figure in Canada than in the United States.

The USWA in Canada has made U.S.-Canada wage parity an issue. Perhaps the most interesting feature of the wage comparisons, however, is the fact that at the very time that the Canadian region made wage parity a major objective and stressed it to the greatest degree in negotiations (1953 to 1958), was the time that the differential in wage rates was again widening. Of importance also is the fact that standards were applied with considerable flexibility. A listing of minimum plant rates at steel firms under USWA jurisdiction in 1962 (Table 5-4) reveals this feature. Thus, wage parity has only been an issue in the central segment of the industry.

THE COLLECTIVE BARGAINING RECORD

Pre-1953 Experience

The formative years of the union saw establishment of the principle of autonomy for the Canadian region, though not complete independence from the Pittsburgh office. This was the clear intention of the international and the desire of Canadian unionists. This is not to say that the USWA in Canada did not often look to the United States and express a desire for U.S. wage standards. There were a number of occasions when such was the case. An examination

Table 5-3

VALUE OF WAGE-FRINGE BENEFIT PACKAGE EACH
BARGAINING ROUND AND IN TOTAL, U.S. AND
CANADIAN BASIC STEEL KEY SETTLEMENTS, 1953-62

United States		Year	Canada	
Total Package	Length of Contract		Length of Contract	Total Package
8.5ª	1 year	1953	1 year	0ª
9	2 years	1954	1 year	7
15.2ª		1955	1 year	13
45	3 years	1956	2 years	33
		1957		
		1958	3 years	27
39	3 years	1959		
		1960		
		1961	3 years	7ᶜ
10ᵇ	2 years	1962		
126.7	Totals			87.0
79.0	Less value of general negotiated wage increases			58.5
47.7	Value of remaining benefits			28.5

a. Reopened the agreement.

b. The value of the 1962 U.S. contract for its first year was estimated at 10 cents an hour.

c. The value of the 3 year agreement signed in Canada in 1961 was valued at 21 cents per hour. The value of 7 cents per hour was allocated to the first year which included a 4.5 cent wage increase.

Table 5-4

MINIMUM PLANT RATES, SELECTED CANADIAN STEEL
COMPANIES, 1962

Stelco	$2.00
Algoma	2.00
Dosco	1.955
Canadian Furnace	1.96
Canadian Drawn	1.955
Burlington Steel	1.955
Stanley Steel	1.80
Manitoba Rolling Mills	1.73
Interprovincial Steel	1.70
Premier Steel Mills	1.69

SOURCE: The files of the National office, USWA, Toronto.

of minutes and proceedings of meetings in the Canadian region and
correspondence in the files of the national office revealed that any
resolutions for wage parity with the U.S. were sporadic and minor,
however. There was interest on the part of Canadian officials in
keeping the international wage differential to a minimum but wage
parity was not set as a major objective. The differential was only
used as a type of yardstick and there was no formal arrangement
between the Canadian and the international office to close the gap
existing between Canadian and American steel wages. Further,
Canadian policy was the outcome of decisions made in Canada. The
following statement, taken from a report by the National Director to
the National Advisory Committee, summarizes the policy of the
USWA during this period in the clearest terms:

> Although wage-hour policy developed by our union in the United
> States is certain to be reflected, to some extent, in Canada, Canadian
> Steelworkers have been given autonomy and the responsibility of deve-
> loping and implementing the wage-hour policies appropriate to their
> needs.[8]

This was in face of the fact that the union in the U.S. was,
since its origin, a highly centralized organization. In Canada, however, a definite policy of non-intervention on the part of international
headquarters was established. Although there may not be a complete
explanation for this policy, certainly there were several contributing
factors. Firstly, the entry of Canada into the European conflict in
1939 laid the groundwork for such a relationship. A report by the

---

8. Report of C. H. Millard, National Director, to the National Advisory
Committee, Toronto, December 14, 1946 (in the files of the Canadian office).

Canadian region regarding the second convention of the SWOC held in 1940 in Chicago stated:

> Because of the emergency situation confronting us by war, any attempt made at this period by the International Office to determine organizational, and wage policy for Canada might be seriously misconstrued as interference in our national affairs. It will be therefore necessary for the International Office to apply its constitutional jurisdiction with sufficient flexibility so as to permit the Canadian Regional Director the responsibility of making and undertaking important decisions affecting the Canadian membership of our organization . . . .
>
> The matter of greater responsibility resting on the Canadian leadership, to cope with problems of particular concern in our Dominion was dwelt on. Those present appreciated the difficulties which had arisen owing to the fact that Canada was at war . . . .
>
> It was suggested that our officers might consider . . . the holding of a national convention of Canadian SWOC Lodges, for the purpose of determining a policy in accordance with the needs of the Canadian . . . steel workers and nation as a whole.[9]

Secondly, there can be no doubt that autonomy was one of the early goals of the Canadian region as the following statement from a report concerning a conference of the SWOC in Canada indicates:

> The Regional Secretary pointed out to the delegates that the practice of Local union officials sending their communications and their problems to the International Office and not to the Canadian Regional Office, only demonstrated to the International, that we were not prepared to exercise our autonomy in most matters, of strategy and policy, as affects us in Canada. It was generally agreed that hereafter complaints and problems would be raised with the Canadian office — and if this office could provide no satisfaction it would take up the matter with the International. Such a practice would tend to strengthen the autonomous character of our organization in Canada.[10]

Thirdly, while there were sporadic resolutions during this period to obtain U.S. wage standards they were submerged, particularly during the war years, by more basic union goals such as the forty-hour week, union security, corporationwide and industrywide bargaining, and greater organizational efforts.

The period of 1940-50 involved two distinct sub-periods in collective bargaining experience — the war years of 1940-46 and the postwar years of 1947-50. During the war years, due to wage and price controls in each country, normal collective bargaining was pre-empted and hence international pattern-bargaining even if desired could not be attained. The union, instead, turned their attention, among other things, to equalizing Dosco and Ontario rates.

---

9. Digest of Proceedings, Second Wage and Policy Convention, Steelworkers Organizing Committee, Chicago, May 21-24, 1940 (in the files of the Canadian office).

10. Commentary and Discussion at Amherst Steel Conference, Amherst, Nova Scotia, March 4-5, 1939 (in the files of the Canadian office).

From 1947 to 1950, the dates and amounts of the settlements in the Canadian and United States industries were significantly different. The meetings and conferences of the union in Canada revealed they were reacting to inflation and new wage patterns set within Canada. In the words of the Research Director in Canada: "During the early postwar years the pressures to increase wages were independent of those in the U.S. With full employment and inflation the emphasis was simply to get wages up."[11]

The variation in wage increases in the U.S. and Canada from 1947 to 1952 is illustrated in Table 5-5. For comparison purposes wage changes at U.S. Steel and Stelco were used. The differences in timing and wage changes between the countries is evident. In no instance were there any similarities. Up until 1950, it can be concluded that collective bargaining in Canada was carried out in a manner clearly independent of U.S. influence. There had been no plan of coordinated action with the International, no marking of time for U.S. settlements, and no concerted attempts to obtain parity with U.S. rates. The year 1951, however, saw a change in the policy of the Canadian region. Wage parity with the U.S. industry became one of its official goals.[12] This was highlighted with the passage of the following resolution at their annual policy conference:

> Since the Canadian cost-of-living now exceeds that in the United States, there is no valid argument for continuing lower wages in Canada. We will seek the same as the best rates existing in American industry in our new contracts.[13]

At the same conference it was decided that the union would press for the introduction of a job classification program similar to the Cooperative Wage Study Manual which had been worked out in the United States industry.

Two developments probably accounted for this change in emphasis on the part of the union in Canada. Firstly, wage parity with the U.S. basic steel industry had almost been achieved by 1951. The international wage differential had increased sharply by 1947. It had then decreased steadily until, in 1951, the common labor rate at Algoma was $1.29 compared with $1.31 at U.S. Steel. This had come about without any planning on the part of the Canadian region and during a period when bargaining in Canadian steel was

---

11. Interview with H. Waisglass, Research Director, USWA, Canadian Office, Toronto, November 2, 1964.

12. A point of interest is the fact that at the time the Canadian region set international wage parity as a major objective national wage parity had been lost. The Dosco rate had dropped 11 cents below the Algoma and Stelco rates.

13. Minutes of the National Policy Conference, Vancouver, B.C., September 15-16, 1951 (in the files of the Canadian office).

Table 5-5

GENERAL WAGE RATE CHANGES, BASIC STEEL
INDUSTRY, U.S. AND CANADA, 1947-52

Effective Date	U.S. Steel	Stelco	U.S. Steel	Stelco
	¢	¢	%	%
April 1/47	12.5		13.0	
April 1/48		16.5		21.3
July 16/48	9.5		8.7	
April 1/49		10.0		10.7
April 1/50		8.0		7.7
Dec. 1/50	12.5		10.5	
Sept. 1/50		5.0		4.5
April 1/51		10.0		8.5
March 1/52	12.5		9.5	
April 4/52		16.5		13.0
Total	47.0	66.0		

SOURCE: The files of the National Office, USWA, Toronto.

independent of that in the United States. Secondly, in the metal
containers industry the USWA in Canada with the cooperation and
aid of the international, had been successful in having the Canadian
locals at American and Continental Can (both U.S. owned) included
in the U.S. master agreement. Both of these instances acted as a
catalyst and no doubt encouraged the union in Canada to push for
wage parity in basic steel and other industries they had organized.[14]

With the establishment of a common labor rate of $1.435 in
1952 at Stelco and Algoma, wage parity, at the common labor rate
level, had been achieved for the two largest Canadian steel firms.[15]
In addition to the accomplishment being, to some degree, a matter of
circumstance, it was also somewhat illusory. CWS had been negotiated in the U.S. industry in 1947. Since that time there had been
four increases to the increment between job classes so that by 1952
the increment stood at 5.5 cents. In Canada, during the same time

14. Part of the 1951 resolution stated — "We propose where possible to
include Canadian workers in (U.S.) master agreements . . . ."

15. The Dosco common labor rate remained below those of the Ontario
firms.

there had been no significant additional increases to workers in the higher classifications. The result was wage parity at the unskilled labor rate but a widening of international differentials above this rate. Additionally, the 1949 U.S. reopener had resulted in the introduction of pension and insurance plans, while in Canada there had been a 10 cents per hour increase and no large changes in pensions. In short, it can be concluded that the decrease in the international differential at the lowest classification was won at the sacrifice of smaller fringe increases and a wider international differential for the higher classifications. Put another way, the U.S. and Canadian segments of the union had been distributing the packages won in their respective countries in a different manner, with the emphasis in Canada almost entirely on general wage increases.

Despite the fact that wage parity with the U.S. industry had become a definite goal of the Canadian region, this objective did not play a major role during the 1952 negotiations. This in spite of the fact that wage parity at the job class 1 level was achieved in this round. The two major objectives of the union were the achievement of the CWS program and the establishment of wage uniformity within Canada.[16] Wage parity with the U.S. industry was not specifically asked for during the negotiations.

The two most important factors governing the specific achievement of international wage parity in 1952 were the existence of a cost-of-living clause in the Canadian industry and the re-introduction of wage controls in the United States. During the 1952 negotiations in the United States, wage and price controls were in effect and the resulting two-year settlement, reached in July after a strike of approximately 60 days prior to which the President had seized the mills, called for a modest general increase of 12½ cents. The increase set a rate for job class 1 in the U.S. of $1.435. In 1951, a cost-of-living clause had been included in the Stelco agreement. This had resulted in a cost-of-living bonus of 9 cents per hour before the time that a Canadian settlement was even approached in 1952.[17] Canadian negotiations had paralleled those in the U.S. and after the U.S. settlement was reached a 16½ cent international differential remained. To obtain wage parity with the U.S. industry necessitated only a 7½ cent increase plus the incorporation of the 9 cent cost-of-living bonus into base rates. The pattern settlement at Stelco in August of 1952 provided for this. The U.S.-Canada wage differential, therefore, quite clearly defined the Canadian settlement.

---

16. *Steel Labor* (Canadian edition), April 1952, p. 7.
17. The union had negotiated the 9 cent increase at Algoma under a wage reopener.

At the National Policy Conference held in September, after the signing of the 1952 contracts, a resolution was adopted to continue the campaign to raise all rates to the level of the U.S. industry. By far the most significant achievement in 1952 for the Canadian industry was the establishment of the CWS program at the plants of the two Ontario producers. This came five years after it had been instituted in the U.S. industry.[18] The report of the Canadian USWA Industrial Engineering Department to the 1952 National Policy Conference contained the following message:

> Last year's Policy Conference adopted a policy of establishing wage parity through the Cooperative Wage Study program . . . . Agreements incorporating it have been reached with Stelco and Algoma and negotiations with Dosco are still going on . . . .
> Parity with the U.S. base rates has been achieved; in future we must strive to attain parity in all job classes.[19]

At the same time, the following resolution, adopted at the 1952 Conference was of interest and a portent for future bargaining:

> This Policy Conference reaffirms the traditional position of the Steelworkers in Canada, which has been recognized by International Convention resolution, that in all matters of contract policy, legislative and political action we shall continue to exercise our autonomy.[20]

Collective Bargaining 1953 to 1962

Table 5-6 indicates the timing of the key settlements in both countries from 1953-62. The timing of the agreements in the two countries in 1954, 1955, and 1956 is too close to ignore. It suggests that there may have been some forces towards a common orbit if only in time.

Table 5-7 compares the U.S. key bargain and the agreements at the Steel Company of Canada over the 1953-62 period in terms of yearly negotiated absolute and percentage wage changes (excluding cost-of-living adjustments). The wage changes at the other two organized integrated Canadian basic steel producers are not included in the table. At Algoma they would be substantially the same and at Dosco would show an even greater deviation. On a yearly basis, with the exception of 1954, 1959, and 1962 the Canadian increases varied significantly in absolute amount from the U.S. key bargain. In 1962 they were similar only in that no increases were provided for in

---

18. The CWS program took three years to work out after the 1952 agreement, but provision was made for full retroactivity. It was also introduced into the Dosco mill with a retroactive date of 1953.

19. Proceedings of the National Policy Conference, Toronto, September 19-20, 1952, p. 2 (in the files of the Canadian office).

20. *Ibid.*, p. 4.

Table 5-6

DATES OF USWA KEY SETTLEMENTS, BASIC STEEL, U.S. AND CANADA, 1953-62

Year	United States	Year	Canada
1952	Two-year agreements	1952	Two-year agreements
1953	June 12 (reopening)	1953	Reopening — no agreement
1954	June 30 (two-yr. contract)	1954	August 31 (one-yr. contract)
1955	July 1 (reopening)	1955	July 23 (one-yr. contract)
1956	July 27 (3-yr. contract)	1956	July 28 (two-yr. contract)
1957		1957	
1958		1958	Oct. 15 (3-yr. contract)
1959	Jan. 4 (1960) (3-yr. contract)	1959	
1960		1960	
1961		1961	Dec. 4 (3-yr. contract)
1962	March 28 (2-yr. contract)	1962	

SOURCE: The files of the National Office, USWA, Toronto.

Table 5-7

YEARLY GENERAL NEGOTIATED INCREASES, U.S. KEY BARGAIN AND THE STEEL COMPANY OF CANADA, 1953-62

	1953	1954	1955	1956	1957	1958	1959	1960	1961	1962
(cents per hour)										
U.S. Pattern	8.5	5	11.5	7.5	0	7	7	7	7	0
Canadian Pattern	0	5	7	10	8	5	7	10	4.5	0
(percent)										
U.S. Pattern	5.9	3.3	7.3	4.5	0	3.8	3.3	3.3	3.2	0
Canadian Pattern	0	3.5	4.7	6.4	4.8	2.9	3.9	5.4	2.3	0

SOURCE: The files of the National Office, USWA, Toronto.

either country. In percentage terms, in no year were the increases between the countries the same.

Table 5-8 demonstrates in an even clearer manner the general lack of similarity between the settlements in each country. Rather than comparing yearly changes, it compares total negotiated general wage increases each bargaining round in each country and reveals that, with the exception of 1954, the Canadian pattern was not similar to the pattern in the United States. When Canadian and U.S. contracts expired in different years during the period 1958 to 1962 there was, further, no international pattern-following on a delayed basis. In the case of 1954 where the absolute changes were the same, the Canadian settlement was a compromise solution to break a seven-months impasse and was largely the consequence of a conciliation board report and provincial mediation. The U.S. pattern of 5 cents may have had an "expectations" influence, however.

Table 5-9 compares fringe changes contained in the U.S. and Canadian key bargains. The table can be summarized simply — the Canadian pattern has displayed only slight similarity to U.S. fringe changes (bordering on the insignificant) and total gains were much larger in the U.S. There were a number of occasions when changes were made in the same benefit or benefits in both countries. However, in such cases the changes were not the same. For example, in the 1954 round in both countries changes were made in the insurance and pension plans. The changes had to be tailored to existing company plans and manifested no similarity to one another. Again, in the 1956 round, shift premiums were increased in both countries but in Canada the increase was 1 cent (making the premium 7 and 9 cents, depending on the shift); in the U.S. the afternoon shift premium was increased by 2 cents to 8 cents, the night shift premium by 3 cents to 12 cents. In the same round there were changes in the pension plan on both sides of the border but the changes were in no way related. Of the three rounds where direct pattern-following in fringe benefits was possible (1954, 1955, and 1956), there was only one instance where such could be inferred. In the 1956 round, premium pay for Sunday work was added in the pattern settlements in each country. The benefit provided in Canada, however, was much smaller than the benefits in the U.S. industry. The latter not only added the benefit but added two further increases to the provision within the life of the contract.[21]

Final testimony to the independence of bargaining in fringes was the provision for a medical centre included in the pattern-setting

---

21. One international pattern-following benefit at Dosco not present at Algoma and Stelco was the SUB plan obtained in the 1957 contract.

Table 5-8

TOTAL NEGOTIATED INCREASES, AND TOTAL NEGOTIATED INCREASES EACH BARGAINING ROUND, U.S. AND CANADIAN BASIC STEEL KEY SETTLEMENTS, 1953-62

United States			Year		Canada	
Total Package		Length of Contract		Length of Contract	Total Package	
¢	%				¢	%
8.5[b]	5.9[b]	1 year	1953	1 year	0[b]	0[b]
5	3.3	2 years	1954	1 year	5	3.5
11.5[b]	7.3[b]		1955	1 year	7	4.7
21.5	12.8	3 years	1956	2 years	18	11.6
			1957			
			1958	3 years	24	13.8
14	6.6	3 years	1959			
			1960			
			1961	3 years	9.5	4.9
0	0	2 years	1962			
			1963			
79.0	55.1	Total negotiated general increases (including cost-of living adjustments) — 1953-63			63.5	44.3

a. Excluding changes in the increment between job classes.
b. Reopened the agreement.
SOURCES: The files of the National Office, USWA, Toronto; U.S. Bureau of Labor Statistics, *Wage Chronology — U.S. Steel Corporation, 1937-64* (Report No. 106).

Table 5-9

MAJOR FRINGE BENEFIT CHANGES, U.S. AND CANADIAN
KEY BARGAIN, 1953-62

Provision	U.S. Key Bargain	Canadian Key Bargain
	1953: Nil	1953: Nil
Insurance Benefits Plan	1954-55: Total insurance cost increased from 5¢ to 9¢, one-half to be paid by company, and company to pay full costs of administration. Life insurance increased by $1000 to new range of $3000 to $5500. Sickness and accident benefit increased by $14 to $40 a week. Hospitalization entitlement increased by 50 days to 120 days.	1954: Provision for 2¢ to improve existing plan and incorporate it into the agreement. New agreement to be jointly administered. Cost to be borne jointly with company paying 53%. Life insurance of $2500, $1250 at retirement at no cost to employee. Sickness and accident benefits of $30 per week up to 26 wks. 70 day hospitalization plan — $9 a day plus $180 for extras and $3 a call for Doctor's calls in the hospital to a maximum of $210; $90 for maternity care; surgical expenses up to $300. No coverage for dependents.
Pension Plan	Primary pension benefits raised from $100 per mo. including social security to $140; maximum entitlement qualification increased to 30 yrs. Minimum pension for permanent disability raised from $50 to $75 per mo.	
Shift Premiums		1955: Increased from 5¢ and 7¢ to 6¢ and 8¢ for afternoon and night shift, respectively.
Holiday Pay		Double time and a half for work on statutory holidays.
Pension Plan		A greater voice for the union in administering the pension plan. Added survivor's benefits and other minor improvements.

Table 5-9 (continued)

Provision	U.S. Key Bargain	Canadian Key Bargain
Shift Premiums	1956-58: Increased to 8¢ on the afternoon shift and 12¢ on the evening shift effective July 1, 1958.	1956-57: Increased from 6¢ and 8¢ to 7¢ and 9¢ for afternoon and night shift respectively.
Premium Pay for Sunday	Added: Effective Sept. 1st, 1956 — a premium of 10% for Sunday work. Effective July 1st, 1957 a premium of 20% for Sunday work. Effective July 1st, 1958 a premium of 25% for Sunday work.	Added: Premium of 15¢ an hour for Sunday work.
Paid Holidays	One additional paid holiday (total of 7). Holiday pay increased: On July 1st, 1957 double time and one-tenth; on July 1st, 1958 double time and one-quarter.	8 paid holidays will be paid for regardless of the day they fall on.
Pension Plan	Minimum monthly pension increased to $2.50 a mo. for each yr. of service up to 30, plus social security benefits. Minimum monthly pension prior to age 65 for permanent disability increased. Early retirement benefits and deferred vested rights added.	Maximum pension increased to $110 at age 65 after 37 yrs. of service; minimum of $60 after 20 yrs. of service. This is a pension of $3 per mo. for each yr. of service up to 37 yrs. Previously $2.50 for each yr. of service up to 37 years. Provision for total and permanent disability pension and early retirement benefits.
Insurance Benefits Plan	Hospital and surgical benefits improved without additional employee contributions. Life insurance schedule increased by $500. Sickness and accident benefits changed from $40 a wk. to graduated schedule of $42 to $57 per wk.	
Jury Duty Pay	Employee to receive difference between 8 hrs. average straight-time earnings and payment for jury service.	

Table 5-9 (continued)

Provision	U.S. Key Bargain	Canadian Key Bargain
Paid Vacations	Effective Jan. 1st, 1958, one-half wk. of additional vacation pay for employees in the 3-5, 10-15, and over 25 yr. brackets.	
Severance Allowances	Employees eligible for allowance to have option within 30 days after shut-down either to be treated as on layoff (and hence eligible for SUB) or to accept the severance allowance.	
Supplemental Unemployment Benefits	52-wk. SUB plan applicable to employees with 2 yrs. seniority. An amount which when added to State unemployment benefits will be the smaller of 65% of employee's (after tax) wkly. straight-time wages for 40 hrs., or $25 a wk. for the maximum duration of State unemployment benefits and $47.50 thereafter, with $2 additional for each dependent, up to 4.	
Paid Vacations		1958-60: Added: 4 wks. after 25 yrs. service.
Insurance Benefits Plan		Increased: Life Insurance from $3000 to $3500; Sickness and accident benefits from $35 to $40 per wk. up to 26 wks.
Insurance Benefits Plan	1959-61: Insurance program to be non-contributory and benefits improved. Life insurance increased by $500; Sickness and accident benefits increased by $11 a wk.	

Table 5-9 (continued)

Provision	U.S. Key Bargain	Canadian Key Bargain
Pension Plan	Minimum monthly pension at age 65 increased to $2.60 a mo. for each yr. of service up to 35 yrs., plus social security benefits. Minimum monthly pension prior to age 65 for permanent disability increased to $100 less any social security disability benefits payable. Added: Special retirement benefit — a special lump-sum payment on retirement equal to 13 wks. vacation pay reduced by pay for vacation previously taken in calendar yr. in which retirement occurs. Liberalization of early retirement provision.	
Insurance Benefits Plan		1961-64: Added: Medical centre — company to contribute additional 4¢ to group insurance plan, effective Jan. 1st, 1963. Additional 4¢ will be used to improve existing plan or for financing union sponsored medical centre, with choice up to individual employee. Life insurance increased from $3500 to $5000. Sickness and accident benefits increased from $40 to $45 a wk. up to 26 wks.
Pension Plan		Normal retirement benefit increased from $3 to $3.15 for each mo. of service up to 40 yrs. of service; reduction of the normal retirement age from 68 to 65; $15 a mo. deduction at age 65 discontinued.

Table 5-9 (continued)

Provision	U.S. Key Bargain	Canadian Key Bargain
Paid Vacations	1962-64: Increased to: 1 wk. after 1 yr. of service; 2 wks. after 3 yrs.; 3 wks. after 10 yrs.; 4 wks. after 25 yrs.	
Supplemental Unemployment Benefits	Size of benefits increased to: 24 times straight-time hrly. earnings, plus $1.50 a wk. for each dependent up to 4. Total maximum wkly. benefits — $43.50 while State benefits are paid and $66 thereafter.	
Short Workweek Benefits	Added: Any employee on short time in any week to receive his standard hrly. wage rate for the difference between 32 hrs. and the no. of hrs. for which he is paid.	
Moving Allowance	Added: For long-service employees who accept job transfers under an inter-regional preferential hiring program.	
Savings and Vacation Plan	Added: Provides supplemental vacation and retirement benefits, in 2 ways. (1) employee will be entitled to 1 wk's. vacation pay for ea. 5 yrs. of service prior to Jan. 1st, 1961, payable only at retirement. Benefit reduced by 10% for ea. 3 mos. after the employee becomes entitled to such pension and does not retire. (2) plan provides that as funds become available employees will become eligible, in order of their length of continuous service for a vacation benefit consisting of 1 wk. of vacation for every 2 yrs. of credited service subsequent to Jan. 1st, 1961, subject to certain min. hrs. requirements.	

Table 5-9 (continued)

Provision	U.S. Key Bargain	Canadian Key Bargain
Savings and Vacation Plan	Employees may take extra vacation benefits through 1 of 3 options; (a) vacation time off during current or following yr.; (b) at a later time but no sooner than 24 mos. after date of entitlement; or (c) receive the benefit as a lump-sum payment at retirement or termination of employment or in the event of a special hardship such as extended unemployment or illness.	

SOURCES: The files of the National Office, USWA, Toronto; U.S., Bureau of Labor Statistics, *Wage Chronology — U.S. Steel Corporation, 1937-64* (Report No. 106).

Algoma contract of 1961. There was no precedent for this in the contracts of U.S. basic steel. Local 2251 (Algoma) prior to 1961 had studied the possibilities of such a program. After extended discussions within the local union and consultation with the Canadian office, the representatives of the local examined other group practice prepayment plans and held a two-day conference in 1959 with consultants from Canada and the United States. The local union did arrange to have the assistance of consultants from international headquarters but that was the extent of the part played by U.S. representatives.[22]

The 1962 U.S. settlements reflected a change in emphasis. With heavy layoffs and a decline in the labor force, the total package was made up of provisions to create employment and cushion the hardships of unemployment (increased supplementary unemployment benefits, the addition of short workweek benefits, moving allowances, and a savings and vacation plan). The change in emphasis was not reflected in Canada.

The overall assessment would certainly have to be that binational pattern bargaining is not well developed. At the same time,

---

22. Submission of the USWA to the Board of Conciliation (Algoma), Sault Ste. Marie, Ontario, November 14, 1961, p. 37 (in the files of the Canadian office).

the analysis of negotiations does indicate that U.S. wage and price movements are watched carefully by both sides. There have been bi-national influences that cannot be ignored and which indicate that the U.S. industry serves as an appropriate benchmark for both labor and management.

1953 Reopenings

The 1952 contracts between the Steelworkers and the major steel companies in the U.S. were reopenable on or before May 1, 1953, "with respect to general and uniform changes in wage rates" only. The clause included the right to strike or lockout if no agreement was reached by June 30, 1953. In Canada, too, the reopener at Stelco and Algoma was limited to wages only, but no strike or lockout provision was included.

At Stelco and Algoma negotiations began in late May and then stalled while the settlement in the U.S. industry was being worked out. Following an 8½ cent pattern in the U.S., it was obvious that this would become the minimum target of union negotiators at the two Canadian firms, given their goal of wage parity.[23] Negotiating committees for the basic steel locals held a joint meeting in Toronto in July and agreed that the 8½ cent U.S. pattern "was the minimum increase acceptable in negotiations now under way".[24] The statement issued at the meeting underlined an intention of "working towards parity with the standards prevailing in the United States industry where increases of 8½ cents had already gone into effect this year".[25] Both companies refused any increase, however, and without the right to strike the union was unable to obtain any concessions from either company.

1954

The U.S. negotiations, which began on May 18, were much shorter than those in Canada. Agreement at U.S. Steel was reached on the expiration date — June 30. The pattern called for a 5 cent increase.

It took seven months of negotiations and conciliation before settlement was reached at Stelco. The union applied for conciliation services in April. At this point the company had held that, because of economic conditions, there was "no justification for any further

23. *Toronto Globe and Mail,* June 13, 1953, p. 1.
24. *Steel Labor* (Canadian edition), August 1953, p. 1.
25. *Ibid.*

increases in wages or fringe benefits this year".[26] The company proposed that the union withdraw its demands and that the agreement be renewed for one year, "with only such changes as may be required for clarification purposes and which may result from the Cooperative Wage Study program".[27]

Both parties refused to change their positions despite the efforts of Ontario's chief conciliation officer during five meetings held jointly with the parties in late April and early May. In the latter month, at the time U.S. negotiations were just beginning, the Ontario Department of Labour was asked to set up a conciliation board. There were fourteen issues in dispute and all fourteen were referred to the board. (Algoma negotiations, which began about a month after those at Stelco, had also reached a stalemate and a conciliation officer had been called in during May.)

Settlement in the United States had already been reached by the time the board began sessions in the Stelco dispute. The hearings started on July 13 and ended July 22 without any concessions by either side, although direct efforts by the board chairman to settle the dispute had been made during the hearings.[28] An additional month elapsed before the board made recommendations for settlement to the parties.

Released on August 24, the report did not result in agreement and the union set a strike deadline of August 31.[29] The board chairman, notwithstanding the fact that he had "come to the conclusion that no substantial wage increase at this time should be allowed,"[30] recommended a 5 cent general wage increase to settle the dispute. Both the company and union nominees to the board dissented from the report but signed it in any case to make it effective.

The company and the union immediately reopened talks. On August 26, Stelco made an offer of a 2½ cent wage increase plus a new welfare plan which would involve an additional 2 cents per hour. The union turned the proposal down. With the possibility of a strike fast approaching, Ontario's chief conciliation officer rejoined the negotiations in the role of a mediator and a settlement of 5 cents was

26. Brief of the Steel Company of Canada to the Conciliation Board, 1954, Exhibit 7 — Letter to the President of Local 1005 from Mr. H. J. Clawson, Director of Industrial Relations, The Steel Company of Canada (in the files of the Canadian office, USWA).

27. *Ibid.*

28. *Steel Labor* (Canadian edition), August 1954, p. 1.

29. Union officials had been given the right to call a strike in July but under the Ontario labor laws could not strike until 7 days after receipt of the conciliation board report.

30. *Toronto Globe and Mail,* August 25, 1954, p. 1.

arrived at on August 31, after several days of concentrated negotiations.

Conciliation talks at Algoma had broken down on July 7 and union officials had immediately applied for a conciliation board. At the same time Dosco negotiations had been carrying on without conciliation, but had also bogged down. With the signing at Stelco on August 31, Algoma promptly accepted the pattern but it was not until December, and after conciliation board hearings, that Dosco agreed to the 5 cent pattern. Throughout the negotiations with Dosco the company had asked for special treatment and was given such by the union. The terms of the agreement were retroactive to October 3 rather than April 1, as had been the case at Stelco, and called for an increase of only $\frac{3}{4}$ of a cent, rather than 2 cents, for welfare which had been provided in the Canadian pattern agreement. Additionally, Dosco had signed a 2-year rather than a 1-year contract.

The reasons for the long delay in the negotiations are impossible to pin down but certainly it is unlikely that the delays were desired by the union. They had applied for conciliation in early April and for a board in May, but it was not until mid-July that the conciliation board began hearings. At no time was it indicated that the union was trying to link their settlements to the pattern in the U.S. The ultimate acceptance by both parties of a 5 cent settlement was simply a face-saving compromise, recommended by the conciliation board and resulting from mediation attempts on the part of the Province's conciliation officer to avert the possibility of a strike. Adverse economic conditions had hardened the industry's bargaining stance and the parties had come closer to an industry-wide strike than at any time since 1946. What does seem likely, or at least possible, is that the conciliation board was influenced by the U.S. settlement in its recommendations and this may have ultimately appeared reasonable to both parties for precisely that reason.

1955

The 1955 negotiations, as far as timing is concerned, were almost an exact repetition of those in 1954 in both countries. The 1954 agreements in Canada had been for one year while in the United States two year agreements had been signed with a reopener provision after June 30, 1955.

Negotiations at Stelco began on February 25, four months before those in the U.S. At that time the union did not specify a definite wage increase but indicated that they expected, as a minimum, a wage increase which would restore wage parity with the

United States at the common labor rate level.[31] Their additional demands were much the same as those put forth in 1954, which had not been supported by the conciliation board of that year — an increase in shift premiums; improvements in holiday pay; increased vacations; higher pensions; that the company pay the entire cost of the employee's hospitalization, surgical, and medical insurance; and elimination of the differentials between the company's basic steel operations and its fabricating plants.

Negotiations broke down in April and the union applied for a conciliation officer at Stelco. Talks with Algoma once again had started a month after those at Stelco and had also proceeded to conciliation.[32] Efforts by the chief conciliation officer in Ontario failed to resolve any of the issues at Stelco and all of the points in the dispute were referred to a conciliation board.

The time expiring between the request for conciliation and the appointment of a board followed the pattern of 1954, with board hearings for the Stelco dispute not beginning until mid-July, two weeks after the establishment of the U.S. pattern. The three-man board, at the suggestion of the union, tried but failed to bring about an agreement even before the hearings began through private consultation.[33] This attempt failing, the board began formal hearings.

With agreement in the United States on July 1, and an increase in the price of steel of $7.35 a ton announced by major steel makers, the union apparently felt that Stelco would be willing to make an offer to resolve the deadlock and take advantage of the price increase in the United States.[34] The National Director stated: "We have no illusion that the company will take advantage of the price increase put into effect in the U.S."[35] There was no attempt on the part of the union, however, to obtain the U.S. pattern. The unions demands in face of an 11½ cent increase in the United States remained unchanged, with the wage request continuing to be unspecified at the conciliation board hearings.[36]

Formal hearings ended on July 21 and the board chairman expressed the hope that settlement could be reached before the

---

31. *Steel Labor,* (Canadian edition), April 1955, p. 2.
32. Dosco, having a two-year contract, was not involved in the talks.
33. *Toronto Globe and Mail,* July 19, 1955, p. 32.
34. *Ibid.*
35. *Ibid.*
36. During the board hearings National Director Millard declared that the union would abandon its *long-term* goal of wage equality with the United States if the company would undertake not to increase steel prices. This the company refused to do, the Director of Industrial Relations at Stelco declaring — "We obviously cannot negotiate our prices with the union." (*Toronto Globe and Mail,* July 21, 1955, p. 7.)

board wrote its formal report. Negotiations continued immediately after the hearings and agreement was announced by the chairman of the conciliation board on July 23. The settlement was largely shaped by informal board proposals. The chairman stated: "I am very pleased to say that after a week of negotiations, the negotiating committee of local 1005, United Steelworkers of America and the Steel Company of Canada, have agreed to proposals of the Conciliation Board as a full settlement of all matters in dispute between them."[37]

The agreement having been fashioned by the board, it is not surprising that there was little similarity in the Canadian and U.S. pattern settlements. Even without the conciliation board, however, the agreements would likely have been quite different due to the fact that the union made no attempt to obtain the U.S. pattern. At the same time it is difficult to assess who was responsible for the inordinate length of negotiations — the union, the company, or the conciliation procedure. Of the two parties, certainly the company would have to assume a large part of the responsibility. In a period of favorable economic conditions the company had made no offer to the union to resolve the monetary issues. Significantly, their first offer was not made until the board hearings were completed, i.e., until the U.S. wage and price increases were clearly defined. Of interest was the fact that in applying for a conciliation board in May, the union "served notice on Ontario's Minister of Labour that the long, drawn-out conciliation board procedure just won't do in basic steel . . . ."[38] They pointed out that the Ontario Labour Relations Act calls for a lapse of fourteen days between the time a board is set up and its report is issued and asked that the dispute be expedited within those time limits. It is therefore conceivable that, if either party were to blame, it was the company rather than the union which marked time waiting for developments in the U.S. industry to be finalized.

The Stelco settlement for 7 cents was a one-year agreement retroactive to April 1. Algoma had followed the Stelco pattern in August, with the agreement retroactive to May 1. It expired two years after the retroactive date but had a reopener in 1956. The two-year agreement at Dosco signed in 1954 was due to expire on March 31, 1956.

1956

Canadian bargaining followed the pattern set during the previous two rounds. Negotiations were held throughout the spring at Stelco.

---

37. *Toronto Globe and Mail,* July 23, 1955, p. 1.
38. *Steel Labor* (Canadian edition), July 1955, p. 4.

The parties finally called in a conciliation officer. The company authorized the officer to offer the union an agreement to run for three years from the date of signing. It was to contain an increase of 5 cents an hour in each year and an immediate increase of 1 cent per hour in shift premiums. The union rejected the proposal which was substantially below an offer made by the U.S. industry in June — a 65 cent package over a five-year period. With no further progress a conciliation board was set up in June several weeks before a U.S. strike. At the same time negotiations without conciliation were continuing at Algoma under the terms of a reopener, and at Dosco.

Board hearings did not get under way until mid-July at a time when the U.S. industry had been on strike for two weeks. Just prior to the board hearings the local union membership at Stelco had authorized the union to take strike action, if necessary, and there was speculation that a Canadian strike would soon accompany the one in the United States.[39] All of the issues in dispute were again referred to the board with three of them — incentives, pensions, and the elimination of geographical differentials within the company's plants — being the major points upon which agreement was apparently held up.[40] None of the three were related to any which were at issue in the United States.[41]

One demand had been added by the Canadian region which clearly reflected the influence of their international affiliation. They had added premium pay for Sunday work which had been included in the U.S. list of demands formulated by the Wage Policy Committee on May 16. There was no indication that this was a major point of disagreement between the parties in Canada.

Interestingly, there may have been some bargaining influence from the United States manifested on the company's side. In both countries the emphasis of the industry was on a long-term contract. At the beginning of negotiations there was no indication that Stelco would seek a long-term contract but in the United States it became evident that this was to be a major condition for agreement as far as the industry was concerned. Stelco, in turn, made this a specific issue in Canada, during the conciliation hearings.

With the assistance of the Federal Mediation and Conciliation Service joint negotiations in the United States were resumed on July 12. A memorandum of agreement with U.S. Steel and the

---

39. *Toronto Globe and Mail,* July 4, 1956, p. 4.

40. *Steel Labor* (Canadian edition), July 1956, p. 1.

41. There was disagreement in the U.S. on incentives but the issue involved was quite different from that at stake in Canada, the dispute in the latter case being related to the Cooperative Wage Study program.

eleven other big producers on a three-year contract was signed on July 27. The conciliation board hearings at Stelco opened on July 18 with the company maintaining a very fixed position.[42] The board hearings lasted ten days and resulted in a settlement without a board report only one day after the U.S. steel strike was settled. The Canadian pattern was followed by Algoma within the next few days.

It is difficult to speculate regarding the impact of the U.S. settlement on Canadian negotiations. A strong argument can be made that there was little impact. In the first place it would have been difficult, if not impossible, to apply the U.S. pattern to the Canadian situation so quickly[43] and, secondly, while a memorandum of agreement had been signed on July 27, a return to work in the United States was delayed until early August to allow the parties to work out the details on certain items, such as the SUB plan. Thirdly, the most convincing evidence was that the terms of settlement in the U.S. and Canada were not the same and the U.S. agreements were to run for three years while the Stelco agreement was for only two years. Fourthly, a break in the Canadian negotiations came three days before the settlement in the U.S. with the possibility that settlement would follow shortly thereafter. The impasse was broken after there was a breakthrough concerning the CWS administrative agreement, along with concessions by the company on pensions that Stelco previously had maintained were not negotiable.

At the same time the correspondence in timing was too close to write off as coincidence. The company, or both parties, were probably waiting for the situation to be clarified in the U.S. The union had charged during the conciliation hearings that the company "is stalling for the outcome of the U.S. steel strike".[44]

Prior to the U.S. settlement, and conciliation hearings in Canada, the union and Dosco had signed a one-year contract. The agreement, reached on July 3 was not considered a pattern settlement and did not resolve the impasse at Stelco and Algoma. The agreement, which the union considered substandard, was signed, according to the National Director, in "consideration of Dosco's special financial picture".[45] The company had agreed to review the relationship between its wage rates and those at the other two firms

---

42. Submission and exhibits of the Steel Company of Canada to the Conciliation Board, 1956 (in the files of the Canadian office).

43. Just before settlement was reached in the United States it was reported that a U.S. settlement could actually have a delaying effect in Canada, the assumption being that either one of the parties or both of them might want to follow the U.S. pattern. (*Toronto Globe and Mail*, July 26, 1956, p. 9.)

44. *Toronto Globe and Mail*, July 17, 1956, p. 1.

45. *Toronto Globe and Mail*, July 19, 1956, p. 1.

after agreement had been reached in the rest of the Canadian industry.

1958

In 1958 there was a slackening of steel demand in both the United States and Canada. In the steel negotiations of that year, a twelve-week strike occurred at Stelco.[46] Algoma, which normally had waited for Stelco to set the Canadian pattern, settled first and the agreement became the basis of eventual settlement of the Stelco strike. Although there were no parallel U.S. negotiations, Canadian bargaining was more lengthy than in the past.

With the Stelco agreement terminating on April 1, 1958, the union notified the company, on February 1, of its desire to negotiate revisions in the collective agreement. Meetings were subsequently held at the end of February, throughout March, and through the first two weeks in April. By mid-April, after having gone through two months of negotiations, little or no progress had been made. On April 16, the union filed a request to the Ontario Minister of Labour that conciliation services be made available to assist in breaking the impasse. The request was granted on April 23 and the parties met with the conciliation officer three times during May. The conciliation officer was not able to bring about a settlement.

Conciliation board hearings began in Hamilton on July 2 but collapsed a week later without settlement. The conciliation board report, with the union nominee dissenting, recommended no increase in wages or fringe benefits.[47] The union negotiating committee immediately rejected the report, held a strike vote, and upon receiving authority to call a strike, did so.

Stelco virtually shut the door on a settlement on any terms other than a 5 cent offer.[48] In addition, the company made it clear that their offer was contingent on an agreement effective for one year from the date of signing, rather than being retroactive to the expi-

---

46. Honoring a verbal commitment made at the signing of the 1956 agreement, Dosco, in July 1957, agreed to put into effect a 2 cent increase to keep the Ontario-Nova Scotia differential at a specified level. The increase was made retroactive to August 1956. In August 1957 they signed a two-year agreement, not following the 1956 Stelco pattern, but including SUB. The company again guaranteed to pay whatever additional increase necessary to prevent the Stelco-Dosco wage gap going beyond 6 cents. The 1957 agreement had an expiration date of July 31, 1959.

47. The key paragraph in the conciliation board report stated it "would not be justified in recommending any general wage increase or changes in respect of the other monetary demands at this time" because of the inflationary impact.

48. *Toronto Globe and Mail,* August 14, 1958, p. 1.

ration date of April 1.[49]   One of the complaints of Stelco officials
was that the August 1 expiration date at Algoma gave them a four-
month advantage, not to mention the even greater concessions made
to the Dominion Steel and Coal Company.

Conciliation board hearings opened at Algoma on October 3.
An agreement was reached by October 15. The settlement formula
was based on the unanimous recommendations of the conciliation
board which, in contrast with the Stelco board, had recommended a 27 cent package including wage increases of 24 cents
over a three-year period with the first wage increase retroactive
to August 1.

New talks to end the Stelco strike began on October 20. It
was with reluctance and some delay (November 3) before the Steel
Company of Canada settled for basically the same terms, ending the
strike in its 86th day.[50] It took 11 days of negotiations and mediation
by Ontario's chief conciliation officer to settle the strike even after
the pattern had been set at Algoma. The Stelco negotiations in
their final stages had bogged down over an argument on the content
and cost of improvements to the Algoma welfare plan and over the
application of the wage increase.

At no time throughout the entire eight-months of negotiations
and the twelve week strike had an international pattern-following
demand been a barrier to settlement. Supplementary unemployment
benefits, won in the United States and in many Canadian industries
by the USWA and other unions, had been demanded by the Canadian region. While it was a serious demand in early negotiations it
was never a contentious issue, and had not, of itself, prevented a
settlement.

Stelco had obtained one concession. Under the terms of the
agreement the expiration date of the new contract was August 1,
1961, to bring it into line with the Algoma termination date. The
first wage increase was retroactive to August 1. The company paid
for this concession, however, by agreeing to pay $24 in back pay to
each employee in order to cover the four month period from April
1, 1958, when the contract expired.

1961 and 1962

A wide difference in expiration dates between the Canadian
and U.S. industries continued when an industry-wide agreement was

---

49. *Ibid.*, p. 2.

50. This made it the longest steel strike in Canadian history, the previous
mark being 81 days in 1946.

signed in the U.S. on January 4, 1960, after a 116-day strike. The new settlement was to be in force through December 31, 1962 on pensions, insurance, and supplementary unemployment benefits and through June 30, 1962 on other matters. The 1961 Canadian round was therefore isolated from any immediate collective bargaining developments in the U.S. Industry.[51]

The 1961 negotiations in Canada were much the same as those in the previous four rounds, taking five months and the two stages of the conciliation procedure to consummate a pattern agreement. Negotiations opened at Stelco on June 6 and at Algoma shortly thereafter. Settlement came at Algoma on December 4 and was followed by Stelco on January 8.[52] As in 1958 Algoma appeared to be considerably more flexible in their negotiations than Stelco. The agreements, however, once more were the outcome of joint sessions between the parties and conciliation boards set up in each dispute.

Rounding out collective bargaining over the 1953-62 period was a U.S. settlement, reached peacefully in March 1962. USWA demands in the United States were tailored to ease the employment consequences of technological change and lower steel demand, developments which have not been felt to nearly as great an extent in the Canadian industry.

AN ASSESSMENT OF U.S. INFLUENCE AND USWA POLICY IN STEEL

It has been maintained throughout the chronological narration of negotiations that the Canadian region of the USWA was not responsible for the long delays in negotiations in the 1954, 1955, and 1956 rounds which resulted in the Canadian pattern being arrived at shortly after the determination of the key settlement in U.S. basic steel. Or, if any responsibility rested in part with the union, their responsibility was minimal. From an analysis of the negotiations there were a number of reasons which, *in toto,* led to such a conclusion.

    1.   There was no indication of any intention to wait for U.S. negotiations to be completed before bargaining in earnest in Canada,

---

51. In October 1959, Dosco agreed to a 30½-cent package which provided for wage increases totalling 21 cents between August 1, 1959 and July 31, 1961. Rates at the Dosco plant remained 6 cents lower than those for the Ontario producers. To make sure that the gap would not be widened, union negotiators again obtained a written commitment guaranteeing further increases for the Sydney workers if rates at the other plants went up when the new contracts were negotiated.

52. With Dosco employment having declined drastically (a decrease in the payroll from 5500 employees to 2000 employees since 1961) the company did not sign an agreement until August 1963 with the wage increase not effective until August 1, 1964.

either in policy statements and remarks at the National Policy Conferences, or in union actions and statements during negotiations.

2. The union made no attempt to have the expiration dates of the Canadian basic steel contracts more closely conform to those in the U.S. industry and in the last two rounds had agreed to expiration dates vastly different from those in the United States.

3. The length of the 1958 and 1961 negotiations were drawn out in a similar manner despite the fact that there were no parallel negotiations in the U.S. industry in either instance. This was the case in later rounds as well.

4. It was the intransigence of Stelco, particularly in 1955 and 1956, when economic conditions in Canada and the industry were buoyant, which, as much as any other single factor, delayed settlement and forced conciliation. They made little effort to resolve the disputes, making few realistic counter-proposals until conciliation board hearings. One reason must have been their reluctance to set the Canadian pattern without first knowing the wage and price developments established in the U.S. which they may have used as a guideline. In 1958 and 1961 they were successful in passing the pattern-setting burden to Algoma who proved to be more flexible in negotiations. Thus, if there were any attempt to mark time waiting for the establishment of U.S. wage-price developments, some responsibility would seem to lie with the industry.

Throughout the period Canadian demands were very similar from one round to the next, were quite unlike those in the U.S., with the exception of the 1953 round, and were very little affected by U.S. industrial relations developments. There were some areas of influence but they were minor. Given the impossibility of isolating Canadian basic steel bargaining from all innovations in United States' labor relations practices (e.g. SUB) the degree of independence demonstrated was impressive. There were surprisingly few references to U.S. fringe benefits at the National Policy Conferences and, as a generality, it can be said that the Canadian region followed the broad changes and developments in the U.S. industry in their policy resolutions, but that was all.

The institution of the Cooperative Wage Study program in Canada, five years after it was developed in the U.S. industry and with lower increments, typifies one type of U.S. influence felt in Canadian basic steel. While it became the policy of the Canadian region to obtain CWS in the late 40's, they never really pushed for it until 1952.

A similar policy has been followed in the case of supplementary unemployment benefits. Although SUB spread into some other Canadian industries quickly after its inception in the United States, in basic steel it had only been obtained by 1962 at Dosco where unemployment has been particularly severe. Otherwise the Canadian region, while they included it in their list of demands, had not given it high priority in steel negotiations. The 1960 National Policy Conference resolved "that SUB be made one of our major objectives in the next basic steel negotiations".[53] In the 1961 negotiations, however, SUB was not a high priority demand.

There have been other minor manifestations of influence derived from U.S. developments and there will no doubt be others in the future. One of the most interesting resolutions was the following, adopted just after the 1959 U.S. steel strike which included the famous clause 2B issue:

> Whereas the Steelworkers in the United States were on strike for 116 days to maintain the "2B" clause in their collective agreements . . . . Whereas many of our collective agreements in Canada do not contain such a clause; Be it resolved that the Steelworkers in Canada negotiate in their collective agreements a clause similar to the "2B" clause in the U.S. Steelworkers contracts.[54]

To date, however, this has not been an issue in Canadian bargaining.

In summary, the union's basic Canadian steel policy, other than the demand for wage parity, has been formulated independently and, taken as a whole, has reflected developments south of the border only in minor ways. The policy of the Canadian region on parity, however, requires some explanation.

Parity of wages with the United States had become the goal of the Canadian region in the early 1950's It continued to be so throughout the period analyzed, despite the fact that the parity obtained in 1952 was quickly lost in basic steel. It is clear, however, that the USWA in Canada was using the wage parity argument simply as a yardstick in arguing for higher wages. U.S. wages were used, along with other data and comparisons, in their repetitive demand for a "substantial" wage increase in each bargaining round. In asking for a wage increase the union's line of reasoning in their conciliation briefs was very similar from one round to the next, each time adding further data and modifications. They consistently maintained the following logic:

> Since Stelco is by far the largest steel producer in Canada, the other three producers follow Stelco's wage and price trends. On prices, Stelco follows the steel industry in the U.S. On wages, Stelco lags far behind, and the gap between Stelco and U.S. wages in primary steel has been widening over the past few years . . . . It should be emphasized that steel wages in Canada are lagging behind the industry in the U.S. while Canadian steel prices have been keeping up with, or ahead of U.S. steel prices. Canadian steel prices have been closely related to U.S. steel prices in spite of the fact that physical production of Canadian steel

---

53. National Policy Conference, United Steelworkers of America, April 22, 1960, Montreal, p. 10 (in the files of the Canadian office).

54. *Ibid.*

labor has been increasing much faster than in the U.S., and in spite of the fact that manhour output at Stelco is now as high or higher than all but a few of the plants in the U.S.[55]

It is clear that wage rates in the U.S. steel industry were simply being used as a benchmark by the Canadian region. Had the benchmark not been U.S. steel rates some other yardstick would have been used, perhaps a Canadian industry paying higher wages than in basic steel. That the benchmark used was American steel rates is not surprising considering that rates of pay in basic steel are already close to the highest of any paid in Canada. One of the union's briefs reported:

> We are not seeking parity in Canadian and American wage rates merely for its own sake. The United States steel industry provides the most useful and practical "bench-mark" (to borrow a term from job evaluation) on which the most valid comparisons can be made for the purpose of establishing wage rates. No other industry, in Canada, the United States, or elsewhere, can provide a more useful, valid, or practical "bench-mark" for this purpose.[56]

Their other briefs throughout the period contained similar comments.

Further, with the exception of 1953, the union made it clear that their immediate objective was to reduce the disparity, complete wage parity being only a long-term goal. This was made clear in their brief to the 1954 Stelco conciliation board.

> It should be pointed out, however, that the Union is not asking for parity at the present time. If all of the Union's wage requests were granted in full Stelco wages would still be 5 cents per hour below the U.S. rates. [p. 14.]

At no time were concerted actions taken even to close the existing gap.[57] Additionally, as the disparity between U.S. and Canadian wages increased from its low point in 1952, the intensity of the wage parity argument diminished proportionately. This confirms to some degree an earlier contention that one reason for the adoption

55. Submission of the United Steelworkers of America to the Board of Conciliation (Stelco), Hamilton, Ont., July 2, 1958, p. 10 (in the files of the Canadian office).

56. Submission of United Steelworkers of America to Board of Conciliation (Dosco), Sydney, N.S., October 28, 1954, p. 3 (in the files of the Canadian office).

57. An anonymous interview at the Steel Company of Canada largely confirms this conclusion. The official interviewed stated — "It (wage parity) has not been a serious demand at Stelco and hasn't been a key factor in negotiations . . . . At the same time, demands such as that for wage parity have not been dropped early in negotiations . . . . They have been pursued by the union but not with extreme vigor and never to the point of a strike." He maintained, however, that the union marked time waiting for the U.S. industry to settle before bargaining seriously. (Interview at the Steel Company of Canada, November 4, 1964.)

of the wage parity objective in the early 1950's was due to the small differential in Canadian and U.S. rates which had developed by 1951.

The attention given to the wage parity objective by the Canadian region hit a peak in the 1952-54 period. During this time it found a prominent place in addresses by Canadian officials at the annual policy conferences. By 1958, wage parity was so far out of reach that it was receiving less emphasis. The goal continued to be "to reduce the wage disparity," and the union continued to use the argument in conciliation briefs. Wage policy resolutions, however, contained less and less reference to the goal until, by 1961, no mention was made of wage parity in the policy resolutions. The argument was re-introduced in the 1966 negotiations. Again, a similar thing had occurred. U.S. contracts did not expire until 1968 and the major emphasis in several previous U.S. rounds had been on fringes. As a consequence, the job class 1 rate at Stelco and Algoma was within 18.5 cents of the U.S. rate. Projected to 1966 it would have been 24.5 cents. The Steelworkers asked for precisely that amount. The settlements at both companies resulted in parity of rates (not earnings) by 1968, but only under the assumption that U.S. negotiations would result in no wage increases. Also, while there was a strike at Stelco, it had nothing to do with parity. Stelco had agreed to the wage increases early in negotiations.

The periodic use of U.S. steel wages as a standard constituted the only significant aspect of coercive comparison. The orbit at the local level was restricted, for the most part, to Canada. Also, at no time did American union officials take part in Canadian basic steel negotiations. Their only visits to Canada were as invited guests, generally as speakers to the National Policy Conferences. McDonald visited Canada in this capacity only once (1960), while Secretary-Treasurer Abel fulfilled such a commitment several times (1955, 1957, 1961) over the ten-year period. In all instances the remarks of these officials were of a very general nature, with little specific reference to Canadian steel bargaining. The election of McDonald in 1952 as President and Mahoney as National Director in 1956 did not change the relationship of the Canadian region to the international.

An examination of the proceedings of the International Conventions over the ten-year period revealed little in the way of reference to the Canadian region. There is generally one resolution regarding the Canadian region, which invariably extends felicitations to the membership in Canada and congratulates the Canadian leadership for a job well done.

The general independence of the Canadian region is to some extent a reflection of the lack of coercive comparisons by the Canadian rank-and-file. The complete explanation, however, is contained in a complex set of factors. Again, it is probably attributable to a number of institutional and economic forces. Part of the relationship is traceable to the early history of bargaining initiated during the war years. Secondly, the initial desire for autonomy by the Canadian region and locals has been perpetuated.[58] Significantly, the largest local (1005) and the oldest local (1064) have been strongly independent. For example, local 1064 submitted the following resolution at the 1957 National Policy Conference:

> Be it resolved that our national officers take steps to impress upon our International leadership the fact that Canadian Steelworkers are sufficiently mature to take direction of their own affairs without prejudice to the existing brotherly relation between Canadian and American Steelworkers.

Centralization of power, therefore, which exists in the U.S. section of the union, has not made itself felt in Canadian bargaining.

With none of the major firms being U.S. owned there are different wage payment systems (incentives being far more important in the U.S.) and a set of fringes different in substance and design. This makes any linkage difficult and there is no U.S. transmission agent on the corporate side. One Canadian official stated: "In the auto industry the lines for transferal are direct. In steel this is not so; any influence in steel has to be more indirect."[59] The importance of this is illustrated in the bargaining relationship established by the USWA at one small (40 employees) non-integrated mill which is U.S. owned. Union Drawn, located in Hamilton, as noted earlier is owned by Republic Steel. The Canadian region, with the assistance of the International, at Republic negotiations in 1954 successfully negotiated to have the subsidiary's employees directly tied in with the U.S. contract. There is a pass-on of U.S. wage and fringe benefit standards and the contract has been signed at the same time as

---

58. For example, an interesting episode occurred at the International Convention which displayed the Canadian region's strong feelings on the question. The International Executive Board had submitted a resolution for convention adoption, that would have made the Canadian Director an appointee of the international rather than by election of the Canadian membership. This resolution was passionately debated, Canadian delegates voicing strong opposition. To the embarrassment of McDonald, who had backed the motion, it was defeated by the Convention. (See *Proceedings of the Eighth Constitutional Convention of the United Steelworkers of America,* Los Angeles, September 1956, pp. 336-343.)

59. Interview with H. Waisglass, Research Director, USWA, Canadian Office, Toronto, November 2, 1964.

those in U.S. basic steel.[60] The key factor is the direct corporate channel which the Canadian region uses. The union, however, confirmed that there was little resistance by Republic to the arrangement. Indeed, it is possible that the company was not at all concerned. A Canadian union official related the following:

> In 1956 or 1959, I'm not sure which, we had pretty well cleared up everything at Republic. Mahoney said to McDonald, "We've got to get more in Canada." McDonald replied, "Well you keep your people out on strike and we'll see what we can do." The result was that an extra nickel was given at Union Drawn. When everything was resolved Republic asked that the men start going back to work immediately "and that includes Canada". McDonald agreed. Neither of the top [U.S.] negotiators knew that Canadians weren't on strike. The local hadn't even gone through the necessary legal arrangements.[61]

In any case, the lack of corporate ties mitigates wage or pattern standardization. This was reinforced further by industry resistance to the application of U.S. wage standards. This would seem to be traceable, at least in part, to U.S. penetration of the Canadian market. The testimony of the President of Stelco before a Royal Commission indicates their concern.

> The payment of wages at or about the U.S. scale by a few Canadian industries which find their principal market in the U.S. exerts great pressure upon those Canadian industries mainly dependent upon sales in the relatively small and far-scattered domestic market.
> In other words, Canadian sales of vitally needed raw or semi-processed materials to a largely assured and protective foreign market tend to have the effect of raising the production costs of those companies which sell mainly in the open and hence more competitive Canadian market.[62]

This, along with the existence of a "low-wage" marginal firm (Dosco) and a non-union firm (Dofasco), undoubtedly restricts the union. The special treatment that was given to Dosco made it more difficult to apply U.S. standards to the other two major firms. Dofasco generally follows the Stelco pattern but a union official stated: "We always have to consider the Dofasco situation."[63]

---

60. Both the USWA Canadian Research Director and an interview at Stelco confirmed that the direct pass-on to Union Drawn has had little influence on bargaining at Stelco. There was a shift from wage disparity with Stelco in 1951 ($1.27 at Stelco compared with $1.17 at Union Drawn) to a minimum plant rate advantage of 24 cents in 1962 (including an 18.5 cent cost-of-living bonus).

61. Interview with Eamon Park, Assistant to the National Director, USWA, Canadian Office, Toronto, May 27, 1966.

62. Brief presented to the Royal Commission on Canada's Economic Prospects by the Steel Co. of Canada, Ltd., Hamilton, Ont., January 1956, p. 38.

63. Interview with H. Waisglass, Research Director, USWA, Canadian Office, Toronto, November 2, 1964.

At the same time it seems clear that the industry considers U.S. wage and price movements as a possible barometer for Canadian adjustments. In reference to this, an interesting revelation was made by the union in the 1958 Stelco conciliation hearings. The company had asked that the effective date of the settlement be August 1, 1958 rather than the expiration date of the contract — April 1. The USWA indicated that when they had agreed to move the date forward at Algoma the company offered a *quid pro quo* in the form of additional increases for the advance. The brief then added:

> In addition, it was done at the request of the Company, who advanced as one of their reasons that they could not adequately judge the situation until they knew the U.S. settlements . . . and until they knew the U.S. price adjustments.[64]

The defining of Canadian increases by U.S. wage levels in 1952 and 1966, and the common orbit in time in 1954, 1955, and 1956 would then seem to be a manifestation of this. Although quite temporal and minor, they do suggest a definite bi-national influence generated, however, as much by company as union observations.[65]

The nature and scope of the product market, therefore, seem to have a dual effect, accounting for the ambivalent demeanor of the companies. On the one hand, imports partially account for employer resistance but, at the same time, the overlapping product market, accompanied at times by price leadership from the U.S. for some products, is the most logical explanation of corporate behavior. While evidence is lacking, prices in the U.S. and Canada are exactly the same, or nearly so, on some steel products and Canadian firms do absorb freight to meet U.S. competition at most Canadian consuming points.[66] It is a natural extension for the two major companies to at least consider U.S. wage developments as a barometer.

---

64. Reply of the union to the Submission of the Steel Company of Canada, Hamilton, Ontario, July 8, 1958, p. 4 (in the files of the Canadian office).

65. Why the correspondence in timing became so precise between 1954 and 1956 and why it broke down thereafter is not clear but it did so when there was a shift to long term contracts in both countries. Stelco, it will be recalled, proposed a contract length similar to that in the U.S.

66. Royal Commission of Canada's Economic Prospects, *The Primary Iron and Steel Industry*, pp. 23, 24.

CHAPTER 6

THE IRON ORE INDUSTRY

INDUSTRIAL BACKGROUND

An understanding of collective bargaining in the Canadian iron ore industry necessitates, first, a rather thorough examination of the development of the industry — its relatively late but explosive growth, the multifarious and complex corporate relationships which exist in the industry, and its confluence to the U.S. and Canadian basic steel industries.

Not only does Canada possess immense reserves of direct-shipping ore but it also has vast reserves of low to medium grade ore that can be processed to upgrade the iron content. Despite the existence of such reserves and knowledge of them, it has only been within the last fifteen years that Canada's iron ore output has expanded to significant proportions. For example, Canada's total output up until 1924, when production ceased temporarily, amounted to no more than six million tons. This delay in the development of Canadian iron ore reserves is directly traceable to the discovery of deposits of high grade direct-shipping ore on the Mesabi Range in the U.S. These deposits south and west of Lake Superior were easier to mine and, as a consequence, interest in Canada's iron ore potential waned. After these important areas were opened up in the 1890's, few steel companies, either in Canada or the United States, were even remotely interested in searching for alternative sources of supply. Here, only a few miles from cheap water transportation, lay what seemed at that time to be almost inexhaustible tonnages of direct-shipping ore. Very little effort was needed to move it by water into the industrial heartland of the continent. As a result, the steel mills around Chicago, Pittsburgh, Cleveland, and Hamilton and Sault Ste. Marie in Canada, turned to the Lake Superior iron ranges as their source of supply.[1] The iron ore market therefore has always been a continental one. Early international shipments, however, travelled from the United States to Canada.

Some sixty years later the U.S. situation began to change. This change, one which compelled a larger resort to foreign sources of supply, was in response to requirements of the U.S. steel industry. Following World War II only a handful of companies were protected by extensive iron ore holdings on the Mesabi range. Most had less

---

1. John Davis, *Mining and Mineral Processing in Canada* (Ottawa: Queen's Printer, 1957), pp. 52-53.

than ten years of direct-shipping ore in sight. It was this latter group that first began to look elsewhere. Because of similar geographical conditions, and the possibility of transporting Canadian ore to mills over internal lines of supply, interest in Canadian ore began to revive.[2] Although these companies also turned to other countries as possible sources, notably Venezuela, they concentrated on Canadian exploration because of the advantages of geographical location and a stable political climate. The result of these developments has been a rapid rise in Canada's iron ore productive capacity.

The pattern of iron ore supply to North America, therefore, has undergone a major transformation since the mid-1950's. From being a small exporter in 1950 Canada has become one of the leading iron ore exporting nations. In absolute figures, from 1950 to 1962 Canadian iron ore shipments increased from 3.2 million tons to a high of 24.9 million tons. Most of its output is for foreign consumption. The largest increase in productive capacity has been, and will continue to be, in the remote Quebec-Labrador area. A major development in iron ore shipments has been the sizeable increase in U.S. imports and the predominant place of Canada as a supplier. The United States, which now imports about one-third of its total consumption, increased its imports fourfold, and Canada now supplies 50 per cent. The following illustrates the growth in this relationship: in 1955 Canada supplied 43 per cent of total U.S. imports as compared with only 16 per cent in 1953. Latin America and particularly Venezuela account for most of the remainder with small amounts from Africa. United States mine production decreased from 98 to 72 million tons during the period, with exports increasing from 2.5 million to 5.9 million tons. Interestingly, most of the exports went to Canada, although the latter became a net exporter in 1953.[3]

With regard to Canada's exports, the principle consuming areas in addition to the United States are Britain, Western Europe, and Japan. But, because of the "captive" mines[4] situation which prevails in Canada, all but a minimal portion of Canada's exports go to the United States. In 1953, in terms of the percentage of total output, the United States took approximately 43 per cent of total Canadian exports, and almost 80 per cent by 1962. The volume of the exports to the United States rose from 1.8 million tons in 1953 to 13.7 million tons in 1956, and 16.9 million tons in 1962.

---

2. *Ibid.*
3. R. B. Elver, *The Canadian Iron Ore Industry in 1962,* Mineral Information Bulletin MR 67, Mineral Resources Division, Department of Mines and Technical Surveys (Ottawa: Queen's Printer, 1963).
4. A mine which is a subsidiary of a basic steel company with the latter taking all or most of its output is referred to, in the union vernacular, as a captive mine.

It became increasingly apparent, even before World War II, that growing steel demands would soon require additional sources of ore due to the steady depletion of domestic reserves.[5] The Lake Superior position weakened in the 1950's and imports from Canada and Venezuela grew rapidly. The same companies operating in Canada and Venezuela continued to operate in the district, but during this period complaints were heard from the area regarding low wage competition from Canada and Latin America.[6] In the 1960's, however, these charges began to disappear when the district assumed new competitive strength by establishing large scale plants to produce pellets from low-grade deposits. This development was responsible for major transformation of the Lake Superior district. The Mesabi continued to be the major U.S. source of both crude and usable ore. More than 70 per cent of the crude and usable ore produced in the U.S. was mined in the Lake Superior area in 1959. The U.S. settlements applied to this area, therefore, are the ones most likely to affect Canadian iron ore collective bargaining.

In contrast to the United States with its major iron deposits in the Great Lakes area, there are both large and small iron mines scattered across the Canadian Shield from the southeastern tip of Manitoba all the way to the Atlantic Coast of Labrador. Formations like those which have been so prolific in Minnesota occur again just north of that state in Northwestern Ontario, 150 miles west of Port Arthur. This is known as the Steep Rock Lake area. A second large body of deposits is found in the northern Quebec-Labrador region. This belt commences in central Quebec and continues northward along the Quebec-Newfoundland border to Ungava Bay. A third deposit is found at Wabana off the coast of Bell Island in Newfoundland. Additional ore of commercial value is found in scattered sections of Ontario. For example, ore is being mined in areas north

---

5. Bethlehem Steel Company, *Memorandum submitted to the United States Tariff Commission in Connection with Investigation of Iron Ore Imports Under Section Seven of the Trade Agreements Extension Act of 1951* (January 1960), p. 7.

6. Because of the expansion of the Canadian and Venezuelan industries fears were expressed in the United States that the domestic industry was being adversely affected. In response to this the U.S. Tariff Commission, under a resolution presented by the Senator of Minnesota, held preliminary public hearings in January 1959 on the effects of such competition. In October 1960 the Commission held additional public hearings to determine whether, owing to the customs treatment accorded under the *General Agreement on Tariffs and Trade,* iron ore imports had seriously injured the domestic industry. No restrictive measures were recommended, however, since that time, various Senate committees have been requested to initiate one or more forms of protection against imports. The Steelworkers, representing the iron miners, was under pressure at that time to find solutions to alleviate the employment situation on the Mesabi Range.

of Sault Ste. Marie and Sudbury, and in Southeastern Ontario. These *in toto* are the most significant areas as far as current iron ore production is concerned.

The first Canadian iron range to divert popular attention away from the main American iron ranges was Steep Rock. Despite early knowledge of iron bodies in the area, it was not until the 1930's that initial development began in this area and not until 1945 that shipments of ore commenced. Most of its output is shipped to the U.S. The Canadian iron ore industry actually had its beginning in 1939 when Algoma Ore Properties Ltd. (a subsidiary of Algoma Steel) brought its Helen Mine into production.[7] It too, is located in an area adjoining the upper Great Lakes. Four-fifths of its ore is shipped to the United States; the remainder is transported to the parent company's mill at Sault Ste. Marie.

Beginning in the 1950's and continuing to the present, the nature of the industry has changed with an influx of U.S. steel corporations which have developed captive mines in Ontario and Quebec. A case in point is the Marmoraton mine located in Southeastern Ontario. A subsidiary of Bethlehem Steel Corporation, Marmoraton ships iron ore pellets to Bethlehem's plant at Lackawanna near Buffalo, N.Y. It is by no means typical of the type of U.S. investment in Canadian iron ore, however. Many of the projects are of a joint nature; that is, a number of U.S. steel companies jointly finance development with iron ore shipments being in proportion to capital investment. The corporate link, therefore, between U.S. steel companies and Canadian iron mines is often quite nebulous. A few details on the sources of capital are necessary to clarify the degrees and diverse types of control which exist in the industry and affect labor-management negotiations in Canada.

Steep Rock Iron Mines is controlled by American interests. Premium Iron Ores Limited is the exclusive sales agent for Steep Rock and it in turn is owned by Cyrus Eaton and Cleveland Associates. It has no direct relationship with any U.S. basic steel companies.

Inland Steel Company also has large iron ore reserves in the Steep Rock area consisting of the "C" zone of Steep Rock Iron Mines. This was leased on a royalty basis for 99 years. Inland's

---

7. The Wabana Mine in Newfoundland has produced continuously since 1895. Its principal customer was the parent Dominion Steel and Coal Corporation, with only about one-fifth of its output exported, mainly to Western Europe. Its output was not large, and in 1966 the mine was closed. The beginnings of a Canadian iron ore industry are traced to Algoma Ore Properties due to the fact that Newfoundland was not a part of Canada until 1949.

operations are managed by the Caland Ore Company, a wholly-owned subsidiary of Inland Steel.

The Iron Ore Company of Canada brought the large Labrador-Quebec deposits into production in 1954 to supply primarily American companies which financed the development — Hanna Coal and Ore Corporation, Republic Steel Corporation, National Steel Corporation, Armco Steel Corporation, Youngstown Sheet and Tube Company, and Wheeling Steel Corporation. It has several mines operating in the Quebec-Labrador area with management of the mines in the hands of Hollinger-Hanna Limited, a U.S. controlled corporation.

As noted, Bethlehem Mines Corporation brought its Marmora, Ontario, mine into production to supply the Lackawanna mill of its parent company, Bethlehem Steel Corporation. The mine began operations in the early 1950's.

Lowphos Ore Limited, a wholly-owned subsidiary of National Steel Corporation has developed an iron ore property at Capreol, 35 miles north of Sudbury, Ontario. Shipments began in 1958. The property is operated by M. S. Hanna Company (Cleveland) as agent for Lowphos Ore.

Quebec Cartier Mining Company at Lac Jeannine and Gagnon, Quebec, is a wholly-owned subsidiary of U.S. Steel Corporation. Initial production occurred in 1961.

In 1958, the Steel Company of Canada, together with Pickands-Mather of the United States and Jones & Laughlin Steel Corporation undertook a joint development of Hilton Mines, 35 miles northwest of Ottawa. This ore is shipped to both American and Canadian steel mills.

The ownership of iron ore resources in one country by basic steel producers in the other is by no means one-sided. The Steel Company of Canada, from the day of its inception, has drawn the bulk of its iron ore from jointly-owned mines in the United States. Algoma Steel Corporation has purchased about two-thirds of its iron ore from U.S. companies. This is a logical consequence of the company's location close to established American sources. The remainder of its iron ore requirements is provided by its subsidiary at Wawa, Ontario, north of Sault Ste. Marie. Dominion Foundries and Steel at Hamilton had not acquired control of its own sources of iron ore but purchased American ore on a long-term contract basis. Dominion Steel and Coal Corporation was the only major Canadian firm which obtained all its raw materials in Canada.

It is apparent from the foregoing examples that the structure of the Canadian iron ore industry is an integral part of the basic steel industry, especially in the United States, and to a much lesser extent in Canada. It is also clear that the corporate connection between U.S. steel corporations and their subsidiary mines is often quite complex. Only in the case of Marmoraton Mines and Quebec Cartier Mining is the U.S. corporate link unobstructed by multiple ownership and intermediary managing companies.

Capital expenditures in setting up and operating an iron ore mine are immense. Transportation costs similarly are very significant. Labor costs as a percentage of total costs are, therefore, minimal. Heavy investments in plant and equipment are involved. Though they vary, depending on the nature of the deposits, the extent to which they require on-site treatment, and the need to install new transportation facilities, they often run into hundreds of millions of dollars. Capital outlay is equal to, or larger than, those required in the establishment of most other types of mining enterprises. Capital outlay per ton of initial capacity has varied from a low of around $10 per ton (Steep Rock) to upwards of $25 per ton (Quebec-Labrador). At Marmoraton Mines, the most notable operation in the collective bargaining sphere, capital outlays per ton of capacity have been estimated to range from $50 to $60 due to the fact that it produces specially prepared pelletized iron ore concentrates.

COLLECTIVE BARGAINING PROCEDURES

There is a single union in both countries. All of the iron ore mines in Ontario, Quebec, Labrador, and Newfoundland are organized by the United Steelworkers of America. The same situation prevails in the U.S. The major difference was a substantial lag in the unionization of Canadian mines. Organization in the United States culminated in the early 1940's, while in Canada it was not until after World War II that Steep Rock and Algoma were unionized followed by Wabana in 1949. The other mines in Canada were organized as they came into production in the mid- and late-1950's and early 1960's.

There is one similarity between the iron ore and basic steel cases regarding collective bargaining — the procedures followed in the Canadian industry bear little resemblance to those followed in the U.S. The greater part of American iron ore is mined either by subsidiaries or divisions of the major American steel companies. As a result, collective bargaining in iron ore takes place simultaneously with that in basic steel.[8] The pattern for basic steel is the pattern for iron ore. In some instances the iron mines are represented in steel company negotiations. A consequence of this is that wages, hours, and working conditions at iron ore mines are similar to, in some instances identical with, those at the basic steel companies. As an example, the United States Steel Corporation owns the Oliver Iron Mining Division, and the Steelworkers negotiate a separate agreement covering the iron miners at the same time that they negotiate for the company's steelworkers. The basic provisions of the steel agreement are adapted to any special conditions that apply in iron ore and, in addition, matters are considered in iron ore which have no relevance to steel. Certain provisions of the contract — those governing wages, pensions, insurance, supplementary unemployment benefits, for example — apply to all of the units of the company including the Oliver Iron Mining Division. In other instances — the Bethlehem Steel Company is an example — a single agreement covers the basic steel plant(s), the iron ore mines, and other operations as well. This particular procedure played a considerable role in Canadian negotiations at Marmoraton Mines, Bethlehem's subsidiary. The union also represents miners for the independent or managing companies and these contracts too, are negotiated simultaneously and are influenced by the same conditions. The iron miners at various times in the U.S. have gone on strike at the same time as workers in the steel industry.

The policy followed in the U.S. of linking iron ore negotiations to those in basic steel has its roots in industry practices developed before the union existed. In arguing for a wage increase (before the War Labor Board in 1943) similar to that granted to "Little Steel", the union pointed out that during the pervious twenty years the wage increases and decreases in cents per hour had been the same and made on precisely the same dates for both the iron ore miners in the Lake Superior region and the steelworkers in the basic steel industry.[9] During the postwar years complete parity of rates between U.S. iron ore and basic steel did not exist. An inequity fund was set up in the early 1950's, however, and complete equality of rates between the two sectors was achieved.

The situation in Canada is quite different. Negotiations are independent and separate from those in Canadian basic steel except at the Algoma interests. Bargaining takes place on a mine by mine

8. Testimony of Meyer Bernstein, International Affairs Representative, United Steelworkers of America, before the United States Tariff Commission, Iron Ore Hearing, October 18, 1960 (in the files of the National Office, USWA, Toronto), p. 1.

9. *Steel Labor* (USWA, Pittsburgh), January 22, 1943, p. 9.

basis with no efforts, thus far, to co-ordinate demands through an iron ore council or committee. The actual negotiating is done by a local committee headed by the local's president with the national director, or the director of District 5 or 6, plus staff representatives from Toronto acting in an advisory capacity. These latter groups, to a limited extent, act as an agent to tie together the negotiations. But there is no formal framework for accomplishing this. By design, they have achieved at least a limited degree of success in co-ordinating their bargaining efforts with those in the U.S. industry, however, and are more likely to push for greater co-ordination on this front than within Canada.[10]

The lack of bargaining symmetry within Canada and attempts by the USWA to obtain some co-ordination *internationally* were the dominant characteristics for the entire analysis period.

U.S.-CANADA WAGES

Table 6-1 lists the labor rates at the leading mine in the U.S. and various mines in Canada. Table 6-2 lists the absolute and percentage differentials of common labor rates between the selected Canadian mines and Oliver, which is located on the Mesabi Range. They reveal that, from 1952 to 1962, the union has achieved some success in pursuit of U.S. wage rates. But the results vary widely. By 1962, at two operations in Canada — IOCO and Lowphos — labor rates had been established which exceeded the comparable U.S. rate. The base rate in 1962 at Oliver was $2.10 compared with $2.14 at IOCO's operations and $2.125 at Lowphos. With the inclusion of the 18.5 cent cost-of-living allowance in the U.S. rate, however, no top-paying mine in Canada had a common labor rate equivalent to the Mesabi Range level. Parenthetically, in 1963 and 1964, wage increases were negotiated at Lowphos and the IOCO operations leading to labor rates of $2.175 and $2.28, respectively. There were no increases in the United States. By 1964, therefore, the differential was only half a cent for IOCO but a differential of 11 cents still remained at Lowphos. As of 1962 the union had achieved the greatest degree of success at Marmoraton where the differential, including the cost-of-living allowance, stood at 4.5 cents. This was maintained through 1965 and basically the same situation prevails today.

Table 6-1 also reveals the considerable variability of wage rates in the Canadian sector. Over the ten-year period the relative U.S.-Canada differential at the labor rate level (including cost-of-living allowance adjustments) had actually increased or remained stable at

---

10. See *Steel Labor* (Canadian edition), May, 1959, p. 2.

Table 6-1

COMMON LABOR RATES, OLIVER IRON MINES AND
SELECTED IRON MINES IN CANADA, 1953-62

Year	Oliver[a]	Marmoraton[a]	Steep Rock	IOCO	Wabana	Hilton	Algoma	Lowphos
1952	$1.435	$1.07	$1.29		$1.145		$1.40	
1953	1.52	1.30	1.39		1.28		1.40	
1954	1.57	1.40	1.44		1.28		1.45	
1955	1.685	1.515	1.46		1.39		1.50	
1956	1.82	1.685	1.55	$1.55	1.40		1.635	$1.81
1957	1.96	1.87	1.785	1.70	1.52		1.715	1.88
1958	2.12	2.075	1.82	1.75	1.56	$1.60	1.785	1.95
1959	2.13	2.085	1.855	1.85	1.56	1.65	1.855	2.025
1960	2.20	2.155	1.925	2.07	1.58	1.71	1.955	2.105
1961	2.285	2.24	2.005	2.07	1.61	1.76	1.955	2.125
1962	2.285	2.24	2.005	2.14	1.61	1.76	2.00	

a. Includes cost-of-living bonuses.

SOURCES: The files of the National Office, USWA, Toronto; USWA Pittsburgh Office.

Steep Rock, Wabana, Hilton, Algoma, and Lowphos. At each of these mines the absolute differential had increased.

The rates at each of the U.S. controlled firms exceeded those of firms controlled by Canadian interests. It should not be inferred from this, however, that if the industry was entirely U.S. controlled, all wage rates would have approached the U.S. level. The Wabana mine was plagued throughout by economic difficulties necessitating a weaker stand by the USWA regarding wage increases. This unquestionably would have been the case regardless of who had controlling interest. The wages at Hilton Mines also significantly lagged behind most of the industry. While Stelco owns a share of the mine, so too do U.S. interests — Pickands-Mather and Jones & Laughlin Steel. In the same area Jones & Laughlin owns Adams Mine where wages are at the Hilton level, far below U.S. rates. Lastly, rates at Algoma, an all-Canadian owned operation, were only half a cent behind those at U.S. controlled Steep Rock. In 1963 Algoma rates exceeded those at Steep Rock by 1.5 cents and then, in 1964, again trailed the latter by only half a cent.

At none of the mines had increment parity been achieved with Oliver Iron Mines. The greatest degree of success was achieved at

Table 6-2

ABSOLUTE AND PERCENTAGE DIFFERENTIALS IN COMMON LABOR RATES, BETWEEN OLIVER IRON MINES AND SELECTED IRON ORE MINES IN CANADA, 1953-62

Year	Marmoraton[a]		Steep Rock		Algoma		Wabana		IOCO		Lowphos		Hilton	
	¢	%	¢	%	¢	%	¢	%	¢	%	¢	%	¢	%
1953	22.0	14.5	13.0	8.6	12.0	7.9	24.0	15.7						
1954	17.0	10.8	13.0	8.3	12.0	7.6	29.0	18.5						
1955	17.0	10.1	22.5	13.4	18.5	11.0	29.5	17.5						
1956	13.5	7.4	27.0	14.8	18.5	10.2	42.0	23.1	27.0	14.8				
1957	9.0	4.6	17.5	8.9	24.5	12.5	44.0	22.4	26.0	13.3	15.0	7.6		
1958	4.5	2.1	20.0	14.2	33.5	15.8	56.0	26.4	37.0	17.4	24.0	11.3	52.0	24.5
1959	4.5	2.1	27.5	12.9	27.5	12.9	57.0	26.8	28.0	13.1	18.0	8.4	48.0	22.5
1960	4.5	2.0	27.5	12.5	24.5	11.1	62.0	28.2	13.0	5.9	17.5	7.9	49.0	22.3
1961	4.5	1.9	28.0	12.3	33.0	14.4	67.5	29.5	21.5	9.4	18.0	7.8	52.5	23.0
1962	4.5	1.9	28.0	12.3	28.5	12.5	67.5	29.5	14.5	6.3	16.0	7.0	52.5	23.0

a. Includes cost-of-living bonuses.

SOURCES: The files of the National Office, USWA, Toronto; USWA, Pittsburgh Office.

IOCO where the differential was only one-tenth of a cent. The Marmoraton increment between job classes had moved to within seven-tenths of a cent of the U.S. increment,[11] and within eight-tenths of a cent at Lowphos. At most of the remaining mines, including Steep Rock, the increment was 6 cents, a full cent below Oliver. The exception was at the Hilton Mine which had an increment of 5.5 cents. The actual movement of differentials for jobs above class 1 can be seen in Table 6-3.[12] While increment parity was not a fact in 1962, from the selected base years to 1962 the international differential had narrowed in absolute and percentage terms for the more highly skilled classifications. The narrowing was slightly greater than that at the labor rate level. One reason was the combination of job classes 1 and 2 in the U.S. in 1956. The result was a reduction in the number of job classes by one. The greatest reduction in the international differential in the skilled classifications occurred at IOCO and Marmoraton. In any case, the wage picture is one of great diversity but with at least some mines having wages close to the U.S. level.

THE COLLECTIVE BARGAINING RECORD

The settlements at all of the major mines in Canada were considered. Emphasis was on their relationship or lack of it, in substance and time, to the leading U.S. producer — Oliver Iron Mines. The latter is the pattern-setter for the Lake Superior iron ore ranges[13] and for the entire U.S. industry. This amounts to a comparison with U.S. Steel. Since 1952, the dates of settlement and contract provisions at the parent company and Oliver have been essentially uniform.[14] Due to the affinity between basic steel and iron ore settlements in the U.S. and the integration of the U.S. steel industry and Canadian iron ore, it is the key bargain arrived at in steel which

---

11. By 1965 the increment at Marmoraton was only .3 of a cent below that at Oliver.

12. While the number of job classifications varies from mine to mine in no case is there a classification higher than 20. Using job classes, 1, 8 and 16, therefore, should be an adequate representation of the wage structure.

13. The Lake Superior district includes the Mesabi, Cayuna and Vermillion ranges in Minnesota, the Gogebic range in Michigan-Wisconsin, and the Menominee and Marquette ranges in Michigan.

14. In 1952, the union successfully argued before the U.S. Wage Stabilization Board that, with respect to the iron ore wage structure, the Board should "restore the parallel to the steel wage structure which existed over an extended period before 1947 . . . ." Press Release: From V. Sweeney, USWA, Hotel Statler, New York, N.Y., February 14, 1952 (in the files of the National Office, USWA, Toronto), p. 2.

Table 6-3

ABSOLUTE AND RELATIVE DIFFERENTIALS IN JOB
CLASSES 1, 8, AND 16[a] BETWEEN OLIVER IRON MINES
AND SELECTED IRON ORE MINES IN CANADA —
SELECTED BASE YEAR TO 1962[b]

	#1		#8		#16	
	1954	1962	1954	1962	1954	1962
Oliver[c]	$1.57	$2.285	$1.955	$2.705	$2.395	$3.265
Marmoraton[c]	1.40	2.24	1.68	2.618	2.00	3.122
Absolute diff.	.17	.045	.275	.087	.395	.143
Relative diff.	10.8%	1.9%	14.1%	3.2%	16.5%	4.4%
	1956	1962	1956	1962	1956	1962
Oliver[c]	$1.82	$2.285	$2.198	$2.705	$2.702	$3.265
Steep Rock	1.55	2.005	1.90	2.425	2.30	2.905
Absolute diff.	.27	.28	.298	.28	.402	.36
Relative diff.	14.8%	12.3%	13.6%	10.4%	15.0%	11.0%
	1955	1962	1955	1962	1955	1962
Oliver[c]	$1.685	$2.285	$2.105	$2.705	$2.585	$3.265
Algoma	1.50	2.00	1.85	2.455	2.25	2.975
Absolute diff.	.185	.285	.255	.25	.335	.29
Relative diff.	11.0%	12.5%	12.1%	9.2%	13.0%	8.9%
	1957	1962	1957	1962	1957	1962
Oliver[c]	$1.96	$2.285	$2.35	$2.705	$2.87	$3.265
IOCO	1.70	2.14	2.12	2.623	2.60	3.175
Absolute diff.	.26	.145	.23	.082	.27	.09
Relative diff.	13.3%	6.3%	9.8%	3.0%	9.4%	2.8%

a. Job Class # 1 — Janitor; Job Class # 8 — Truck Driver; Job Class
16 — Shovel Operator.
b. The base year used in each case was the year in which CWS was introduced in the relevant Canadian mine.
c. Includes cost-of-living bonuses.
SOURCES: The files of the National Office, USWA, Toronto; USWA Pittsburgh Office.

is of most concern to the union in Canada when dealing with iron ore producers.[15]

Pre-1953 Experience

As stated in the basic steel chapter, the USWA in Canada firmly established their autonomy from the international office. A definite policy of non-intervention on the part of international headquarters was laid down in the postwar years. An analysis of collective bargaining in Canadian iron ore from 1945 through 1952[16] indicates complete independence of action on the part of the Canadian region. No influences of either a direct or indirect nature were felt from the U.S. An examination of collective agreements over the period substantiates a statement, made by the Research Director in Canada, that: "During the early postwar years the pressures to increase wages were independent of those in the U.S. With full employment and inflation the emphasis was simply to get wages up."[17] Union wage policy was dictated by this concern plus an additional factor. From 1945 to 1952 the Canadian region was negotiating initial agreements at Steep Rock, Algoma, and Wabana. Emphasis was on union security and other provisions to consolidate the union's foothold in the industry.

---

15. The comments with regard to Oliver Iron Mines were substantiated as follows by a U.S. union staff officer — "You are correct in assuming that the former Oliver Iron Mining Co. has been the pattern setter in the Iron Ore Mining Industry in the United States . . . . Oliver Mining Co. has been, over the years, a close follower of the pattern set in U.S. Steel's Basic Steel operations. These facts are readily apparent from the *U.S. Steel Wage Chronology* . . . . The major divergence in our bargaining pattern occurred in 1946, when we settled our steel strike and left Oliver out on strike. It took almost another month of strike to secure the same gains in Oliver that we had earlier secured in the Basic Steel operation of the Corporation. We have never permitted a repeat of this performance. We have, instead, insisted on an economic settlement with Oliver at the same time as the steel settlement. There was a long delay in Oliver in getting an agreement on our CWS Job Classification Program. This led to certain differences in the wage portion of the economic settlements in 1947, 1950 and 1952. The 1952 settlement, however, put the same job class scale in Oliver as in the Basic Steel Operations effective as of July 1, 1953. At one time, Oliver had a different shift differential arrangement of 5 cents on the second shift and 5 cents on the third shift. This was, however, shifted over to the steel pattern of 6 cents and 9 cents in the 1952 settlement." (Correspondence dated June 9, 1966 to the author from Mr. Otis Brubaker, Director, Research Department, USWA, Pittsburgh, Pa.)

16. The analysis starts in 1945 due to the fact that this year marked the beginning of collective bargaining in Canadian iron ore at Steep Rock Iron Mines.

17. Interview with H. Waisglass, Research Director, USWA, National Office, Toronto, November 2, 1964.

The 1945 agreement at Steep Rock simply incorporated existing wage rates (approved by the National War Labour Board). It established a labor base rate of 64 cents per hour and provided union security in the form of dues checkoff. Similar procedures were followed when the union negotiated the initial agreements at Algoma and Wabana in 1949 and 1951, respectively. The union, throughout the early postwar years, in all the industries in which it had organized was emphasizing the union shop, the 40-hour week and shift premiums, in addition to wage increases.[18] Standard contract provisions were their objectives with little attempt being made to follow events south of the border.

Table 6-4 presents the wage changes from 1947 to 1952 in the two countries, in absolute terms. Table 6-5 presents similar data in percentage terms. The outstanding features of both tables are the large degree of variability in the wage changes at the three Canadian mines, and the complete lack of relatedness between the increases in the U.S. and Canada. Table 6-6 reveals, however, that despite the fact that there was no union attempt to narrow the international differential or link their negotiations to those in the U.S., the Steep Rock-Mesabi Range differential had decreased over the six-year period. After 1947, when there was a return to free collective bargaining in Canada, the wage increases were significantly higher than in the U.S. But, unlike the steel industry, wage parity had not been obtained at this point with a 14.5 cent differential at the labor rate level still existing.[19]

In 1951 there was a major change in union policy. With the narrowing of the international differential in the steel industry, wage parity became a goal of the Canadian region. At the same time it was decided that the introduction of job evaluation in the form of CWS, which had been introduced in the U.S., would become a priority item. Of even greater importance to the Canadian iron ore situation was the following resolution at the 1951 Canadian Conference:

> We propose where possible to include Canadian workers in master agreements negotiated by our union with parent firms in the United States.[20]

At that time only Steep Rock was owned by U.S. interests and the corporate link was such that it was difficult to tie Canadian negotiations to any in the United States. In the following year, however, Bethlehem opened their mine in Marmora and the union

---

18. *Steel Labor* (Canadian edition), November 1949, p. 1.

19. The labor rate at Algoma Ore Properties had advanced to $1.40 by 1952, leaving only a 3.5 cent gap.

20. *Steel Labor* (Canadian edition), November 1951, p. 1.

Table 6-4

YEARLY ABSOLUTE GENERAL WAGE CHANGES —
CANADIAN AND UNITED STATES IRON ORE INDUSTRIES,
1947-52

Year	U.S. Key Settlement	Steep Rock	Algoma	Wabana
1947	12.5	6		
1948	9.5	25		
1949	—	9	9	
1950	12.5	4	5	
1951	—	10	15	
1952	12.5	11	20	14
1947-52	47.0	65		

SOURCES: USWA Pittsburgh Office; the files of the National Office,
USWA, Toronto.

Table 6-5

YEARLY PERCENTAGE[a] GENERAL WAGE CHANGES —
CANADIAN AND UNITED STATES IRON ORE INDUSTRIES,
1947-52

Year	U.S. Key Settlement	Steep Rock	Algoma	Wabana
1947	13.0	9.4		
1948	8.7	35.7		
1949	—	9.5	9.9	
1950	10.5	3.8	5.0	
1951	—	9.3	14.2	
1952	9.5	9.3	16.7	14.0

a. Percentage of the labor rate.

SOURCES: USWA Pittsburgh Office; the files of the National Office,
USWA, Toronto.

Table 6-6

ABSOLUTE AND PERCENTAGE WAGE DIFFERENTIALS — UNITED STATES MESABI RANGE[a] AND STEEP ROCK IRON MINES, 1947-52

Year	U.S.	Canada	¢	%
1947	$1.09	$ .70	39.0	35.7
1948	1.185	.95	23.5	19.8
1949	1.185	1.04	14.5	12.2
1950	1.31	1.08	23.0	17.6
1951	1.31	1.18	13.0	9.9
1952	1.435	1.29	14.5	10.1

a. Oliver Iron Mining Company.

SOURCES: USWA Pittsburgh Office; the files of the National Office, USWA, Toronto.

signed a first agreement in 1953. It was at this operation, with its distinct U.S. corporate connection, that the union attempted most seriously to implement such a policy. There were also other examples of bi-national influence in other segments of the industry.

Collective Bargaining 1953 to 1962

Table 6-7 lists the dates of signing of the major Canadian iron agreements and those for U.S. basic steel. With the exceptions noted, Oliver dates were identical with those of the latter. Two observations should be made. First, there is general dissimilarity between U.S. and Canadian settlement dates. Second, the Marmoraton dates coincided closely with those in the U.S.

Not surprisingly, because of the diffuse nature of the negotiations, settlements within Canada and between those on the Mesabi Range varied widely. Table 6-8 compares the yearly increases at selected companies in Canada and Oliver Iron Mines. There was a broad range of increases in Canada and in only isolated instances were similar increases provided for in the same year. The dissimilarity was also apparent in terms of total general wage increases by wage round (Table 6-9). A comparison on a lagged basis also shows little relationship between the settlements.[21] There was, however, a connection between the settlements at Marmoraton and those

---

21. A comparison in percentage terms did not show any more uniformity.

Table 6-7

DATES ON WHICH AGREEMENT WAS REACHED — UNITED STATES BASIC STEEL (KEY AGREEMENT) AND MAJOR CANADIAN IRON ORE COMPANIES, 1953-62

Year	U.S. Basic Steel	Canadian Iron Ore	
1953	June 12 (reopening)[a]	March 6	— Steep Rock
		June 30	— Marmoraton
		October 14	— Algoma Ore
1954	June 30	June 30	— Marmoraton
		November 29	— Algoma Ore
		December 17	— Steep Rock
1955	July 1 (reopening)	July 1	— Marmoraton
		October 18	— Algoma Ore
1956	July 27[b]	April 4	— Wabana
		May 2	— Steep Rock
		August 3	— Marmoraton
1957	Nil	February	— Algoma Ore[c]
		February 27	— Wabana
		June 18	— Lowphos
		June 21	— Steep Rock
		October 23	— IOCO
1958	Nil	September 26	— Hilton
1959	Nil	January 9	— Algoma Ore
		January 21	— Steep Rock
1960	January 4	January 4	— Marmoraton
		January 30	— Wabana
		February 16	— Caland
		March 3	— Lowphos
		March 8	— IOCO
		May 1	— Quebec Cartier
		December 12	— Hilton
1961	Nil	Nil	
1962	March 31[d]	April 13	— Marmoraton
		May	— Algoma Ore[c]
		August 28	— Steep Rock
		December 13	— Lowphos

a. Date of signing for Oliver Iron Mines was June 16, 1953.
b. Date of signing for Oliver Iron Mines was August 3, 1956. Individual contracts for basic steel were not signed until this date as well.
c. Specific date not available.
d. Date for signing for Oliver Iron Mines was April 6, 1962.

SOURCES: USWA Pittsburgh Office; the files of the National Office, USWA, Toronto.

Table 6-8

NEGOTIATED GENERAL WAGE INCREASES BY EFFECTIVE DATE, OLIVER IRON MINES AND SELECTED CANADIAN COMPANIES, 1953-62[a]

(cents)

	1953	1954	1955	1956	1957	1958	1959	1960	1961	1962
Oliver	8.5	5.0	11.5	7.5	7.0	7.0		7.0	7.0	
Marmoraton	23.0	10.0	11.5	17.0	11.5	11.5		7.0	7.0	
Steep Rock	4.0	5.0	2.0	9.0	23.5	3.5	3.5	7.0	8.0	
Algoma	5.0		5.0	13.5	8.0	7.0	7.0	10.0	4.5	
Wabana	12.5		11.0	1.0	12.0	4.0		2.0	3.0	
IOCO					15.0	5.0	10.0	22.0	7.0	7.0
Lowphos						7.0	7.0	7.5	8.0	2.0

a. Excludes cost-of-living allowances.

SOURCES: The files of the National Office, USWA, Toronto; USWA, Pittsburgh Office.

Table 6-9

NEGOTIATED GENERAL WAGE INCREASES by WAGE ROUND AT DATE OF AGREEMENT, OLIVER IRON MINES AND SELECTED CANADIAN COMPANIES, 1953-62

(cents)

	1953	1954	1955	1956	1957	1958	1959	1960	1961	1962
Oliver	8.5	5.0	11.5	21.5	27.0		18.5	14.0		
Marmoraton	23.0	10.0	11.5	40.0	18.0		24.0	14.0		
Steep Rock	4.0	5.0	2.0	9.0	16.0					9.5
Algoma	5.0		8.5							
Wabana		12.5		1.0	30.0			5.0		
IOCO								22.0		21.0
Lowphos								21.5		

SOURCES: The files of the National Office, USWA, Toronto; USWA, Pittsburgh Office.

in U.S. basic steel, and, therefore, at Oliver. The increases at Marmoraton were larger through 1958 in order to close the international wage differential. Also, IOCO and Lowphos in the 1959-60 round settled for a total increase similar to that granted at Oliver in 1956. There was also some resemblance between the IOCO settlement in 1961 and the January 4, 1960, settlement at Oliver. Both provided for annual 7 cent increases but at IOCO there was an additional increase of 7 cents effective in 1963. There seemed to be some trend toward an international orbit, therefore, in segments of the industry.

As far as wage changes for workers in classifications above Job Class 1 were concerned, this depended entirely on the changes to the increment under the CWS system. Table 6-10 compares the changes in the increment at Oliver and selected Canadian companies. The changes in the increment within the Canadian industry and in comparison with Oliver were not related, other than the changes at Marmoraton and Oliver in the 1960 round.

A comparison of fringe benefit changes is contained in Table 6-11. This table only compares changes at Oliver, Marmoraton, Steep Rock, and IOCO but the inclusion of all Canadian iron ore producers would not change the conclusions evident from a perusal of the table. It adequately reflects the lack of relatedness, internationally (with the exception of Marmoraton) and nationally. Marmoraton, after 1954, experienced a direct pass-on of all but a few minor benefits which were negotiated in U.S. basic steel. The changes, therefore, were almost identical to the changes at Oliver. For the rest of the industry fringe benefit changes varied widely from company to company.

1953

Bargaining in the U.S. began May 15 and a general wage increase was announced on June 12, 1953. Two weeks later an agreement was worked out for Marmoraton Mines which was in no way similar to U.S. contract *changes*. The negotiations were of importance, however, because of the degree of U.S. involvement, on the part of both the union and management.

When negotiations were in the initial stage at Marmoraton the national office wrote to the international for copies of the Bethlehem agreements covering its U.S. iron mines. In addition, they requested any further information they could use with regard to pension and welfare plans.[22] During negotiations the union proposed to the com-

---

22. National office correspondence dated May 22, 1953, to Otis Brubaker, Research Director, USWA, Pittsburgh, Pa. (in the files of the National Office, USWA, Toronto).

Table 6-10

CHANGES IN AND LEVELS OF THE INCREMENT BETWEEN JOB CLASSES, OLIVER IRON MINES AND SELECTED CANADIAN IRON ORE MINES, 1953-62

Year	Oliver		Marmoraton		Steep Rock		Algoma		IOCO		Lowphos		Hilton	
	Inc.	Level	Inc.	Level	Inc.	Level	Inc.	Level	Inc.	Level	Inc.	Level	Inc.	Level
1953	1.0	5.5		4.0										
1954		5.5	1.0	5.0		5.0		5.0						
1955	.5	6.0	.4	5.4	.25	5.25	.5	5.5						
1956	.3	6.3	.3	5.7	.5	5.75		5.5						
1957	.2	6.5	.3	6.0	.1	5.85		5.5						5.5
1958	.2	6.7		6.0	.15	6.0	.5	6.0		6.0		5.0		5.5
1959		6.7				6.0		6.0		6.0	.5	5.5		5.5
1960	.2	6.9	.2	6.2		6.0			.3	6.3		5.5	.4	5.9
1961	.1	7.0	.1	6.3					.3	6.6		5.5	.3	6.2
1962		7.0					.5	6.5	.3	6.9		5.5		6.2

SOURCES: The files of the National Office, USWA, Toronto; USWA Pittsburgh Office.

Table 6-11

A COMPARISON OF FRINGE BENEFIT CHANGES, OLIVER IRON MINES AND SELECTED CANADIAN IRON ORE COMPANIES, 1953-62

Oliver	Marmoraton	Steep Rock	IOCO
1953: Nil	1953: 6 paid holidays Vacation pay — 2 after 5 3 after 15 Shift premiums: 6¢; 9¢ Severance pay — 4 wks. pay after 2 yrs.; 2 mos. after 10 yrs.	1953: Nil	
1954: Insurance Benefits: increased min. from $2000 to $3000; increased max. from $4500 to $5500. Accident and sickness benefits: increased by $14. Hospitalization: increased by 50 days. Pension plan: benefits increased.	1954: Nil	1954: Nil	
	1955: Nil	1955: Nil	
1956: Added: pay for Sunday work. Added: additional ½ wk. vacation pay for 3 but less than 5, 10 but less than 15, and 25 or more yrs.	1956: Same Same	1956:	

Table 6-11 (continued)

Oliver	Marmoraton	Steep Rock	IOCO
Added: 7th paid holiday.	Same	Added: 2 more paid holidays.	
Shift premiums: 8¢ and 12¢ rather than 6¢ and 9¢.	Same		
Life insurance benefits: increased. Sickness and accident benefits: increased. Hospitalization: improved. Surgical benefits increased.	Same		
Pension plan: benefits increased. Added: early retirement. Added: deferred vested rights.	Same		
Added: supplementary unemployment benefits.	Same		
Added: jury duty pay.			
		1957: Shift premiums increased from 3¢ to 5¢ and 7¢.	1957: Sunday premium — 15¢; Shift premiums — 5¢ and 9¢.
		Welfare plan: improved — company to pay ½ cost of providing Blue Cross comprehensive and PSI for employees and dependents; $2000-life insurance.	Paid vacations — 2 wks. after 1 yr. 2½ wks. after 2 yrs. 3½ wks. after 3 yrs. 4 wks. after 4 yrs.

Table 6-11 (continued)

Oliver	Marmoraton	Steep Rock	IOCO
		1959: Life insurance increased by $1000; Accident and sickness benefits increased by $3.50.	1959: Vacation pay increased: — 18 days after 1 yr. 23 days after 2 yrs. 28 days after 3 yrs. 33 days after 4 yrs. 2¢ for improving Health & Welfare Plan.
1960: Insurance Benefits Plan: Changed to all company-paid; Life insurance increased by $500; Accident and sickness benefits increased by $11.	1960: Same		
Pension plan: Normal retirement benefits increased; Minimum monthly pension prior to age 65 for permanent incapacity increased.	Same		
Early retirement benefits increased; Added: special retirement benefit — 13 wks. less vacation previously taken in calendar year in which retirement occurs.			
1962: Vacation pay changed — 1 wk. for 1 but less than 3 yrs.; 2 for 3 but less than 10; 3 for 10 but less than 25; 4 for 25 or more yrs.	1962: Same	1962: Vacation Pay added — 3 wks. after 15 yrs. Pension plan improved.	1962: Nil

Table 6-11 (continued)

Oliver	Marmoraton	Steep Rock	IOCO
Savings and Vacation Plan: Plan to provide retirement savings and supplemental vacation benefits.	Same	Shift Premiums increased from 5¢ and 7¢ to 6¢ and 8¢.	
Increased early retirement benefits.	Same	Accident and sickness benefits increased by $10.	
SUB — contribution of company increased and benefits improved.	Same		
Added — short week benefit.	Same		
Added — moving allowance.			

SOURCES: The files of the National Office, USWA, Toronto; USWA Pittsburgh Office.

pany that they put into effect the same kind of contract as was in effect for Bethlehem's iron ore operations. Specifically, they suggested that the contract covering its miners at Cornwall, Pennsylvania, be used. The company, before the threat of a strike was imminent, agreed to use that agreement as a basis for negotiations. Many of the issues, both monetary and non-monetary, were resolved through this device. Using the Cornwall agreement the following matters were settled — union recognition; union security; a 40 hour week; shift premium of 6 cents and 9 cents per hour; time and a half for hours worked in excess of 40; payment for 6 statutory holidays; one week's vacation after one year's service, 2 weeks' after 5 years' service, and 3 after 15; seniority rules; safety regulations; and severance pay. All were identical to the U.S. provisions. On the wage issue, however, the company would not agree to pay the same rates as they were paying in the U.S. They stated that they would be willing to settle on some figure between $1.435 (the U.S. base rate) and the company offer of $1.20.[23]

23. This information was obtained from *Report on Negotiations,* Director of District 6, USWA, May 1953 (in the files of the National Office, USWA, Toronto).

Negotiations entered the first stage of conciliation but an agreement was worked out before the conciliation board stage was reached and about two weeks after negotiations were concluded in U.S. basic steel. The increase agreed upon only established a base rate of $1.30, 10 cents below that at Algoma Ore Properties, and an increment of 4 cents (1.5 cents below that in the U.S.). Of importance was the fact that details of the final settlement were worked out when union negotiators met top company officials in the United States after the negotiations had reached the conciliation stage.[24] An agreement in the United States at Bethlehem was delayed until the Marmoraton agreement had been worked out.

> Co-operation between union negotiators in the United States and Canada contributed very considerably to the success of the negotiations. Before agreeing to a settlement with Bethlehem Steel (the parent company) in the United States, union negotiators there made arrangements for District Director Larry Sefton to present the case of the Canadian workers to top management.[25]

Also notable was the company's celerity in agreeing to use a U.S. contract as a model for Canadian negotiations.

An additional benefit to the union arising from the parent-subsidiary relationship, was the quick implementation of CWS at Marmoraton. When negotiated in the Canadian basic steel industry it took approximately two years to work out the details. At Marmoraton it was introduced within a few months. The major reasons were obvious. In working out the job classifications and slotting of jobs, the union in Canada negotiated with local management, but with constant recourse to top management at Bethlehem. They used the Bethlehem CWS manual as a model.[26] To facilitate their plans for future international pattern-bargaining the union actually "gave up a little in placing jobs in classifications so that they would be the same as at Bethlehem making a tie-in in the future possible."[27]

1954

The key development in Canada once more occurred at Marmoraton. Negotiations paralleled those in the U.S., agreement coming on the same day, but with a 10 cent general increase — 5 cents more than in the U.S. This additional amount was granted by the company to commence the elimination of the Canada-U.S. differential.[28]

---

24. *Steel Labor* (Canadian edition), July, 1953, p. 1.

25. *Ibid.*, p. 1.

26. Interview with Pat Tirrell, Industrial Engineering Department, National Office, USWA, Toronto, May 26, 1966.

27. *Ibid.*

28. *Steel Labor* (Canadian edition), November, 1954, p. 1.

Previously they had agreed, as a matter of policy, to close the differential.[29] Negotiations on wages and other important sections of the contract took place at the international level as they had in the previous year.[30] Despite the 10 cent increase, the Canadian base rate was 17 cents below the U.S. level.

1955

The union took further steps at Marmoraton in 1955, when they were successful in having the workers at that mine directly included in the U.S. negotiations. To ensure this the Director of District 6 was sent down to Pittsburgh during U.S. negotiations to sit in on wage policy committee meetings. At the final sessions the National Director also went down to Pittsburgh.[31] The Marmoraton workers were not included in the master agreement but did receive the 11½ cent increase granted to U.S. workers plus an additional cent on the increment between job classes. The increases took the form of a direct pass-on to the company's Canadian labor force. The increase left the Canadian common labor rate 17 cents behind its equivalent in the U.S. A differential also still remained in the increment (5 cents in Canada compared to 6 cents in the U.S.) but that differential had been narrowed by half a cent due to the fact that the U.S. increment was only raised by half a cent.

1956

With the expiration of two-year contracts on June 30 in the U.S., negotiations were under way on May 28. Unable to come to an agreement by the termination date a strike began on July 1. A memorandum of agreement was signed on July 27 but a return to work was delayed until early August to allow the parties to work out the details of certain items. The policy of having the local union at Marmoraton represented on the international bargaining committee by the national office continued with the result that a further breakthrough for the union was achieved.[32] Of further interest was the fact that the Canadian local walked out with U.S. workers when the international decided to strike on July 1. The U.S. workers actually stayed out only one additional day to pressure Bethlehem management on the Marmoraton situation.[33]

---

29. Interview with Eamon Park, Assistant to the National Director, National Office, USWA, Toronto, May 27, 1966.

30. *Steel Labor* (Canadian edition), November, 1954, p. 1.

31. *Ibid.*, August, 1955, p. 4.

32. *Ibid.*, September, 1956, p. 4.

33. Interview with Eamon Park, Assistant to the National Director, National Office, USWA, Toronto, May 27, 1966.

When the strike ended the Canadian workers had obtained a larger increase than the U.S. settlement called for — 17 cents in 1956, 11.5 cents in 1957, and 11 cents in 1958 opposed to 7.5, 7, and 7 in the United States in the same years. In both countries job classes 1 and 2 were combined. The wage increases resulted in narrowing the international differential to 4.5 cents by 1958 ($1.91½ in Canada, $1.96 in the U.S.). All other contract provisions, except the increment provisions, were in line with the settlement in the U.S.

There were just two other agreements signed in Canadian iron ore in 1956. Just as negotiations started in the U.S. in May, a settlement was worked out at Steep Rock calling for increases of 13 to 37 cents per hour plus the Co-operative Wage Study with 5 cent increments. At Wabana in April a 21 cent increase was negotiated but it was to be effective only when daily production reached 14,000 tons a day. This latter condition was never reached.

1957 to 1958

With the signing of a three-year agreement at Bethlehem's Marmoraton operations there were no further developments during 1957 and 1958 at that company. The activities in Canadian iron ore during this period were, nevertheless, of interest.

Contracts were signed in February of 1957 at Algoma and Wabana. The agreement at Algoma contained little of interest except that the wage increases granted kept Algoma rates, at that point, ahead of all those in the industry including those at Marmoraton. The most important feature at Wabana was a clause which provided that, barring circumstances beyond the company's control, there would be no reductions in the existing work force between 1957 and 1961 — provided production held at about 12,000 tons a day.[34] The wage increases included in the agreement still left Wabana rates well below the industry level. The settlement illustrated the union's flexibility and differences in approach when faced with different economic circumstances.

A different set of circumstances faced the union at Steep Rock. At that time Steep Rock was the largest iron ore development in Canada and, of course, just a relatively few miles away from the U.S. Mesabi Range. In June of 1957 a substantial package was negotiated — better than 45 cents over a two-year period — but it was ratified by the membership of Local 3460 by only a slim majority.[35] The cause of the dissatisfaction was that the

---

34. *Steel Labor* (Canadian edition), April, 1957, p. 3.
35. *Ibid.*, July, 1957, p. 3.

agreement still left Steep Rock rates throughout the entire job structure behind those at the Marmoraton operations. The latter was now looked upon as the pace-setter in Canada. Additionally, it did not include the SUB plan granted at Marmoraton and in the U.S. industry. The result was that the union considered the possibility of tying the Steep Rock negotiations to those in the U.S. industry in 1959. The agreement signed called for an expiration date which closely approximated the ones in the U.S. industry. Just prior to the Steep Rock agreement an initial contract had been signed at Lowphos. Its expiration, too, was similar to those in the United States. This prompted the following statement by the Canadian region:

> Contract expiry date . . . just like that negotiated at Lowphos near Sudbury, ties closely with the big U.S. iron ore negotiations in the spring of 1959. There is no doubt that the heat will be on then to eliminate even more differentials between Steep Rockers and iron ore unionists employed in mines a few miles south below the border.[36]

In 1957 the union successfully organized the labor force of the Iron Ore Company of Canada in the Quebec-Labrador region. Certified as bargaining agent in early September the union signed the initial agreement a month later. There was no relationship between the terms and any others either in Canada or the U.S. Despite the fact that the development is U.S. controlled, negotiations took place on site and involved only Canadian officials although Canadian management may have contacted their head office in Cleveland.[37] As in the other mines the one instance of U.S. influence was an agreement to institute the CWS program within a year. The base rate established was comparable to those in the rest of the Canadian industry.

1959 to 1960

After a contract renewal was signed at Algoma in January 1959 settlements were reached at Steep Rock, Construction Aggregates, and Canadian Charleson in June and July while negotiations were underway in the U.S. The latter Canadian settlements were all similar. The package at Steep Rock provided 28 to 31 cents per hour over a three-year period. The negotiations took place at a time when there were cutbacks in production in the Steep Rock area.[38]

---

36. *Ibid.*
37. In an interview with the author, the Assistant to the National Director in Toronto stated that at IOCO local negotiations proceed up to a point but before a settlement is reached telephone calls are made by the company to Cleveland.
38. The workweek had been cut to four days at Steep Rock in 1958. The reduction was due to American mills operating at 52 per cent of capacity.

When negotiations began in May of 1959 in the U.S., Canadian delegates from Local 4854 at Marmoraton sat in on the bargaining with Bethlehem. When a strike was called in the U.S., the labor force at Marmoraton also walked off their jobs.[39] When agreement came in January 1960 in the U.S. the Canadian operations of Bethlehem received similar increases in terms of both wage and fringe benefit changes. The general wage increases received plus the effective dates were identical. They were not included in the master agreement, however.

Two other agreements signed in March of 1960 were also part of the 1959 round. Settlement at Lowphos was delayed until the strike ended in the U.S. Final negotiations took place between U.S. company officials of National Steel, Canada's national director and a union committee from Local 5500. It "provided a striking demonstration of the complete co-ordination of union forces from the local union level, to the national and international level,"[40] according to the union. The settlement reached in March, not patterned after the U.S. strike settlement, provided for 22½ cents in general wage increases. This resulted in the highest labor rate in Canada if the cost-of-living bonus at Marmoraton is excluded.

The Iron Ore Company of Canada opened a new mine at Carol Lake, Labrador in 1959 with the USWA gaining recognition in October of that year. The workers at this operation were included in the IOCO master agreement which was renewed with significant changes on March 8, 1960. The wage increases established a labor rate of $2.14 in 1961 compared with $2.10 in the U.S. While not directly related to the U.S. settlement, representatives from the locals had sat in on the culminating U.S. negotiations.[41]

At Lowphos, then, the previous agreement had expired in June of 1959 but the union and company marked time until after the January 4 (1960) U.S. settlement. The contracts at IOCO expired in October of 1959 and they, too, were not renewed until March of the following year. The reasons for the delay in both instances were the same and indicate the effect that international corporate integration was beginning to have on Canadian union policy and iron ore negotiations. According to the union there were a number of factors contributing to the inordinate length of the negotiations. Firstly, they did not want to force a settlement in Canada until one came in the U.S. because of the effect it could have had on the U.S. situation. Secondly, they felt that they could do better by waiting for the U.S.

---

39. This despite the fact that in Canada the Marmoraton strike was declared illegal.

40. *Steel Labor* (Canadian edition), April, 1960, p. 1.

41. *Ibid.*

pattern to be set. Thirdly, and perhaps of most importance, because the U.S. mills were closed down, the bargaining position of the union at these mines (with almost all of their output going to U.S. mills) was extremely weak.[42] Both parties, therefore, waited for the U.S. dispute to break and then began bargaining in earnest.

1960 to 1961

In Canada during 1960 and 1961 there were two mines at which the USWA gained bargaining rights and signed initial agreements. In addition there were two contract renewals. A new mine was opened by Caland Ore and an agreement signed in February, 1960. The terms provided little of interest for this analysis. The only other agreement in 1960 was a thirty-month renewal on January 30 at Wabana where unemployment was still a problem.[43] Wage rates continued to fall far behind the rest of the industry with the new agreement only calling for a 5 cent increase.

There were no significant developments in 1961. Only two agreements were signed. A new two-year agreement was signed at Hilton Mines, and Quebec Cartier, owned by U.S. Steel, signed an initial contract. The rates established at that point were well below the top industry level.

1962

In contrast to the difficulties experienced in reaching agreement in 1959, the U.S. steel companies initialled a memorandum of understanding on March 31, 1962 — three months before the 1960 agreement was scheduled to expire. The contract for Oliver Iron Mines was signed on April 6. The settlement, to run for two years, was made up entirely of fringe benefits. The major item was a savings and vacation plan established to provide supplemental vacation-retirement benefits. The package was quite small totalling approximately 11 cents.

All of the benefits gained in the U.S. settlement were passed on to the Marmoraton workers with the effective date — July 1, 1962 — being identical to that in the United States. The union continued to look upon this as a tool to give them leverage at other U.S. subsidiaries. The following quotation illustrates this:

> The Steel union's success in winning the vacation plan may be the way for getting similar concessions from other iron ore firms which are

42. Interview with H. Waisglass, Research Director, USWA, National Office, Toronto, May 27, 1966.
43. In May, 1959, 550 employees had been laid-off by the company.

owned by U.S. concerns such as Lowphos Iron Ore at Capreol and the Iron Ore Company of Canada at Schefferville, Quebec.[44]

Collective bargaining for the 10-year period was completed with the signing of agreements at Algoma, Steep Rock and Lowphos in May, August, and December respectively. None of these displayed any similarity to the Marmoraton agreement, although the package at Steep Rock was made up entirely of fringe benefits.

AN ASSESSMENT OF U.S. INFLUENCE AND USWA POLICY IN THE IRON ORE INDUSTRY

The policy of the USWA towards the Canadian iron ore industry can best be described as heterogeneous. The fact that the industry was still basically in its formative years with the union facing a different set of variables at each company resulted not only in a diverse, but an indeterminate and opportunistic set of policies, as well. Despite a many-sided approach, union policy was not an incongruous mixture without a common denominator. Underlying the differences in policy toward individual iron ore companies is an awareness of U.S. labor developments in the industry which has left its mark on general union policy. In an article in 1959 National Director, William Mahoney stated:

> Much of our iron ore development is closely related to the industry in the United States — Steep Rock, Lowphos, Iron Ore Company of Canada, to mention a few of our U.S. connections, while bargaining up to now has been confined to Canada. Hilton Mines is operated by Pickands-Mather a U.S. company even though Stelco is a half owner of the mine. Marmoraton Mine is a subsidiary of Bethlehem Steel Company. All of this is worth considering in connection with negotiations going on in the United States in the basic steel industry chains, and including the mining operations in the U.S. The effect of these negotiations cannot be over emphasized to Canadian members of our union . . . .[45]

In 1951 the USWA enunciated a general policy which included a push for wage parity with related U.S. industries, job evaluation at all plants under their jurisdiction by using the Co-operative Wage Study, and a form of continental bargaining where applicable.[46] In the iron ore industry union policy was influenced by U.S. developments and, in a number of instances, in significant ways.

The transmission of CWS *per se* to both the Canadian iron ore and steel industries can be described as of little significance as

44. *Steel Labor* (Canadian edition), June, 1962, p. 12.

45. *Ibid.,* May 1959, p. 2.

46. National Policy Conference, USWA, September 15-16, 1951, Toronto (in the files of the National Office, USWA, Toronto), p. 1.

far as international pattern-bargaining is concerned. It was introduced to Canada with a notable lag and with lower increments between job classes than in the U.S. It was of importance, however, to
overall union strategy in iron ore and demonstrated the effective
use made by the union of U.S. ownership. The introduction of CWS
at Marmoraton opened the way for the present arrangement of including Marmoraton workers in the Bethlehem chain negotiations.
With regard to the introduction of CWS a union staff officer stated:

> Bethlehem Mines at Marmora, is a subsidiary of the Bethlehem Steel
> Corporation in the U.S. and it should be noted in passing that *the
> Program at this mine was completed under the terms of the Agreement
> covering the program with the parent company.* The first instance was
> in the case of the Union Drawn Steel plant in Hamilton which is
> a subsidiary of Republic Steel Corporation. *Certainly this is a step in
> the process of tying the negotiations in these two plants into the master
> negotiations which take place between these Corporations and our
> Union in the U.S.* This serves the three fold purpose of supporting and
> maintaining the standards established by the members in the U.S.
> sections of these Corporations of furthering the policy of eliminating
> any rate of pay differentials in various sections of the Corporations
> and of giving our members in these plants in Canada the advantage of
> the bargaining strength of our brothers in the U.S.[47]
> [Italics added.]

The degree of success achieved at Marmoraton with regard to
the third 1951 policy declaration was outstanding. This, to a large
extent, was due to effective action taken by the Canadian union.
Throughout the period delegates from Local 4854 and the Director
of District 6 or an official from the National Office participated in
negotiations with the Bethlehem Corporation. There has always been a
separate agreement covering Marmoraton but with the provision that it
will have the same termination date as the U.S. master agreement and
the same effective date for contract changes. After negotiations are
completed in the U.S. a letter is sent to the Marmoraton local detail-
ing what changes were worked out in the U.S. applicable to Local
4854.[48] While the union took effective actions to ensure such an
arrangement, their ability to apply the policy is accountable to the
fact that it is basically in tune with management policy.

There is no evidence to suggest that the company put up much
resistance to the arrangement proposed by the union. This was

47. Report to Staff Meeting, USWA Department of Industrial Engineering,
Hamilton, Ont., January 29, 1955 (in the files of the National Office, USWA,
Toronto).

48. It has been noted that most benefits at Marmoraton are identical to
those in the U.S. There are some differences, however, due to the fact that the
mine is in Canada. The Marmoraton pension plan is the same as that in the
U.S. but the offsets for government pensions are different because of the
differences in Federal legislation. Similarly, the welfare plans are not identical because of legisation in Ontario.

confirmed in interviews with Canadian union officials.[49]   The reason for the company attitude is probably partially contained in the administrative area. It is undoubtedly much easier and perhaps less costly for the company to include the Marmoraton workers in U.S. negotiations.   Marmoraton is the only Canadian subsidiary of the company so that, rather than providing a well-trained industrial relations staff in Canada, it simplifies matters to centralize policy in the U.S.[50]   It was noted that Bethlehem signs a master agreement with the USWA which covers employees in a number of U.S. industries. This was a significant determinant of union policy. Bethlehem provided a situation where the U.S.-Canada corporate link was distinct and identifiable. It was a simple matter for the union to send representatives to the U.S., sit in on Bethlehem negotiations, and ask for U.S. wage standards. Decision-making is at that level on the company side and international bargaining was a natural consequence.   It was simply an extension of current practices followed by the parties in dealing with each other in the U.S. This, plus the strategic element, no doubt accounts for the ready agreement on the part of the company to the union suggestion to use the Cornwall, Pennsylvania, agreement as a benchmark during 1953 negotiations. A Canadian union official succinctly summed up the situation with the following statement: "They are not going to let a little operation like Marmoraton distort policy that may be used against them in U.S. negotiations."[51]

The policy the union followed in developing the CWS program was symptomatic of the situation. According to the union, when the program was constructed the negotiations were between local management and Canadian union officials but constant recourse to U.S. management was necessary throughout the process.[52] "Local people at Marmoraton just couldn't make decisions because of corporate structure. We found it necessary to talk to U.S. management."[53] In order to be in a position to tie-in Marmoraton negotiations with those of the parent firm in the future, the union agreed to conform

---

49. Interviews with J. Norton, E. Park, and P. Tirrell, National Office, USWA, Toronto, May 26 and 27, 1966.

50. One manifestation of such centralization is the resolution of fourth stage grievances.   The Marmoraton contract provides that — "Except as otherwise agreed by the Company and the Union, meetings which shall be required under this Step No. 4 shall be held at Marmora, Ontario, within 60 days."   According to Eamon Park, Assistant to the National Director, however, most of the grievances which reach stage 4 must be resolved with the company in the U.S. at the latter's request.

51. Interview with P. Tirrell, Department of Industrial Engineering, National Office, USWA, Toronto, May 26, 1966.

52. *Ibid.*

53. Interview with H. Waisglass, Research Director, USWA, National Office, Toronto, May 27, 1966.

to the Bethlehem CWS manual even though it meant that, in a limited number of cases, jobs were placed in lower classifications than ordinarily would have been agreed to by them.

There are three other factors which help explain Bethlehem's acceptance of the tie-in arrangement. Firstly, wages, as a percentage of total costs, are relatively low, and capital expenditures are extremely high at Marmoraton. Secondly, there are only 250 employees in the Marmoraton labor force which constitutes a minute proportion of Bethlehem's total work force of over 90,000 hourly-paid employees. The cost to Bethlehem of providing U.S. wages and benefits to Marmoraton employees is exceedingly small when considered on a company basis.[54] Thirdly, a shortage of labor in the industry provides an appropriate background.

The union has attempted to pave the way for similar arrangements at some other U.S. controlled mines. The lack of success in the rest of the industry has been just as notable as the Marmoraton achievement, notwithstanding their introduction of CWS to the industry and the close to parity wages which they have achieved at some mines. They have not even pressed vigorously for the Marmoraton arrangement at the Lowphos, Caland, IOCO, Quebec Cartier, or Adams operations. There seem to be a number of reasons for this. The most basic one is that because the mines do not compete with each other, there is no pressure on either the union or management to be industry oriented in their wage policies. In addition, there are institutional dimensions to be considered.

Firstly, there is no other corporate link as direct as the one between Marmoraton and Bethlehem, with the exception of the Quebec Cartier - U.S. Steel relationship. In each of the other cases the mines are controlled by a multiplicity of interests, are not captive, or there is no direct link between operating management and management in U.S. basic steel. Steep Rock, for example, is not a captive mine and Caland is simply a leased property within the Steep Rock development. Lowphos while owned by National Steel is managed by the M.S. Hanna Company; IOCO by Hollinger-

---

54. A USWA Canadian official tells of an amusing incident in which he was involved which suggests another possible factor — lack of company information regarding their Canadian operations. In his words — "In 1956 we reached a settlement at Bethlehem but it took two weeks to get the contract language. At Bethlehem, Malony [union] said, 'Get the Canadian situation straightened away'. The U.S. workers stayed out an additional day to pressure Bethlehem on the question of Canadian operations. We spend the whole day working out Marmoraton terms. After agreement was reached the company negotiator turned to me and said, 'Where is this Marmoraton place anyway'." Interview with Eamon Park, Assistant to the National Director, National Office, USWA, Toronto, May 27, 1966.

Hanna; and the Hilton and Adams Mines by Pickands-Mather. This type of corporate relationship has been influential in inhibiting the union from expanding the area of direct impact of U.S. settlements to international dimensions.[55]   Although Quebec Cartier has the same type of U.S. parentage which prevails at Marmoraton, it is a late arrival to the industry and policy centralization does not seem to be as great as at Bethlehem.

The second reason is traceable to union policy in Canada. The union, by choice in many cases, has settled for a variety of benefits within the industry in response to the different situations its membership faces at specific mines. The result is that at certain operations it is not feasible to follow the U.S. pattern. This is the case at IOCO. There, they have negotiated the highest shift and Sunday premiums in the Canadian industry. Due to the fact that work at IOCO mines is scheduled around the clock, seven days a week, this is an important feature to the employees. Also, high on the priority list to a labor force working in an isolated area are annual paid vacations. They have, therefore, negotiated the most liberal regular paid vacations at IOCO for either the Canadian or U.S. industries.   The company has also agreed to provide free transportation by train for employees, their family, and car from Wabush Lake and Schefferville to Seven Islands when an employee takes his vacation.   This pragmatic approach is attributable in part to the autonomy which locals have in determining demands. "When National officers negotiate with a company they must get a mandate from the local involved."[56]   The result is a lack of fringe uniformity within the industry in Canada and little resemblance to U.S. practices. This makes any systematic tie-in difficult.

Interviews at the National Office revealed other reasons for the lack of a U.S. tie-in at specific mines. These reinforce the above two.   Again, it is apparent that in some cases the union does not have the power or, in others, the desire to bring about such a relationship.   The situation at Steep Rock was described this way:

> The Steep Rock establishment first of all is not a captive mine. It is, of course, a Cyrus Eaton interest but from the beginning we couldn't tie-in with his U.S. steel interests.   Really it's an historical situation more than anything else.   Also, you have the influence of Algoma.   The settlement there influences negotiations at Steep Rock. This also extends to Lowphos.   Both of these factors exert some influence.   Also, it's hard to develop the militancy of miners at Steep Rock to back a policy of tying-in with the United States.   They were

55. This was substantiated in an interview with the USWA Canadian Research Director.

56. Interview with H. Waisglass, Research Director, National Office, USWA, Toronto, May 27, 1966.

> mostly farmers. You have to look at Caland within this context, as well.[57]

Another official stated:

> Steep Rock is a Cyrus Eaton outfit. They've been able to resist any such arrangement. It's been an up and down situation and this, as much as anything else has prevented a closer relationship with the U.S. We have never tried to relate Caland to Inland. One reason is that CWS in the U.S. [Inland Steel] is a bit different.[58]

In addition to the Algoma settlement influencing Lowphos, it was felt that a propitious occasion for pushing for international bargaining at the latter had not yet arisen. Originally, it was felt that the mine at Capreol would be a short-run operation, with a life expectancy of approximately ten years. This factor has restrained the union to this point.[59]

Two supporting reasons were given for the lack of international pattern bargaining at IOCO and other mines in the Quebec-Labrador area. Here it seemed to be by choice rather than circumstance. Firstly, the union has felt that they can be more effective by negotiating independently, or as an official who had been directly involved in IOCO negotiations said: "We feel we can deliver more outside a U.S. master agreement than we could within it."[60] He did not rule out the possibility of at least limited international pattern bargaining in the future, however. An interesting second element was that of "self-determination" for French-Canadians.[61] International unions, in Quebec particularly, face the problem of economic nationalism. Any strategy leading to a closer tie with U.S. negotiations would have to be considered in this sociological context.

While there has been no extension of the Marmoraton procedure to the rest of the industry, union policy has been affected by the existence of U.S. capital. In essence, *segments* of the Canadian industry are considered by both sides as an extension of the U.S. basic steel industry. Union and corporate policies are basically complementary.

In their negotiations and before conciliation boards the union made frequent reference to labor standards in the U.S. basic steel industry. By no means atypical is the following reference to the Lowphos-National Steel relationship:

---

57. *Ibid.*
58. Interview with Eamon Park, Assistant to the National Director, National Office, USWA, Toronto, May 27, 1966.
59. *Ibid.*
60. Interview with P. Burke, past Director of District 5, USWA, at the National Office, Toronto, May 27, 1966.
61. *Ibid.*

We might point out that this Company in every important respect is part of the U.S. iron and steel industry. It is a wholly owned subsidiary of National Steel Corporation . . . . Since Lowphos was established and functions as an integral part of the parent firm's operations, there is every reason to look to the U.S. industry pattern when wages and other economic benefits are being considered . . . .

There is no logical reason for continuation of these wage differences and our position is that the present negotiations should result in a substantial movement towards parity with U.S. rates . . . .

Since Canadian shipments of iron ore to U.S. mills have been running well ahead of 1961 levels, it is safe to say that Lowphos contributed more than proportionably to the increase in National's revenue and operating profit.[62]

They also use the U.S. pattern indirectly in Canadian negotiations by using Marmoraton as a benchmark. Such references to U.S. practices, directly and indirectly, were not ephemeral; rather, recurrent reference was made to international corporate structure and the significance that this should have with regard to wages and fringe benefits in the Canadian iron ore industry. There was also U.S. influence of a more tangible nature affecting Canadian labor-management relations. The use of U.S. basic steel as a benchmark was just one manifestation and is the least significant aspect. One of the notable features was the variety and broad scope of conspicuous U.S. influence beyond the use of coercive comparisons. The examples given below are illustrative of this.

When CWS was introduced at Hilton it was agreed that, with minor modifications, it would be the same as the manual at U.S. Steel. The agreement was confirmed by correspondence to the national office from Pickands-Mather.[63] Also agreements were delayed at Lowphos and in Northern Quebec until settlement of the 1959 U.S. steel strike. A settlement was dependent on the U.S. situation being resolved. Shortly after contracts were signed at IOCO and Lowphos the Director of District 5 (Quebec) stated:

I may remind you that the United Steelworkers of America has, since its inception, recognized the right of the Canadian locals to set their own policies in matters which are of Canadian concern. These include wages, other contract provisions and legislative objectives.

However, where Canadian locals deal with branches of American industry in Canada and where arrangements are feasible, joint U.S.-Canadian negotiations are held. So, the effects of the victory in the U.S. were felt in District 5 when in March we signed new contracts with the Iron Ore Co. of Canada which is largely controlled by certain American steel companies . . . .

---

62. Submission of the Union to the Conciliation Board, United Steelworkers of America and Lowphos Ore, Ltd., December 12, 1962, pp. 4, 5 (in the files of the National Office, USWA, Toronto).

63. Correspondence to Eamon Park from Pickands-Mather dated September 13, 1958 (in the files of the National Office, USWA, Toronto).

An impressive feature of these negotiations was the solidarity of the IOC locals; the Quebec locals refused to sign their contracts until the IOC-associated Hanna Corporation reached agreement with the local at Lowphos Ore at Capreol, Ont. Here is another clear indication of the value of national and international policy in collective bargaining.[64]

Because of the captive mines situation, therefore, Canadian union policy in the industry considers collective bargaining developments in U.S. basic steel for strategic purposes; and management, in some cases, does so as well. This would seem to result in an occasional timing influence. There are other examples, as well.

When a pension plan was negotiated at Lowphos, and subsequent changes were made to the plan, the details were worked out by the Hanna Mining Company at their Cleveland office as the managing agent for National Steel. This necessitated direct communication between U.S. management and the national office of the union. Because corporate decision-making power resides in the U.S., Canadian union officials must deal with management at that level.

U.S. management of Hanna also played a direct role in the certification of the USWA at IOCO. The procedure involved in gaining certification was long and bitter, due, among other things, to the political climate in Quebec at that time. Local management of the company initially decided to oppose the entrance of the Steelworkers and an independent union was set up in 1954. The USWA successfully organized the dock workers at Seven Islands which gave them leverage in that they could control ore shipments from IOCO's mines. In 1957, according to the union, their certification application was held up by the Quebec government. Under a union threat that they would shut down the company's operations in both countries, a top Hanna executive from Cleveland met with the legal counsel of the USWA, Arthur Goldberg, and worked out the details of the bargaining unit. Certification was granted shortly thereafter.[65] Because of the series of events the union feels that there was an agreement between the company and the Quebec government.

> None of it was out in the open but there must have been an arrangement between the government and IOCO. We talked with McManus [Canadian manager of IOCO] after the meeting between Goldberg and the company in the States. He tried to stall but finally agreed to the terms worked out. He then picked up the phone right in front of us and called Cleveland. We heard him say, 'Go ahead and tell your friend Duplessis it's O.K. to grant certification'.[66]

64. District 5 Report to the National Policy Conference, USWA, April 21-22, 1960, Montreal, Quebec (in the files of the National Office, USWA, Toronto), pp. 1-3.
65. Interviews with Eamon Park and P. Burke, National Office, USWA, Toronto, May 26 and 27, 1966.
66. Interview with Eamon Park, USWA, National Office, Toronto, May 27, 1966.

While not as direct and all encompassing as at Marmoraton, these occurrences clearly illustrate that U.S. influence is present and tangible at other firms in the Canadian industry. The influences clearly take place on both sides. While union wage policy as such is not always affected, decision-making in the U.S. has already had some influence on collective bargaining. Furthermore, the union expects that the Bethlehem-Marmoraton arrangement can and will be extended to other iron ore companies in the future because of U.S. ownership and the continental shipments of ore. The greatest likelihood of international bargaining emerging in future years exists at Lowphos and Quebec Cartier. Both are captive mines involving relatively small numbers of employees (140 and 600, respectively) and at each the union has found it necessary at times to deal with U.S. management. In order to facilitate the possible inclusion of Lowphos in U.S. basic steel negotiations the USWA Canadian Industrial Engineering Department agreed, against their better judgment, to combine job classes 1 and 2 in order to be in line with the practice of National Steel. "We went along with combining job class 1 and 2 at Lowphos for future expediency."[67]

At Quebec Cartier, "U.S. Steel leadership became overt at the first set of negotiations."[68] The union feels that the mine will become the pattern-setter in Quebec. Even though IOCO is the largest producer in Canada it is not a leader in bargaining. If such a pattern does emerge it is most probable that U.S. Steel management will play a greater role in Quebec Cartier negotiations increasing the likelihood of patterns set in U.S. basic steel spreading into the Quebec industry. The degree of U.S. policy control exercised in the industrial relations area at IOCO is already substantial. The union feels that local management have little authority. Major decisions are made in the U.S. "At IOCO and Quebec Cartier there are fairly direct negotiations with local management but they continue only up to the point when the conciliation officer enters and then they make phone calls to 'higher ups' in the United States."[69] Whether the union would want to pursue a policy of international bargaining in the face of anti-international unionism in Quebec is another matter, but it should be noted that they have not ruled out the possibility of trying to apply at least part of the U.S. pattern. The course they expect to follow, however, is to "maintain wage parity and close the fringe benefit gap".[70]

67. Interview with P. Tirrell, Industrial Engineering Department, National Office, USWA, Toronto, May 26, 1966.
68. Interview with H. Waisglass, Research Director, National Office, USWA, Toronto, May 27, 1966.
69. Interview with Eamon Park, Assistant to the National Director, National Office, USWA, Toronto, May 27, 1966.
70. Interview with P. Burke, National Office, USWA, Toronto, May 26, 1966.

Attempts to extend the practice of international negotiations, the pressure for wage parity, and the use of U.S. ownership as a lever, therefore, will undoubtedly continue in the future. The USWA sees such an arrangement not only as having real value but necessary in dealing with U.S. subsidiaries. Additionally, international headquarters has enunciated a policy of dealing with the threat of Canadian imports to its U.S. membership by favoring free trade but at the same time emphasizing the elimination of low-wage competition.

The large increase in iron ore shipments emanating from Canada, coupled with the decline in production and employment on the Mesabi Range, gave rise to complaints from some employees and producers in the U.S. in 1959 regarding low-wage competition from Canada and other countries. Such complaints resulted in hearings on the situation in 1960 before the U.S. Tariff Commission. In a brief presented to the Commission, however, the USWA opposed the imposition of a tariff or quota on iron ore.[71] At the same time the situation has resulted in greater cognizance of the importance of standardizing working conditions in the industry on a North American basis. Specific concern was expressed from the U.S. section of the union and in 1960 the director of District 33, which includes the Mesabi iron ore mines, attended the Canadian National Policy Conference in Montreal. To a group of iron ore delegates he spoke of the need to eliminate the international differential "as uniformity throughout the industry was essential in the interests of workers in both countries".[72] The research director in Canada indicated that "there are informal exchanges of points of view between District 33 and Sefton and Mahoney. But it is not highly structured; it's very casual".[73] Union negotiators in Canada, therefore, are well informed with respect to developments on the Mesabi and the growth of Canada's iron ore industry prompted the Canadian section in 1960 to adopt a resolution to eliminate the international differential at a time when the wage parity objective had diminished in importance in

---

71. Testimony by Meyer Bernstein, International Affairs Representative, USWA, before the United States Tariff Commission, Iron Ore Hearings, October 18, 1960 (in the files of the National Ofice, USWA, Toronto).

The hearings were of some concern to Canada. The *Labour Gazette* reported after the 1960 settlements at Bethlehem, Lowphos, and IOCO which reduced the U.S.-Canadian differential — "An indirect result of the new wage scale may be some easing of pressures from areas in the U.S. that were calling for tariffs against iron ore because it came from what was termed a 'low-wage country'." *Labour Gazette* (Canada, Department of Labour), April 1960, p. 342.

72. Summary of the National Policy Conference, April 21-22, 1960, Montreal, Quebec (in the files of the National Office, USWA, Toronto), p. 5.

73. Interview with H. Waisglass, National Office, USWA, Toronto, May 27, 1966.

basic steel.[74] This policy was re-stated by the national director at a USWA conference in the United States. In part he said: " . . . the only way to protect the interests of the U.S. miners is to make sure that U.S. investors in Canada meet the same standards they must meet in the U.S."[75]

While rising exports to the U.S. have resulted in some additional union pressure to eliminate the international differential, North American wage uniformity *per se* has not been an intransigent policy pursued by the union. Instead, they have taken on each company one at a time and pushed for the highest wages possible in each individual situation rather than unremittingly demanding wage parity in every case, or even the standardization of wages within the Canadian industry. The union apparently adjusts its demands to meet the needs of a particular situation, if the adjustments can be made without a serious threat to the employment in other mines on the continent. At IOCO, where the level of wages increased more than any other company from 1957 to 1962, productivity was extremely high and consequently the impact on labor costs was probably no greater than at most other Canadian firms. The union while driving up the wage level has cooperated in raising the level of productivity.[76] When the focus was shifted to companies with less ability to pay, demands were scaled down considerably.

The lack of co-ordination in the Canadian industry has been noted but cannot be overemphasized in this connection. Even by the late 1960's this situation remained essentially the same. Before co-ordination takes place on an industry-wide basis it will be necessary to achieve greater co-ordination in negotiations at groups of mines. The union has already gone some distance in that direction but their policy so far is to standardize rates by area thus indicating the importance of labor market conditions. All of the mines in the Steep Rock area have similar expiration dates and experience very similar wage changes. The union also follows the policy of having simultaneous negotiations in the Quebec-Labrador area and has established equality of rates in that region. Even this small degree of co-ordination is difficult to achieve and maintain because of the

---

74. Policy Resolutions of the United Steelworkers of America in Canada, as adopted by National Policy Conferences, 1958-62 (in the files of the National Office, USWA, Toronto), p. 7.

75. *Steel Labor* (Canadian edition), September 1960, p. 7.

76. One union official stated — "We developed a training program jointly with IOCO. The labor force there, which is made up of lumberjacks and farmers, is the most efficient in the iron ore industry and that includes the United States. Hell, labor costs there are almost infinitesimal." Interview with P. Burke, past Director of District 5, at the National Office, USWA, Toronto, May 27, 1966.

diffuse labor markets. A second reason is the jealously guarded autonomy of the locals.[77]

With regard to the political aspects of the union's wage policy, the preferences of the membership, because of the autonomy of iron ore locals, undoubtedly played a role. They were of primary importance, however, in determining the particular form of the settlements. It was the union executive, on the other hand, who took the lead and established the Bethlehem-Marmoraton arrangement. The existence of coercive comparisons on the part of the Canadian locals, therefore, did not appear to be that important.

In total, the significant features of USWA Canadian policy have been its flexibility and the use made of U.S. corporate control by the union executive in their negotiations. If a Canadian company is a U.S. subsidiary the union generally attempts to link bargaining in Canada to bargaining with the U.S. parent firm. Their success in achieving such an arrangement has not been confined to the iron ore industry. It is also clear, however, that there must be other favorable circumstances to achieve such an arrangement. They have sought a similar relationship at other U.S. controlled firms and failed. All attempts at Timkin Roller Bearing Company, for example, resulted in absolutely no inroads. Expansion of the area of direct impact of a U.S. settlement seems to go hand in hand with centralization of corporate industrial relations policy. This was the case at Marmoraton and Union Drawn. At Timkin, on the other hand: "Policy is centralized only in the sense that they hate the union, period. They hate it in Canada and they hate it in the United States. As a consequence we've made no headway there."[78]

In iron ore, in addition to U.S. control, the union, therefore, faced other factors which shaped their policy and procedures, viz., the captive mines situation plus free trade which resulted in heavy reliance by the Canadian industry on U.S. basic steel output; the minute labor cost to total cost ratio, the widely divergent ability-to-pay situations. These environmental and economic factors have affected the approach of the union, elicited U.S. influence on Canadian iron ore

---

77. In debating whether there should be an Iron Ore Council in Canada several local representatives raised the question of the infringement of such a body on local autonomy. It was necessary to point out "that the Council would not make hard and fast decisions which could adversely affect any particular local but would coordinate activities in support of over-all objectives." Meeting of Iron Ore Delegates, National Policy Conference, Montreal, Quebec, April 23, 1960 (in the files of the National Office, USWA, Toronto).

78. Interview with P. Tirrell, Department of Industrial Engineering, National Office, USWA, Toronto, May 26, 1966.

labor-management relations, and resulted in increased pressure for U.S. wage parity.[79] Faced with international integration of the corporate side, the international scope of the union was used to a considerable extent while, at the same time, union policy seemed to respond to the economic realities.

---

79. With only one union in the industry it was not possible to make any judgment on the existence of more than one union as a force eliciting union pressure for U.S. labor standards. It is interesting to note, however, that the union used the fact that they had negotiated U.S. benefits in a certification battle with another union in 1965 at Continental Can. They also see the existence of the Extended Vacation Plan at a number of Canadian plants as a strong weapon for organizational purposes.

CHAPTER 7

SUMMARY AND EVALUATION

It is appropriate at this point to draw together all of the material with an overall assessment of the major findings and their implications. It should be stressed that in discussing U.S.-Canada uniformity there is no intended implication concerning the effect of various forces on wages. The emphasis is on inter-relationships in terms of processes and practices only. A further caveat is in order. The limited number of cases examined and the qualitative nature of the data introduced limit the analytical power of the study. Just as basic is the question of whether the relationships will remain basically the same over time and the applicability to other industries. In light of this any generalizations should be construed as tentative.

The purpose of this chapter is, in any case, to bring together the results of the five separate studies in order to analyze them as a whole. Differences in the practice and process of bargaining, and similarities which cut across the cases are set forth. An attempt is made to account for the observed relationships. The chapter is divided along the following lines — (1) a synopsis of the major findings; (2) a discussion of the results; and (3) some concluding observations. Within the first section, the predominant pattern relationships are consolidated in a table. Conclusions with regard to substantive and procedural aspects are specified and discussed. The emphasis then shifts from bargaining practices to the question of bi-national patterns and the length of negotiations and strike activity. The final part of the first section assesses the role of constituent groups in the bargaining process. This includes an evaluation of the compulsory conciliation process as it relates to this study. The emphasis in section two is on the relationships between the findings and the institutional variables discussed in Chapter 1. This is followed by a consideration of intra-organizational and other implications of bi-national bargaining. Attention is then directed, in the final section, to the potential dangers stemming from international pattern-bargaining. The chapter concludes with some random remarks on the issue of international unionism and bi-national bargaining, based on the case studies.

A SYNOPSIS OF THE MAJOR FINDINGS

Pattern Configuration

The variety of experiences between and within the industries is apparent in Table 7-1. There were mixtures and degrees of bi-

Table 7-1

CONFIGURATION AND CONTENT OF BI-NATIONAL INFLUENCE IN INDUSTRIES ANALYZED

PATTERN CONFIGURATION / TYPE OF BI-NATIONAL INFLUENCE	U.S. BARGAINING UNIT	CANADIAN BARGAINING UNIT		
		U.S. PATTERN INFLUENCE		NO U.S. INFLUENCE
		CONSISTENT	SPORADIC	
	A	B	C	D
WAGE AND FRINGE CHANGES I	MARMORATON UNION DRAWN	GENERAL MOTORS FORD CHRYSLER AMERICAN MOTORS	STUDEBAKER	
WAGE CHANGES II		CANADIAN INT. PAPER ONTARIO PAPER COS. QUEBEC PAPER COS.	B.C. PAPER COS.	CANADA PACKERS, BURNS, ET AL DOSCO VOLVO SEGMENTS OF IRON ORE SEGMENTS OF PAPER
TIMING ONLY III			ALGOMA STELCO IOCO QUEBEC CARTIER LOWPHOS	
FRINGE CHANGES IV			SWIFT CANADIAN	

national pattern bargaining, each industry having its own unique characteristics and ensuing bargaining contours. The configuration of U.S. pattern influences varied considerably. The most complete form — expansion of the U.S. bargaining unit to encompass Canadian employees — occurred at Marmoraton in iron ore and at Union Drawn in steel. At the opposite extreme, the pattern in meat packing was divorced from developments in the U.S. Within this context, however, Swift Canadian patterned some of its fringes after those at the parent firm. In between, there were international relationships in the auto and paper industries through pattern-bargaining, and in the central segment of the steel industry. Both U.S. wage and fringe changes were extended into the Canadian auto industry primarily after 1956, while in paper the bi-national relationship was predominantly in terms of wage changes. The manifestaton in steel was confined for the most part to the timing of wage increases. On two occasions outside the central analysis period (1952 and 1966), the U.S.-Canada differential, however, defined the size of the Canadian increase. In addition to the Marmoraton experience in iron ore, the mines in Northern Quebec achieved approximate parity with U.S. mines on the Mesabi Range, and agreement at several mines was delayed in 1959 because of the U.S. steel strike.

It would seem, then, that a stereotyped conception of what constitutes bi-national bargaining escapes rigid generalization. Instead, various structures and permutations are present. The U.S.-Canada relationships can be characterized as strong in paper and in autos (after 1956); fairly strong in segments of steel and iron ore; and extremely weak in meat packing.

Substantive Aspects

Various elements of international standardization in wages, fringes, or both, existed in at least segments of each industry. These are treated below.

Wage Levels and Changes

Wage equality with the U.S. was an issue in the paper, auto, steel, and iron ore industries. It was achieved, but in varying degrees, in segments of each of those industries. It took the form of a conscious movement toward wage parity that was gradual in autos and iron ore. In paper, Canadian common labor rates consistently corresponded to those in specified U.S. regions but they were not equal to those in the highest paying U.S. region (*i.e.,* the West Coast). There was a lack of consistency in steel, but, as noted, on two occasions parity was achieved and then lost. Wage parity at Union Drawn, however, has been maintained since 1954.

From the evidence it would appear that the parity concept is a nebulous one and that great care is required when comparing agreements that are apparently uniform on both sides of the border. An assumption is often made that parity will mean equal real income and identical wage structures. This, of course, need not be the case. The evidence indicates that, where wage equality is claimed, it is really an attenuated version. Firstly, wage levels were transmitted in terms of domestic currency. Union Drawn provided the single case where Canadian rates were equivalent to the highest paying U.S. company when the Canadian dollar was at a premium. To have made exchange rate adjustments to Canadian settlements would simply have added another dimension and complication to negotiations. In any case, the parties did not introduce adjustments.[1] This would seem to indicate that the unions look upon U.S. levels as proper and sellable in Canada, rather than reflecting a desire for equal real income. The administrative and strategic aspects are probably the paramount considerations.

Secondly, within the more limited concept of parity in Canadian dollars, it was not complete in terms of producing equivalent wage structures on the two sides of the border. Common labor rates have most typically been the ones equalized. Marmoraton and Union Drawn constitute the only cases where rates for each job class are the same as in the U.S. In both cases, however, the wage structure is more compressed in Canada, in that no jobs have been slotted in the higher classifications. The auto companies have agreed to wage parity for all jobs but, at this point, only in principle. Also, the U.S. cost-of-living clause has been more liberal. Thirdly, parity in both wages and fringes exists, to date, at only two of the companies analyzed. Again, Marmoraton and Union Drawn, both extremely small in terms of employees, were the exceptions.

Where there has been a substantial U.S.-Canada differential the movement to parity has been gradual. In autos, the movement began in 1964 and presumably will be completed by this year. At Marmoraton it took over ten years to eliminate the international differential. In addition, it has rarely been a permanent phenomenon. Lastly, when achieved at major producers, the standardization has not been complete in terms of covering all companies in an industry.

---

1. The 1967 Chrysler agreement deals specifically with this point. The memorandum states — "Wage rates in plants of Chrysler Canada shall be stated in Canadian currency, and wage rates in plants of Chrysler in the United States shall be stated in United States currency, and it shall be conclusively presumed that said currencies are on a par with each other . . . regardless of the rate of exchange at any given time or from time to time."

In conclusion, American wages provided a target in four of the industries. They seemed to constitute a ceiling, however, rather than a floor and the nominal, rather than the real, diffential was of primary concern.

There were a number of cases where U.S. wage changes defined Canadian wage adjustments. International pattern-bargaining, in terms of wage changes, was well developed throughout two industries — autos and paper. The U.S. pattern was carried predominantly in percentage amount, however, so that the effect on wage structure was not so severe. In one round Canadian steel followed the U.S. pattern but this was limited to a 5 cent increase. At Union Drawn, the absolute and percentage increases were the same as at Republic. This was the only case where it would be accurate to portray a Canadian agreement as a carbon copy of an agreement in the U.S. Pattern plus agreements took place at Marmoraton and at some mines in Northern Quebec.

Three generalizations, therefore, seem appropriate with regard to the wage adjustment aspect. Firstly, agreements in the two countries were rarely identical. Secondly, when U.S. patterns were consistently applied they were conveyed predominantly in percentage amount. Thirdly, pattern plus agreements were not widespread.

Fringe Benefits

Most of the benefits negotiated in the U.S. auto industry were transferred to the Canadian industry. Swift, in the meat packing industry, has a distinctly different array of benefits from the other Canadian packers. Marmoraton and Union Drawn departed in significant ways from the practice in Canadian steel and iron ore in this regard, as well. In both cases, all of the major U.S. benefits were included in the Canadian contract.

Three facts stand out in this area. Firstly, in every case where U.S. benefits were transmitted, U.S. subsidiaries were involved. Administrative advantages, therefore, were probably a primary consideration particularly to the companies. Secondly, while benefits were similar, costs probably were not. Lower base rates in autos and at Swift Canadian and eligibility credits at Marmoraton and Union Drawn would attenuate the cost impact. Thirdly, where applicable, differences in the social security system were taken into account by providing for different offsets. At times there were minor anomalies in Canadian agreements because of international pattern-bargaining. At Marmoraton, for example, the escalator clause was based on the U.S. Consumer Price Index.

Procedural Aspects and the Bargaining Agenda

One of the consequences of international bargaining seemed to be the introduction to the bargaining agenda of issues which would otherwise be downgraded or completely ignored. Although speculative, in some cases the contract talks have probably been tilted more towards fringes than would otherwise have been the case. Benefits such as the extended vacation plan, which was introduced during the U.S. automation scare, have not been high priority demands in Canada but were transferred in any case at Union Drawn and Marmoraton. Moving allowances in autos may be another example. SUB, as well, became an immediate issue after it was negotiated in the U.S. In addition to shifting the content of negotiations, another aspect has been the introduction of U.S. wage adjustment approaches. The CWS program in steel and iron ore, the annual-improvement-factor in autos arrived in Canada shortly after their development in the United States.

A second procedural aspect involved the timing of negotiations. The attractiveness of U.S. settlements as a standard for Canadian negotiators was demonstrated by the timing of agreements and expiry dates in all the industries except meat packing. Again, among and within the four industries, a broad experience was in evidence. At one extreme, the timing was precise by expanding the U.S. bargaining unit (Marmoraton and Union Drawn). At the other, U.S. and Canadian expiry dates were generally dissimilar but with occasional overlap and a consequent delay in Canadian negotiations while the U.S. situation was resolved. This occurred in segments of steel and iron ore. As an added dimension in steel, the date on which yearly increases became effective was changed from March to August to concur with the practice in the U.S. industry. The auto and paper industries remained somewhere in between by providing for U.S. and Canadian expiry dates, which were only one to three months apart.

Another procedural factor much in evidence was the participation of U.S. negotiators on both sides of the table. This is discussed in later sections.

The Length of Negotiations and Strike Activity

From the analysis of negotiations two notable features seemed to be in evidence. These involve the efficacy of the negotiations. Firstly, lengthy negotiations prevailed, particularly in steel and autos, when there was no U.S. pattern to follow. Secondly, there appeared to be a greater incidence of strikes over non-pattern-following issues. Table 7-2 summarizes the results — in meat packing, steel, paper and autos — regarding the length of negotiations and strike

Table 7-2

APPROXIMATE AVERAGE LENGTH OF NEGOTIATIONS
(IN DAYS) AND STRIKE ACTIVITY, KEY NEGOTIATIONS,
MEAT PACKING, STEEL, EAST AND WEST COAST PAPER,
AND AUTO INDUSTRIES, 1953-62.[a]

	Meat Packing	Steel	Pulp and Paper		Autos
			East	West	
Approx. avg. length of negotiations	106(6)	193(5)	80(8)	111(7)	148(5)
Approx. avg. when not following U.S. pattern	106(6)	228(2)	60(4)	235(1)	240(3)
Approx. avg. when following U.S. pattern	—	170(3)	97(4)	90(6)	87(2)
Avg. length between U.S. and Canadian settlements when U.S. pattern set first	—	27(3)	103(4)	35(6)	57(2)
No. of strikes when not following U.S. pattern	—	1	—	1	2
Length	—	74	—	91	109; 148
No. of strikes when following U.S. pattern	—	—	—	—	1
Length	—	—	—	—	2

a. Figures in brackets denote the number of observations.

activity for the key negotiations in Canada. Sufficient data was not available in iron ore for a similar tabulation.

Any firm conclusion is limited by the number of observations. It is interesting to note, however, that negotiations were much longer in steel, autos and in the B.C. paper industry when the parties were not following the U.S. pattern or when one did not exist to use as a benchmark. In the paper industry in eastern Canada the opposite occurred. In cases where eastern firms followed the U.S. pattern, however, negotiations were not unduly long. The average length was approximately the same as in the meat packing industry. The shorter length when not following the U.S. pattern in this case, is also somewhat misleading. When eastern firms were not following the U.S. pattern the continental pattern was set in that region. In these cases negotiations were very short.

When the U.S. pattern was followed the paper and auto negotiations were shorter than the average in meat packing. Steel negotiations were by far the longest, even when there was a U.S. pattern to follow. The parties in steel used conciliation in every round and this probably accounts for the longer length of time. The average length of time consumed after the U.S. pattern was set, was only 27 days in steel, 35 in B.C. paper, 57 days in autos but approximately 100 days in eastern Canada paper. On two occasions, however, negotiations had been postponed in eastern Canada by agreement of the parties.

In the four industries there was only one strike over a U.S. issue. This occurred in the auto industry. It concerned the issue of pension parity. The strike lasted only two days. In contrast, when the parties were not following a U.S. pattern there was one strike in steel (74 days), one in paper (91 days), and two in the auto industry (109 and 148 days). The limited evidence that exists, therefore, supports the view that, for these industries at least, following the U.S. pattern does not result in more intractable negotiations.

The Role of Constituent Groups

The next three sections consider the findings concerning the role and policy of management, labor, and the government. The focus is on the bargaining process.

The Companies

Collective bargaining theory places an important responsibility on unions in the spreading of patterns, and in the case analyses this held true. It seems clear, however, that in cases where pattern relationships existed, employer policies also contributed to the transmission process. At least some company co-ordination with U.S. negotiations was a feature common to each of the cases that entailed concurrent wage changes. The auto companies, notably GM and Chrysler, helped precipitate the transmission process by the active participation of U.S. officials in Canadian negotiations. In 1967, the Canadian package was negotiated entirely by U.S. Chrysler officials in Detroit. In the paper industry, there were various company policies. Apparently, some U.S. subsidiaries were given broad discretion, others were quite centralized. Additionally, as a clearing-house of wage and collective bargaining information for practically all mills on the continent, the Canadian Pulp and Paper Association (in cooperation with the American Pulp and Paper Association) fulfilled the co-ordination function on the employer side. As far back as 1929, Swift had co-ordinated U.S. and Canadian industrial relations policy. It had unilaterally extended some U.S. fringes to the Swift Canadian labor force. During negotiations Canadian officials had to clear wage offers with the parent firm. In steel, the movement of effective dates for wage increases in order to conform with the U.S. date came after a request from Algoma Steel. There was little local autonomy allowed for company negotiators at Union Drawn and Marmoraton. Lastly, there were a number of occasions when local management negotiators in iron ore had to clear wage offers with their U.S. offices.

In no cases where U.S. patterns were followed did management seem to seriously resist. Common bi-national policies seemed to be acceptable to both sides. A large international corporation may prefer to direct Canadian industrial relations policy and probably increasingly so when faced with an international union. It is difficult to say whether corporate centralization preceded union pressures for uniformity in all cases. Centralization on the corporate side, however, seemed to come first. As noted, corporate paternalism at Swift goes back well before the entrance of the union. It was at their insistence that some fringes were tailored after their counterparts at the parent firm. There was apparently little corporate concern or resistance to the transmission of the Bethlehem pattern to the Canadian subsidiary. While the actions taken by the USWA executive fostered and facilitated the arrangement, the corporation was an accomplice; perhaps an unwilling one, although the evidence suggests just the opposite. The collective bargaining policy of the company was decidedly centralized prior to the pass-on and they agreed, without subjection to pressure, to use the U.S. agreement as a standard when negotiating the initial Marmoraton agreement. They agreed early in negotiations and as soon as it was suggested by the union. Although wages at several other iron mines have approached or equalled those in the U.S., the same type of system has not been agreed to, even though U.S. interests predominate in the industry. Significantly, centralized corporate policy was absent at those operations. They are operated by managing companies or owned by a multiplicity of interests.

There did not appear to be resistance in the pulp and paper industry. Indeed, during some periods prior to World War II, the Canadian industry had provided for automatic wage adjustments when a change had been made at a U.S. mill. A discussion and consideration of U.S. conditions, wage changes, and levels by the employers often constituted a major segment of Canadian negotiations.

It was also notable that the first UAW breakthrough as far as international pattern-bargaining is concerned came at GM — one of the auto companies which follows a fairly centralized labor relations course in dealing with its Canadian operations. Until 1964, the Canadian cost of individual items originally established in the U.S. were below those of the U.S. pattern. Oral testimony by auto officials in Canada, it will be recalled, indicated a preference for the international pattern-following system. Also, Chrysler agreed to the wage parity concept in 1967 with little observable resistance.

While Swift Canadian accepted some bi-national uniformity in fringes they resisted any extension of the practice to other areas. When the union approached Swift officials in the U.S. and requested the inclusion of Swift Canadian workers in the master agreement they were turned down. This limited the bi-national relationship to the dimension observed.

In any case, there are grounds for believing that employer actions and policies had a decided impact in shaping bargaining relationships between the two countries.

The Unions

The international unions differed somewhat in the internal processes whereby demands were formulated and in their bargaining practices. The pulp and paper unions were highly centralized in their bargaining activity. The UPWA and the USWA were more decentralized in the U.S.-Canada context. The UAW's position was somewhere in between — demands were formulated in Canada and U.S. officials generally participated in, but did not lead, Canadian negotiations. Certain features, however, cut across union lines.

Firstly, demands were formulated in each union at individual conferences in Canada. There was just one occasion where there appeared to be a direct carry-over of U.S. demands before negotiations began. This occurred within the IBPM in 1946.

At the beginning of the conference a few delegates from Pulp, Sulphite and Paper Mill Workers' locals stated that the International Brotherhood of Paper Makers had already submitted a program to the manufacturers, and these delegates voiced the objection of their locals to a program being submitted before all the locals had had a chance to meet and to draw up a program. Vice-President D'Aoust explained that the Paper Makers had just had their convention; that the delegates from all Paper Makers locals had already prepared their program at Columbus, Ohio, and that this program had been sent to the manufacturers. This came as a distinct shock to the Pulp

> Workers delegates. It presented a completely new situation. It was
> no longer a question of trying to reconcile two different ideas. One
> of these ideas had already been made into a program and had been
> presented to the manufacturers. The Paper Makers stated that this
> program could not be changed. This was their program and it was
> all settled.[2]

In that instance, however, the delegates from IBPM locals adjusted their demands to take into account the desires of the Canadian delegates from other unions. Otherwise, in each union the initial bargaining agenda seemed to be formulated by Canadian delegates.

Secondly, U.S. negotiators participated in Canadian negotiations predominantly when Canadian firms exported substantially to the U.S. That is, they showed little interest in Canadian negotiations unless U.S. members could conceivably be affected by employment shifts due to Canadian competition. The most publicized example of the importance of the product market has, of course, been the auto industry. With the signing of the auto pact, U.S. officials negotiated the key Canadian agreement for the first time. This is probably an extension of UAW policy. They normally pursue the same collective bargaining objectives throughout a given product market. When U.S. officials in the UAW participated prior to the passage of the auto pact, administrative considerations seemed to be of primary importance. They entered negotiations in the late stages and offered their expertise in resolving issues already on the table. They essentially played a "back room" role.

The paper unions have been following a somewhat similar course for years in the primary paper industry. The pressures for uniformity seemed to be particularly embodied at the U.S. leadership level. The presidents of the IBPSPMW and the IBPM participated in a substantial number of Canadian negotiations. On some occasions U.S. officials other than the above would participate. John Sherman, international vice-president of the Pulp and Sulphite Workers on the U.S. West Coast, chaired the B.C. negotiations. His counterpart for the IBPM was also generally present. They often led the negotiations for the union or played a commanding role. Through this process they pursued similar bargaining policies in the two countries. One reason was probably economic. One international official stated during negotiations:

> Competition is an important factor as between Canadian and U.S.
> producers, as well as between east and west. The wage structures

---

2. Ontario Newsprint Conference, 1946, Article 3 (in the files of the Department of Research and Education, IBPSPMW, Montreal, Quebec), p. 2.

of the two countries must be considered and do have a bearing on each other.[3]

The available transcripts of negotiations suggest strategic considerations, as well. The corporations argued that a pattern could not be established unless wages in other regions went up in a corresponding fashion. The following from 1950 negotiations highlights this type of interaction:

> I attended the Conference on the Pacific Coast this year. The employers there have been condemning our unions because of the low rates we agree to in the east. At the conference this year they used me as a machine gun target . . . . I defended our methods of bargaining in the East, but they asked me what I was going to do about Eastern competition.[4]

The policy of the USWA in iron ore was not precisely the same. U.S. officials did the negotiating for Marmoraton Mines, however, and became involved in the late stages of negotiations at several other mines. They did this by way of telephone calls from Canadian negotiators. Also, the Director of District 33 which encompasses the Mesabi Range, visited Canada in 1960 and held policy meetings with the iron ore locals. This may have been in response to pressures from U.S. locals which were concerned with Canadian competition. Just prior to his Canadian visit, a letter from a local to the Director of District 33 read in part:

> Prior to 1955, whenever a mine was closed down permanently, everyone in the community more or less accepted it as being caused by the depletion of a particular ore deposit. Since then, however, attention has been drawn to the importance of iron ore from foreign sources, especially Canada and South America and of course some very justified suspicions have begun to take effect.[5]

The link between the letter and his visit is tenuous but the letter indicated the feelings of the U.S. rank-and-file on the matter of Canadian imports.

USWA leaders have pursued a much less active role in Canadian basic steel. Significantly, the paucity of Canadian steel exports to the U.S. constitutes little danger to the rank-and-file in that country. At no time did they come to Canada to supervise negotiations. This was also the case of U.S. officials in the UPWA.

A third aspect of union policy that was notable was the extent to which negotiators sought the most effective decision-making unit

---

3. Ontario Newsprint and Pulp Conference, Toronto, April 18, 1950 (in the files of the Department of Research and Education, IBPSPMW, Montreal, Quebec).

4. Canadian International Paper Company and Subsidiary and Affiliated Companies, Labor Conference, April 26, 1950 (in the files of the Department of Research and Education, IBPSPMW, Montreal, Quebec).

5. In the files of the National Office, USWA, Toronto, Ontario.

in a firm. In the case of U.S. firms, when labor relations policy for a Canadian subsidiary was formulated in the U.S. office, or at least subject to central consideration, the internationals seemed to find it advantageous to deal with U.S. management. In almost every instance where U.S. union officials became involved in Canadian negotiations the firms involved were U.S. owned. The exception was the pulp and paper industry, but even there U.S. control was of considerable importance to union policy. The basis for an inter-related union policy began in the embryonic stage of collective bargaining, primarily at firms owned or controlled by U.S. interests. The important point is, however, that in many of the U.S. firms the policy makers are in that country. As a bargaining ploy union negotiators would approach these officials rather than those in Canada. The UPWA approached Swift negotiators in the U.S. at one point because of their feeling that company negotiators in Canada did not have the authority to make decisions. The USWA approached officials at Bethlehem and Republic to negotiate for Marmoraton and Union Drawn, respectively. They also negotiated pension plans for several iron ore mines at the parent company. The paper unions followed a similar course over the same issue at Kimberly-Clark. This type of strategy took other forms, as well. The UAW by-passed Ford who set the pattern in the U.S. in 1967 and approached Chrysler on the wage parity issue. The relationship between Ford and Ford of Canada is more tenuous than between Chrysler and its Canadian subsidiary.

A fourth feature that seemed to cut across union lines was that, while the unions used U.S. patterns on many occasions as a standard and lever, they often demonstrated a capacity for compromise and flexibility. Union officials in some cases acted as a moderating influence. In the 1947 Ontario negotiations, for example, a caucus of delegates was held to consider the employers' final offer.

> Vice President D'Aoust spoke of the effect the rejection of the offer would have on the other groups meeting next week. He also spoke of the lost time and earnings due to strikes in other industries. He asked if it was worthwhile to go through all this trouble for $100.00 a year which was approximately 4 cents per hour for that year. It was his opinion that this was all that we could get and suggested the offer be accepted.[6]

Oral testimony from company officials in the auto and paper industries suggested that U.S. union officials, particularly, were somewhat more flexible. Wage parity demands by the UAW and USWA were, more often than not, given lip service but dropped. It

6. Minutes of the Conference held with the Ontario Newsprint Employers at the Mount Royal Hotel, Montreal, April 9, 1947 (in the files of the Department of Research and Education, IBPSPMW, Montreal, Quebec), p. 13.

simply was not feasible for the UPWA to press for U.S. standards and they did not do so. The Canada Packers pattern was established for the central segment of the industry but there were geographical differentials even at the major firms. Faced with well insulated local labor markets and a variety of marginal and expanding mines (the latter with very low labor costs), the policy of the USWA was highly segmented and a considerable variety of wage rates were negotiated. The internationals overall, therefore, did not seem to be excessively rigid.

Wage comparisons of the nature discussed in Chapter 1 did exist. Even in the absence of international unions and U.S. corporations, however, Canadian unionists would probably express some interest in U.S. settlements and wage levels. There exists in Canada what one author has referred to as the "demonstration effect" which leads unions — international or purely Canadian — to inevitably refer to U.S. provisions. The close cultural and economic ties probably give rise to this.[7] The comparisons and other local manifestations of pressure for uniformity in this study took numerous forms. In 1957 the iron ore locals in the Steep Rock area stated that they would attempt to tie their negotiations to those on the nearby Mesabi Range. In 1953 the UAW local in Oshawa refused to ratify an agreement because it did not include wage parity. Comparisons during collective bargaining were often made by delegates from the pulp and paper locals. Examples have already been given but the following from two separate sets of negotiations are quite typical:

> We realize that this is definitely a gift. You are offering it because the employees are not satisfied. Well, 5 per cent will not satisfy them either. We have a problem at Fort Frances. We used to have a joint agreement with International Falls [U.S.] . . . . Then the CIO took over the whole local . . . . At our meetings we constantly face the CIO threat.[8]
>
> That 15% is not a very realistic offer from our point of view because we here in B.C. are faced with the fact that we are living next door to people who are doing exactly the same jobs on the same type of machinery with the same type of skill and in some cases are getting $4.00 a day per man more than we are . . . . Our fellows go down and visit these people every year . . . . Here is another angle of it. These companies in the province of B.C. are not Canadian companies.[9]

7. See S. Jamieson, *Industrial Relations in Canada* (Toronto: The Macmillan Company of Canada, 1957), p. 23.

8. Ontario Pulp and Newsprint Conference, Toronto, Ontario, November 2, 1950 (in the files of the Department of Research and Education, IBPSPMW, Montreal, Quebec).

9. Verbatim report of 1950 Labor Conferences, Vancouver, B.C. — IBPSPMW, IBPM and British Columbia Paper Company Limited, *et al.,* pp. 253-54 (in the files of the Department of Research and Education, IBPSPMW, Montreal, Quebec).

Resolutions at Canadian USWA conferences were submitted by local unions which called for wage parity with the United States. Even in the meat packing industry there was some manifestation of this. In 1953, the Swift Committee "went on record to the effect that they believe they are entitled to American rates of pay . . . ."[10] In proposing an amendment for a substantial wage increase one Swift Canadian local submitted the following resolution three years later:

> Whereas the spread in rates between American and Canadian plants has increased in the past years, Therefore, be it resolved that we demand a substantial wage increase.[11]

The importance of wage comparisons, however, should not be overemphasized. In the meat packing case they did not play an important role in negotiations. In the other cases strategic and administrative factors, and a search for acceptable standards, seemed to be far more important.

The Government

Another institutional factor, government labor policy, affected the practice and process of collective bargaining in two ways. First, wage controls during World War II were not lifted until 1947. They effectively prevented any tie-in with U.S. bargaining so that negotiations during those years were largely unaffected by U.S. developments. Additionally, the structure of bargaining was balkanized during those years because government policy allowed, for the most part, single plant representation only on wage change requests. This helps explain the delay in the emergence of international bargaining arrangements until the late 1940's and early 1950's. After wage controls were lifted, the unions were first concerned with getting wages up and with reshaping the structure of bargaining.

The second is of more lasting importance and deserves more extensive treatment. Compulsory conciliation, particularly when coupled with the multiple *loci* of public policy in Canada, was a pervasive factor in negotiations especially in steel and meat packing, and autos up to 1956. If anything, it made a closer tie-in with U.S. bargaining more difficult to facilitate. It appeared to make the parties more intractable in many instances and caused serious delays in negotiations. Additionally, under some circumstances it seemed

---

10. Correspondence of S. S. Hughes, Assistant Canadian Director, to all Swift Canadian locals and staff representatives (in the files of the National Office, UPWA, Toronto, Ontario).

11. Proposed Amendments to the Swift Contract, April 1956, p. 4 (in the files of the National Office, UPWA, Toronto, Ontario).

to play a negative role. Of particular importance to this study is the question of the attitudes of conciliation boards when the parties are using external standards as referent points and its impact on negotiations, particularly in contrast to international pattern-bargaining.

Firstly, there is little doubt that conciliation procedures can result in long periods of delay. The delays appeared to be the result of difficulties in getting conciliation officers and boards appointed and convened. The Ford and Chrysler disputes of 1954 and 1955 illustrate how the procedure becomes extended. The lapse of time from the application for conciliation services to the issuance of the board's report was six months in the case of Ford and just over five months in the Chrysler case. From data on the other cases these delays cannot be portrayed as atypical. Similar delays existed during various rounds in steel and meat packing. The important feature in the Ford and Chrysler cases is that, in retrospect, the entire process did not seem to aid the parties. At Ford the parties were intransigent throughout post-conciliation bargaining and during most of the 109 day strike. To complicate matters further, board hearings into the Chrysler dispute extended into the period of the Ford strike. This, despite the fact that it was almost certain that the union would not settle at Chrysler without the right to strike or until they had concluded negotiations at Ford.

Secondly, in some cases boards did attempt to find an acceptable solution but in a number of cases they did not. The board report in the 1954 Ford case consisted almost entirely of the board's own recommendations of what the settlement ought to be. The criteria used were completely normative and it concluded that any increase was not justified. There was no reference to any effort to settle the dispute. Similarly, the board appointed in 1958 at Stelco recommended no wage increases because of the potential effect of an increase on inflation. It is not suggested that this was always the case, but the accommodative principle was often laid aside. The interesting fact is that a wage increase was agreed to in both cases. When the board report is considerably different from the final settlement confidence in the conciliation process is bound to be weakened. This is what appears to have occurred in the auto industry in 1956 when the UAW initiated the practice, which was followed in all ensuing rounds, of presenting no brief to the board. Instead, they requested that the chairman report failure to effect a settlement immediately and allow the parties to bargain alone with the right to strike or lockout.

This indicates that a third shortcoming of compulsory conciliation is that the parties often make no attempt to settle issues until the dispute settlement procedures are behind them. Evidence of this is that the conciliation board for Chrysler in 1955 was forced to consider 66 unresolved issues. Throughout, the union did not submit a detailed written brief. In 1956, 100 unresolved issues were submitted to the GM board. All 14 issues involved in negotiations between Stelco and the USWA were referred to the board in 1954. A similar procedure was followed in 1956. It often appeared that there was no effective collective bargaining during the two stages. Backing up this observation is the following statement by the company nominee on the 1951 Ford board who submitted a supplementary report:

> It is obvious that virtually no collective bargaining had taken place between the parties in connection with the present contract renegotiation . . . . Instead of being required to effect reconciliation of residual disputes when all attempts to bargain in good faith have broken down, the board has, in effect, been placed in the position of having to do all the bargaining on all points of disagreement that arose at the time of renegotiation . . . . In attempting to decide matters that the parties themselves should have decided long before intervention became necessary, the board is required to deal with subjects beyond the competence of its members.

The existence of a supplementary or dissenting report, such as the above, points to a fourth weakness. The reports are often not unanimous so that there were occasions when there were dual recommendations. This only leads to confusion. The confusion is compounded when two boards are convened in the same industry and issue reports which recommend substantially different things. The Algoma board in 1958 recommended a 27 cent increase immediately after the Stelco board found that no increase was justified.

Fifthly, when the reports are finally received, they may have the effect of making it more difficult to reconcile differences between the parties. There were cases where one of the parties used a report as a propaganda weapon. This may widen the gap between the parties. Just prior to the Stelco strike in 1958 the company, in a newspaper advertisement, maintained it would not ignore the report of the conciliation board. In the Ford case of 1954 the company published the board's report in full. The union, in 1951, maintained that the report offered extensive proof that the union's demands were "just".

The first stage of conciliation did not demonstrate any more effectiveness. The conciliation officer was often accepted as a perfunctory duty and seemed to be impotent. Generally, when conciliation procedures were initiated the parties went through both stages. Without the pressures generated by economic sanctions there is little incentive to settle at the first stage. An interesting revelation in the iron ore case was that in northern Quebec — "The real negotiations go on where the conciliation officer is not."[12] Because of U.S. ownership, off-site negotiations are apparently the crucial ones. The conciliation officer is, in effect, by-passed. There were few instances in the cases analyzed of settlement under the aegis of a conciliation officer.

The parties often displayed an ambivalent attitude toward the process. Unions, like the UAW, have opposed it because it reduces their control over the timing of strikes. Management for the same reason, is often favorably disposed to using it. The process, therefore, can be misused for strategic reasons. This was highlighted in the 1958 meat packing negotiations when market conditions were soft. It took eight months of negotiations and conciliation before an agreement was reached at Canada Packers. After preliminary meetings with the companies in January, the union called the National Policy Committee to Toronto on March 24. Negotiations were conducted for only five days when the union decided to proceed to conciliation. The key factor was a provision in the contracts signed in 1956 that any negotiated increase would not become effective until August 1, 1958, even though the contracts expired on March 31. Management having made no offer on money items, and with the effective date of any wage increase being already determined, an ideal situation had arisen for the union to use the conciliation procedures to their own benefit. The union's position was clearly summed up this way:

> Bro. Dowling [Canadian Director] said he then advised Mr. Carroll [Canada Packers] that the delegates were going home, and that he intended to make application for conciliation in all provinces. He said we had lots of time and perhaps in this way we would prove the stupidity of this procedure . . . . Bro. Dowling pointed out that we had until August to wait for a wage increase. We could use up the time we have and we will meet after this with the power of a strike vote. It was only then that the Company would really negotiate.[13]

The preliminary and perfunctory step of having conciliation officers appointed in eight provinces was not completed until June. The first conciliation board hearings for Canada Packers in Ontario were not held until August 2. By this time prospects in the industry had improved and a substantial increase was negotiated.

Of relevance to this study is the fact that conciliation was ineffective or not used in the two industries (autos and paper) where U.S. standards are extensively used as relevant referent points. The policy in the auto industry has already been noted. In the paper

---

12. Interview with Eamon Park, Assistant to the National Director, National Office, USWA, Toronto, May 27, 1966.
13. Minutes of Swift Committee meeting, Saturday, March 29, 1958 (in the files of the National Office, UPWA, Toronto, Ontario).

industry, it is the policy of the internationals and the companies to use conciliation as rarely as possible, both parties preferring to settle their differences without outside help. That boards rarely will accept U.S. standards for normative or accommodative purposes is clear from the experience in the five industries. The one exception occurred in steel when the board reluctantly recommended a 5 cent increase in the Stelco negotiations after a similar increase had been granted in the U.S. industry. This became the basis for settlement. There were other cases, however, where boards rejected the counterpart U.S. industry as a benchmark for their recommendations. Addressing itself to this question the Ford board of 1954 stated:

> The true criterion must be the rate of wages paid in Canada in a comparable sphere of industry in a place where economic conditions are similar.

The board appointed in 1953 to resolve the dispute between the paper unions and the Ontario Newsprint Group observed:

> We think it is unwise to attempt to use American precedents when examining wage rates in Canada for so many different conditions apply that such a comparison is unsound.

These remarks are not intended to infer that their judgment was incorrect but merely to point out that this position differed from that of one party or the other, or both.

To conclude, the evidence in the five industries indicates that compulsory conciliation procedures affected negotiation practices and the tone of negotiations. On several occasions, it did seem to introduce rigidities and delays into the bargaining process and certainly more so than union attempts to apply U.S. standards to the Canadian scene.

A DISCUSSION OF THE FINDINGS

The findings do not provide solid answers to the most important forces shaping collective bargaining. Both institutional and economic factors, the external as well as the internal environment, were important. While the existence of common ownership, centralized union policy, and union rivalry assumed prominence in some of the cases, other factors apart from the Ross construct are just as important in understanding the bargaining relationships. In three industries — autos, paper and meat packing — there was historical information available which goes back prior to 1940 when unionism either did not exist (autos and meat packing) or was not a major force (paper). In each of these cases bi-national patterns were a frequent phenomenon. This was limited to fringes in the case of Swift but there was uniformity in wage changes and levels in parts of the auto and paper industries. Laying aside the Swift experience for the moment, the underlying force behind concurrent wage adjustments must be contained in factors other than union policy and orbits of comparison. Reinforcing the pre-1940 data is the fact that there was little management resistance to the pass-on arrangement at Marmoraton. Significantly, in the auto, paper, steel, and iron ore industries price determination from the U.S. is a major feature.[14] As is true of wage adjustments, American price decisions affect Canadian firms but in various degrees. The major U.S. paper companies, for example, have mills in Canada and price leadership affects producers throughout the continent. Major price decisions in the auto industry are apparently made in the United States. The pricing of new Canadian models is done in the U.S. and, in between model years, Canadian officials can only move certain lines by offering rebates to dealers. Canadian steel producers look to U.S. price decisions as a barometer for their own price adjustments. In some cases, as noted, list prices are identical. The fate of Marmoraton, and most Canadian iron mines, is directly tied to the fortunes of the U.S. parent firms. Thus, even though there may not be a direct relationship, the linkage in the product market would clearly have some importance in explaining developments in the labor market. This, of course, is something that Ross has downgraded.

The three institutional factors which Ross has emphasized — common ownership, centralized union bargaining, and union rivalry — assumed some importance as far as the process is concerned. They do not, however, hold up completely under scrutiny. At various levels in the hierarchy of the unions it was true that binational comparisons developed, and this was largely where one would expect on *a priori* grounds. They were probably important in setting targets. But, the question of uniformity in the bargaining process hit in different ways. It was never an issue in meat packing and only sporadically in basic steel. The reasons are difficult to pin-point but a few observations can be made. Because of the dominant size of Canada Packers, and correspondingly the C.P. negotiating committee, the Swift negotiations had a diminished function in union strategy. C.P. delegates to a large extent controlled the policy of the union and, because of its size, the union inevitably selected Canada Packers to set the pattern. Swift offered to take the lead in 1961 but the union simply took their wage offer and "whipsawed" Canada Packers. The result was that U.S. oriented demands formulated at Swift were never presented. The

---

14. Information on pricing in the auto industry was obtained through oral testimony. For the paper and steel industries see Guthrie, *The Economics of Pulp and Paper,* pp. 111, 112; and Royal Commission on Canada's Economic Prospects, *The Primary Iron and Steel Industry,* pp. 23, 24.

Canadian branch of the USWA very early in their existence clearly established autonomy in their relationships with the Pittsburgh office in all matters including collective bargaining. This was by design and was always respected by Phillip Murray. As a consequence, American officials rarely, if ever, visited Canada to supervise negotiations. In contrast, the practice of co-ordinated bi-national wage adjustments in paper dates back to World War I. John Burke, the perennial president of the IBPSPMW, particularly, institutionalized the practice. He had unusual influence with the locals, however, because of his guidance during the difficult 1920's and 30's.

There appeared to be another reason why the question of uniformity hits in different ways. Each union has its own rank-and-file attributes. In the iron ore mines the USWA represents a membership widely dispersed by geography, one with a diversity of preferences and backgrounds and one in which there are decided differences in militancy from local to local. This had an effect on the distribution of the package, and the attitudes toward the international. A uniform program is extremely difficult to obtain even within Canada because of differences in tastes and culture. At the remote Quebec mines, for example, the miners are primarily interested in such benefits as long vacations and transportation allowances. French Canadian nationalism dictates against centralized control over negotiations at the Quebec mines. Oral testimony indicated, as well, that a lack of militancy was another reason why the USWA has not pushed for the Marmoraton arrangement at some of the other mines. On the other hand, the membership in the auto industry is probably at least as militant as the leadership and, although differences in emphasis exist from local to local, they are a comparatively homogeneous group in both countries. This gave the leadership additional leverage, once they marshalled rank-and-file support, and facilitated a common approach.

Wage comparisons did seem to be used most intensively at U.S. owned firms but the latter did not generate uniform wage changes or levels in all cases. It may, however, build in or allow greater degrees of uniformity between U.S. and Canadian settlements in the fringe benefits area. Centralized union bargaining, however, did not seem to be an autonomous variable. Rather, control or co-ordination from the U.S. could be looked upon as an organizational or administrative reaction to other factors. The USWA presents an excellent example. It is decentralized in the U.S.-Canada context in the basic steel industry but centralized for Marmoraton.

Union rivalry is undoubtedly important in some instances. It was not the primal antecedent behind the relationships, however. Internal rivalry was at a peak in the UAW during the postwar years but this did not generate international pattern-bargaining. If anything, the evidence indicates that the internal strife caused the UAW to delay their efforts in that direction. The impact of external rivalry could only be examined in the pulp and paper industry. At times it did appear to magnify the use of bi-national comparisons. Rivalry between the two AFL unions and the CIO and Quebec-based unions, however, was the most bitter in the postwar years. Bi-national patterns had existed long before that and the relationship between U.S. and Canadian settlements actually broke down in the 1950 to 1952 period.

Rather than viewing uniform settlements as the result of union pressures an alternative hypothesis can be suggested. Bargaining, as Reder suggests, takes place within limits which are determined by the economic environment. Within this framework, both sides will use certain bargains as referent points. They may use the same ones. For the company, firms in the same or closely related product market are likely to serve as the appropriate standard. For the union this is also a relevant consideration along with the wages paid at the other plants of the same company. The important point is that the transmission process seemed to be a joint one. It has been stressed that in every case of bi-national influence the evidence was to the effect that U.S. standards were acceptable and assumed prominence for both parties. Their policies seemed to be mutually reinforcing for the most part so that a parallel process exists for both.

From the point of view of the company there can be strategic and/or administrative advantages in following an internationally co-ordinated policy. For example, head office policy could be upset and the firm "whipsawed" in their U.S. negotiations if the subsidiary follows an independent course. Or, in the pulp and paper industry, mills in various regions could be "whipsawed" or a particular firm could obtain a competitive advantage. There are also administrative advantages in having at least some standardization in certain contract provisions. The reasons for Swift's policy with regard to fringes is probably contained in administrative considerations. Baker and France[15] list the following principal factors favoring centralization of insurance and pension plans: (1) the sums of money involved and legal long term commitments; (2) the need for the services of a specialist; (3) the desirability of wide coverage; and (4) desirability of uniformity.

---

15. H. Baker and R. France, *Centralization and Decentralization in Industrial Relations* (Princeton, N.J.: Princeton University, Industrial Relations Section, 1954), p. 148. Slichter, Healy and Livernash, *The Impact of Collective Bargaining on Management,* p. 613, also point out that a reasonably broad unit is required for some fringes.

The uniqueness or focal quality of U.S. settlements takes place in varying degrees at various levels within both union and company structures. It can be further hypothesized that the mechanics take the form of behavioral tactics which are a response, among other things, to the structural arrangements of the other party. The point has already been made that the internationals sought the most favorably disposed decision-making unit of the company.[16] This tends to be the highest unit and in the case of U.S. companies is located in the United States. The experience at Marmoraton, Union Drawn, and the auto companies all illustrate this. It also took place in paper but at a different level because of the regional nature of multi-employer bargaining. The U.S. union leadership took an active role in key Canadian negotiations — ostensibly those where management is most favorably disposed to follow the U.S. pattern. This was successfully carried out in eastern Canada in 1958 and 1959. To facilitate this strategy they also stagger negotiations throughout the continent. By so doing they can enhance the focal quality of key settlements.[17]

Neither side can be pin-pointed as the agent of pattern conveyance. Instead, the initiative probably comes from both sides with the parties adjusting their structures in response to economic and institutional factors. The actual mechanics do not conform to a fixed pattern. They can take the form of shifting Canadian negotiations to the United States. Here, *de facto* supervision from the U.S., which existed in the past, became explicit. Alternatively, U.S. negotiators can exert an on-site influence by playing a "back-room" role in Canada. Or, they can exert an influence *in absentia* as in paper, through the employers' association.

The mechanics may, and the evidence indicates that they do have repercussions in the intra-organizational sense. A movement towards centralized bargaining is typically the result for one party or the other, in some cases for both. The interest of local negotiators may be sacrificed; their function becomes less important. First and second level negotiators may not see eye to eye. The most serious aspect of the wage parity agreement to Canadian officials in one auto firm is the future ramifications as far as their role is concerned. They see an evolution towards the complete centralization of the industrial relations function. Centralization at Swift deprived Canadian negotiators of their effectiveness and undermined their prestige

---

16. This union approach in procedural tactics has been elaborated by Walton and McKersie, *A Behavioral Theory of Labor Negotiations*, pp. 74-75. It is important to note that Walton and McKersie indicate management may attempt to approach higher union officials, as well.

17. This tactic has also been noted by Walton and McKersie, *ibid.*, p. 106.

with the union.[18] Rebellion by the West Coast paper locals in both countries in the 1960's was partially attributable to centralized bargaining. Similarly, Burke's activities, particularly at CIP in 1958 and 1959, caused local friction and dissension. There are advantages which may outweigh this. The achievement of U.S. standards may help the leadership resolve competing pressures. Nevertheless, one of the consequences is that some local unions, just as local managements, may disagree with headquarters on important issues but be forced to accept uniform treatment. Strong local unions may have a particular complaint if they feel they can do better outside an international agreement. Also, to the extent that on-site negotiators do not play as great a role, local issues may be de-emphasized and have later repercussions.[19] Adjustment to local needs sometimes suffers under multi-plant bargaining. In the cases examined, however, an area of local initiative remained in the day-to-day handling of grievances, the application of seniority rules, and so on. The locus of bargaining also varied by issues and in each case a local contract exists which is largely worked out by Canadian officials on both sides.

At the same time, as others have noted, narrowing wage differentials increase the emphasis on the level of work so that the effort bargain may take on more importance.[20] The auto companies agreed to parity but used the occasion to press for improvements in work practices. At their new plants in Canada, Ford and GM have insisted on the "tag relief system" that is prevalent in their U.S. plants, so that the assembly line is not shut down during coffee breaks. In paper, wage uniformity could not be maintained for eastern Canadian mills without union concessions on continuous operations.

SOME CONCLUDING OBSERVATIONS

A few random observations can be made with regard to the issue of international unionism and bi-national wage patterns. Clearly there are potential dangers stemming from bi-national strategies and pressures. Firstly, it can be argued that Canadian sovereignty is threatened because of some extra-territorial decisions on the part of labor and management in the U.S. Secondly, a North American wide strike

---

18. Canadian officials not only had to clear wage offers with the parent firm but it, in turn seemed to withhold information from Canadian officials until the pattern was set by Canada Packers. As a bargaining strategy it had definite advantages in that they never had to set the Canadian pattern. This bargaining gambit is discussed by Walton and McKersie, *ibid.,* p. 316.

19. Reuther ultimately had to face this problem in the U.S. auto industry. See *ibid.,* p. 374.

20. Slichter, Healy and Livernash, *The Impact of Collective Bargaining on Management,* pp. 620-621.

initiated from the U.S. is possible where a continental agreement exists. The importance of both can be grossly exaggerated.

The first involves the presumed danger of issues being resolved outside of Canada by U.S. rather than Canadian personnel. The crucial factor is that collective bargaining is for the two most affected parties — labor and management — unless an emergency situation develops. They must live with the agreement and are most apt to know the conditions of demand and supply for labor. It can be argued that U.S. corporation officials may be more sympathetic to union demands or, that in the interests of industrial peace throughout the corporation they may be more lenient. It is, however, dubious to assume that they will act irrationally. They are in a better position to judge the overall economic position of the firm. Head office officials will, in any case, probably have the final say, even if Canadian officials do the bargaining.

While an international strike is a possibility, continental agreements to this point are very rare and the number of Canadian employees covered is relatively small. They are not in areas which could be designated as public interest situations, or where a strike would lead to an emergency situation. Furthermore, the possibility is only of particular concern to the extent that Canadians are striking over non-Canadian issues or, are ordered out on strike by American officials. There were no cases where either occurred. A most important consideration is that a continental unit can only last as long as it is found to be worthwhile to the parties. Without this ingredient an expanded negotiating unit is not likely to survive internal, let alone, external pressures. To the extent that they do survive, presumably they are of value to the parties.

Overall, international bargaining arrangements are probably a factor bringing stability and a greater degree of industrial peace to an industry. Officials are placed at the bargaining table, whether it is located in the U.S. or Canada, who have the responsibility, authority and experience to break an impasse. Also, because U.S. standards possess focal quality, settlements are likely to be arrived at more quickly.[21] At the same time the locus of decision-making varied with the issues under consideration, a group of dissident locals in the British Columbia paper industry were able to break away from the IBPSPMW in the 1960's, the Abitibi Paper Company objected to being blanketed in a multi-employer unit but successfully disengaged itself, and so on. The structural and procedural arrangements, therefore, seemed to accommodate the interests of constituent

---

21. See Walton and McKersie, *A Behavioral Theory of Labor Negotiations,* p. 124.

groups reasonably well, but at the same time responded to the dynamic institutional and environmental features of particular situations.

The empirical evidence indicates that the internationals do possess some advantages because of their U.S. link. These can be grouped under the headings of available expertise, structural advantages when dealing with U.S. subsidiaries, and access to American funds. The Canadian branches can draw on the experience and research facilities of U.S. headquarters. A thorough knowledge of the policies, provisions, and profit position of U.S. parent firms is available to them at short notice. It is unrealistic to assume, however, that a purely Canadian union would function in isolation from their U.S. counterpart. Next, a Canadian branch has the opportunity of having certain issues resolved at the top level in the U.S., through international headquarters, when subsidiary policy is directed from that country. But any additional power is dependent on the actions of the U.S. membership and it is doubtful that they would initiate or maintain a lengthy strike for their Canadian confrères. There is also nothing to prevent a Canadian union from attempting the same strategy. Lastly, a Canadian branch may have access to U.S. funds to support their members on strike. Actually, there are probably only a small number of cases where U.S. union leaders would tangibly support a set of Canadian demands whose acceptance would require a strike of inordinate length. Employers may credit internationals with more power than they actually possess due to the latter's large (real or imaginary) strike funds and the international link may give the membership confidence. Both of these are of doubtful validity, particularly as time expires, and, in any case, would be very minor advantages. They may also face some disadvantages due to their U.S. link. A purely Canadian replacement would, perhaps, be closer to its membership and able to develop the militancy of the rank-and-file more effectively. The militant Quebec-based unions are a case in point.

Finally, it has been argued that wage parity in the auto industry will cause a surge in demands for parity in other industries. This is unlikely. There may be some increase in wage parity demands but it is doubtful that the issue will be seriously pursued throughout negotiations. The experience in the auto and steel industries over the ten year period are cases in point. Despite autos' important position in the economy, it is even doubtful that it will be pursued where it had not been an issue before. It is not a new issue, but a recurring one and it has always been compartmentalized — one restricted to a few industries. The evidence in this study indicates that the same is also likely to be true of international wage change co-ordination. The future is not therefore likely to be very different from the past.

DATE DUE
